CHAMPION CHARLIE

Also by Michael Clower

Mick Kinane – Big Race King

MAINSTREAM SPORT

CHAMPION CHARLIE

THE AUTHORISED BIOGRAPHY OF CHARLIE SWAN

MICHAEL CLOWER

MAINSTREAM
PUBLISHING

EDINBURGH AND LONDON

First published in Great Britain in 1997 by
MAINSTREAM PUBLISHING COMPANY (EDINBURGH) LTD
7 Albany Street
Edinburgh EH1 3UG

This edition 1999

ISBN 1 84018 260 1

A catalogue record for this book is available from the British Library

Typeset in Sabon
Printed and bound in Finland by WSOY

Contents

Acknowledgements

I would like to thank all those who generously gave up their time to help me with this book. Most are readily identifiable from the text but I would also like to acknowledge the assistance I received from John Randall, Tony Sweeney, Jonathan Williams, the Australian Jockey Club, the Jockey Club, Jockey Club Estates and the Turf Club.

Michael Clower
1 October 1997

Since this book was first published in paperback in September 1998, Charlie Swan has won a second Champion Hurdle on the mighty Istabraq and has successfully laid the foundations of his new career as a trainer.

He has decided to continue riding over hurdles but much of his time and energy is devoted to his rapidly expanding stable at Modreeny, and in his first season as a trainer he sent out the winners of 21 races.

1

For Whom the Bell Tolls

Cheltenham, Wednesday 12 March 1997; 1.40 p.m. Three officials leave the stewards' room, walk past the clerk of the scales and into the noisy, crowded jockeys' room. One of the three, a serious-looking bespectacled figure, calls for the jockeys to gather round.

The other two stand beside him but remain quiet. They are Sir Piers Bengough, the chairman of the acting stewards, and Philip Arkwright who is the clerk of the course. The man who is addressing the jockeys is Patrick Hibbert-Foy, the senior stewards' secretary. All three come from the top public school, smart regiment background that for so long seemed to be of paramount importance in the Jockey Club's selection process. The trio all went to Eton. Arkwright and Hibbert-Foy both served in the 9th/12th Royal Lancers, the former reaching the rank of major and the latter captain. Bengough did rather better. He retired as a full colonel after commanding the Royal Hussars. According to the list of officials given in the racecard, they have all held on to their military titles.

Hibbert-Foy explains that there is a possibility of disruption from animal rights' protestors. He then says what will happen if the protestors succeed in sabotaging any of the fences or hurdles. If the whole obstacle is blocked off, the race is void and the jockeys should pull up. But, if there are arrows indicating that the fence or hurdle should be bypassed, the race will still be on. He explains about the different coloured flags that will also indicate whether the race is on or off.

His audience listens, with varying degrees of concentration. Some are thinking more of the tactics they are going to employ in the first race. A few are still chuckling at one of the many jokes they have just heard. For others his words are a welcome break from an almost unbearable build-up of tension.

The minute Hibbert-Foy and the other two officials walk out of the room, there is a shout of 'Tie up, jockeys'. Seventeen of the riders pick up their helmets. The vast majority of these already have their peak-capped covers on them. But the ribbons that hold the covers in place are loose. Most of the jockeys go to the valets to get them to tie the ribbons tight, and so ensure that the covers do not get blown off as the air rushes past them at over thirty miles an hour throughout the two miles and five furlongs of the Royal SunAlliance Novices Hurdle.

One of the few who does not walk up to the valets is Charlie Swan. He ties up the cap cover himself. Not because he has no faith in those he pays to do the job, but because he knows they are so busy. He does not want to add to their workload.

The twenty-nine-year-old Irish-born jockey has been through this many times before, but he is feeling the pressure even more than he did on the day he had his first racecourse ride fourteen years earlier. The hair beneath the helmet is brown. In the summer it is quickly bleached by the sun and transformed into a golden blond that would be the envy of many a girl. But it would not take many more days like this one to turn his hair prematurely – and permanently – grey. His face is as white as his well-brushed teeth.

Unusually for a jump jockey, he has a complete set. Many of his rivals have taken out their false ones and have carefully wrapped them up into a handkerchief for use later in the day when appearance is a greater consideration than the danger of swallowing them. But Swan's seemingly faultless molars are a tribute, not so much to his toothpaste, as to his dentist. When Desert Lord fell at the final fence in the lead in the Munster National at Limerick in October 1993, his jockey was kicked in the mouth. The blood that he involuntarily spat out onto the green turf contained one of his front teeth. After two months of tiresomely taking out a false one each time he rode, Charlie went back to his dentist and asked for a more practical alternative. The two teeth each side of the gap were filed down and a crown was cemented on top of each stump. A false tooth was joined to the two crowns in what the dental profession call a three-unit bridge.

However, the reason the colour of his cheeks matches that of his teeth has nothing to do with his dentist. It has everything to do with pressure.

Try as he might, he cannot blank out the repeated reminders from his brain. He still has a vivid mental picture of being on the same panel as Mike Dillon, at a pre-Cheltenham preview at Adare in County Limerick eleven days earlier, when the Ladbrokes betting guru said that Istabraq would be the best bet of the meeting. Since then Swan has said repeatedly that the horse he is about to go out to ride has a better chance of winning than any of his other mounts at the three-day meeting.

The previous day has been a disaster. All the favourites were beaten. So too were all the Irish horses, notably Finnegan's Hollow, who was still cruising when he fell heavily with Swan at the third last. Stories of how much the horse's owner, J.P. McManus, lost have spread like wildfire. According to one report the big punter, known to some as the Sundance Kid, had put on £200,000 in the expectation of winning £700,000.

McManus has a reputation for being a good loser, but his jockey detected an unmistakable air of gloom when he joined him in his box in the grandstand after that day's racing. Several of JP's friends and business associates were with him, wealthy men like John Magnier and Dermot Desmond. Swan walked back down the stairs convinced they all intended to try and recover their losses on Istabraq.

What is also running through his mind, like an out-of-control video for which he is unable to find the stop button, is the exchange between John McCririck and Ted Walsh on Channel 4's *Morning Line* earlier in the day. Walsh, asked if he would put his last £40,000 on Istabraq, replied: 'Yes, I would. What is more, I would mortgage my house and put on another £40,000!'

As Charlie Swan prepares to walk out of the jockeys' room and into the parade ring, his leg is pulled for the umpteenth time that day by one of his rivals. 'You'll need to win on this one, Charlie. The whole of Ireland has backed him.' It is all the Irish champion can do to force a smile. To say that the whole thing is getting to him would be the understatement of the meeting. The only good thing is that there is no time for any more cracks.

As the white-faced jockey walks down the weighing room steps and onto the grass of the parade ring, he searches through the sea of faces for J.P. McManus and Aidan O'Brien. What he sees almost stops him in his tracks. Istabraq is dancing around on his toes. On his neck are ominous traces of sweat. He is clearly about to boil over. Racehorses, like most athletes, are brimful of nervous energy. But, if they are to perform to their best, they must keep this in reserve for the race. If they use up even part of it beforehand, they will not win.

11

'Istabraq has got himself very uptight,' Aidan O'Brien mutters as the jockey joins him and McManus. The three men agree that the second the bell sounds for the riders to mount, Swan will take the horse straight out onto the course in the hope that he will relax once he is away from the pressure-cooker atmosphere created by the 43,000 people and all the noise they make. But, seemingly, the bell has already tolled for Istabraq, and for all those who have backed him. By the time Swan is given the leg-up, the edgy bay is sweating profusely.

If it were not for all the money McManus and his friends are putting on the horse, the bookmakers would lengthen his price. But, with almost all the sizeable bets continuing to be for the favourite, they do not dare. O'Brien leads Istabraq down the chute towards the course. The young trainer has his left hand on the horse's rein and his right on the girth. 'When you get him down to the start, Charlie, try to get him relaxed,' are the only words he says. At least out loud. His prayers are silent.

O'Brien lets the horse go the minute he reaches the green grass of the course. It is as well for his grey suit that he does. Istabraq's sweating is more profuse than ever, and it has stretched all the way from his neck to his girth. Swan stands up in the irons and lets the horse break into a canter. A white-coated attendant lets out a roar of disapproval. He yells at Swan that he must take Istabraq down the all-weather strip put in place to save the course from unnecessary wear. The attendant, to his fury, is ignored.

Swan brings his mount to a halt in front of an inspection hurdle. Istabraq stands still, ears pricked, and then begins to look round him. For the first time in more than half-an-hour he relaxes. But this proves to be no more than the calm before the storm. Within five minutes the first of the other sixteen runners reaches the start. Istabraq starts sweating again. Within seconds the latest perspiration has joined forces with the previous ones to produce a soap-like lather on his neck, beneath his number cloth and on each side of the breast plate used to stop the saddle slipping back. The number of horses who have sweated away their chance before a big race to this extent, and still won, can almost be counted on the fingers of one hand.

Charlie Swan, his brain working overtime since he first saw the horse in the paddock, decides desperate measures are called for.

> My plan was to ride him handy but if I do that now he will run
> keenly, and far too freely. He will burn himself out well before

the end. My only hope is to drop him out, and switch him off. It does briefly cross my mind that, if I get beaten riding him like this, the critics will have a field day. But it's my only chance, and it's a pretty remote one at that. But I have none at all if I adopt conventional tactics.

We are called into line, and Istabraq almost boils over yet again. Instead of taking it steady, as I ask him to, he charges forward into the tape. I only just manage to stop him bursting through. We turn and line up again. This time I rein back and Istabraq is caught flat-footed. He has no option but to miss the break, and I anchor him at the rear. By the time we jump the fourth, the flight nearest the stands, I am last and happy to be there. Istabraq seems nicely settled. If only I can keep him switched off.

Going into the next, though, Fred Hutsby on Mighty Moss quickens the pace and I am twenty lengths off the leaders. Soon we are going uphill. Istabraq is making up ground but I let him lob along at his own speed. If you push a horse going uphill, he will run out of steam before the end. And this one has sweated so much he is almost certain to do that without me using up even more of his energy. Once we reach the top of the hill, however, I give him a squeeze. He pings the next. He is going well. I now know he will have enough in the tank for me to be able to challenge when the time is right. But whether he will have enough to do anything more is something I hardly dare think about.

We land over the third last in sixth place, and we are close behind the leaders. For a few strides I push him along. He is a horse who does not do anything quickly, and I have to have him handy when we turn for home. The ground is fast and he will not be able to quicken much on it. Well before we reach the next, he is back on the bridle. Just as well because I've got problems.

Richard Hughes on Daraydan takes over the lead from Mighty Moss on the inside. There is a nice gap for me between Daraydan and Forest Ivory (Richard Johnson) who is several yards wide. Too wide for me to challenge on his outside. But, if he moves in, he could squeeze me out. I am three-quarters of a length behind him and, unless I act quickly, powerless to stop him. I have to get on terms by the time we jump. I kick Istabraq. He responds. Christ almighty. Richard Johnson comes in as we jump and cannons into me in mid-air.

Istabraq's head nods on landing. I can feel his legs slipping from under him as his body is knocked sideways by the impact. I sit like a limpet. And I pray. Somehow Istabraq stays on his feet, but he is half-winded. He has even less chance now. But I have to sit still to give him a few moments to recover. Not as much as I should, though. The race is on in earnest and, if I don't get him going again quickly, the leaders will be gone. Amazingly Istabraq quickens, the final flight looms up and I am going to jump it in front.

I remember Fairyhouse over three months earlier. I left him alone at the last and he fiddled it. I can't afford to do that again. I have to have a good jump to keep me in the lead. I throw everything at him to make up his mind for him. He comes up nicely, and jumps it well. He lands running, but still only just in front. I have the whip out and I use it. I have to keep using it. I can't shake off Mighty Moss. I hit him again. And again. I can see the post drawing near. Twenty yards, then ten, and I know I have it. Thank God.

I can feel the delight flooding through me. I stand right up in the irons and wave my whip in acknowledgement as I realise that all the cheering is for me. I am showing off, but suddenly that's what I want to do. I turn sideways and wave my whip again, but this time at JP and his friends in their box. I know how relieved they will be to have got their money back. But not half as relieved as I am.

2

Bonnie Prince Charlie

We are all, to a greater or lesser extent, a product of our genes.

Students of human genealogy tend to place far less importance on inherited talents than do those who study the pedigrees of animals. If the man who has ridden more Irish jumping winners than any other jockey in history had been a horse, the breeding experts would have had no hesitation in attributing his ability to all the jockeys on his mother's side of the pedigree. Theresa Swan is the grand-daughter of George Chaloner, a successful jockey who later trained at Newmarket and whose father, Tom, rode ten classic winners.

Founding a racing dynasty was the last thing on Tom Chaloner's mind when he forced Macaroni up on the line in the 1863 Derby to snatch a head verdict. Apart from his understandable feelings of jubilation, he was simply glad to get the race over with. It was bucketing with rain and the start of the race had been marred by so many false starts that it would make the 1993 Grand National look like a cake-walk. Charlie Swan's ancestor had been brought up in humble circumstances in Manchester and went into racing on the other side of the Pennines at Middleham in Yorkshire. He was apprenticed to John Osborne and gave his career a kick-start by employing a short-cut used by many before him, and by many since. He married his boss's daughter.

Tom Chaloner may have had an eye for the main chance but he proved to be a jockey of considerable ability. He looked like becoming a successful trainer too, but he died when he was only forty-seven. His widow Ellen, widely known as Nellie, took over her husband's Newmarket stable, even though it was to be another eighty years before the Jockey Club was finally forced by Florence Nagle's High Court action to give trainers' licences to women. Nellie's brother, Johnny Osborne, rode Pretender to win the 1869 Derby and several of her six sons became jockeys. Four of them also trained at Newmarket, although Tom junior did so only until he made so much money on Marco in the 1895 Cambridgeshire that he was able to retire.

George Chaloner won the 1892 Middle Park on the famous Isinglass and was second on Curzon in the 1895 Derby. He had also finished third the previous year. As a trainer, he won the first running of the Coronation Cup and also sent out the winners of the Lincoln and the Royal Hunt Cup. Like Tom junior, though, he packed it in once he had made enough money to do so. That was when he was forty-one and he then bought a substantial farm in Bedfordshire.

His own son, Theresa's father, turned his back on the turf to become a soldier and he was an officer in the Indian Army when Theresa was born in Pakistan in October 1941. Her family moved to Britain shortly after the end of the Second World War, and she was educated at Littlehampton Convent in Sussex. When she left school, she went to the Chiltern Nursery Training College at Caversham near Reading. Her first job was as a nanny in Germany with a family at Wolfenbuttel, some forty miles to the south east of Hanover.

The First Queen's Dragoon Guards were stationed at Wolfenbuttel and several of the young officers were taken with the petite but stunning blonde, none more so than Donald Swan. He asked her out and, as the second date followed the first, Theresa found herself becoming increasingly entranced by the dashing lieutenant with the light brown hair and by his seemingly boundless enthusiasm for life. She was amused by his succession of stories, and by all the arm-waving gestures that accompanied them. That so many of the stories were so obviously exaggerated served only to add to the entertainment and to the appeal of the man who was telling them. One evening he told her about his family history.

> 'Swan is a Scottish name and we came from the Glasgow side,'
> he began as his listener sat beside him, a trace of a smile already
> on her lips. She knew she was going to enjoy this. 'In the Jacobite
> rebellion my great-great-great-great-grandfather backed the
> wrong horse. He was surgeon to Bonnie Prince Charlie and,
> when the Prince's army was routed by Butcher Cumberland at
> Culloden Moor in 1746, surgeon Swan was condemned to death.
> While he was waiting for the executioner, he heard that one of

the English generals was badly wounded. He volunteered to perform the operation. The general muttered through the anaesthetic – half a bottle of whisky – that the execution was to be called off and he later told Swan that he would fix him up with a job. He came from Lincoln and he knew there was a vacancy there. My family remained in Lincolnshire, at Spilsby, until the Second World War.'

At this point the narrator paused. He went to the bar to get himself another drink. When he returned, together with one for Theresa, he asked the blonde if he was boring her. Not at all, she replied, smiling back at him. She was fascinated. She wanted him to continue.

My father, Charles Francis Trollope Swan – Anthony Trollope, the novelist, was another of my ancestors – fought in the First World War in the Rifle Brigade. In the Second he commanded the Black Watch. The regiment was fighting in France and one day my mother was informed that the house and land were being requisitioned for use by the Canadian Army. She was given forty-eight hours to move out. When the war was over, my father sold the place and we lived in Sussex.

'What about you, Donald?' Theresa wanted to know. 'Did you go to school in Sussex? How did you come to be in the army?'

Her new boyfriend explained that he had been educated in Scotland, ironically not all that far from Culloden Moor. He was thirteen when he was sent to Gordonstoun in 1952. These days Gordonstoun has as many girl pupils as boys and, although not much has been done to alleviate the effects of the climate in this remote part of Scotland, the school is a long way removed from the spartan, cold bath and exercise-dominated regime that stamped its character on those who were educated there in earlier years. Some of its pupils, like Prince Charles, who was there a decade later than Donald Swan, hated the place. But for the outgoing, energy-packed army officer's son it was fun.

'I decided I wanted to become an actor.' Theresa's smile broadened. Now she could see where the expansive gestures came from. 'I actually passed into RADA. My sister, Coral, did so too. My father said she could go but he wouldn't let me. He said acting was too dodgy a career for a man. I was sad about that but, looking back on it, I think he was possibly right.

17

Anyway, I then decided on the army and I followed my father's route through Sandhurst. Coral didn't become an actress in the end but she went into the speech and drama side of the business.'

Donald was intrigued to hear about the Chaloners because he was hooked on racing. When the First Queen's Dragoon Guards were stationed in Dorset, he told his commanding officer that he wanted to take up point-to-pointing and he asked him if he knew anyone who would teach him how to ride a racehorse. Lt-Col. Tom Muir was a friend of Toby Balding and he introduced his young subaltern to the trainer one day at Newbury. Most trainers would shudder at the idea of teaching an army officer – unless he had the means to buy decent horses and put them with the trainer concerned. Not so the genial Balding. The would-be amateur rider was told he would be welcome to go and ride out whenever he liked. When the offer was taken up, Balding generously threw in breakfast at Fyfield House, the Weyhill training establishment where he trained a large string, most of them jumpers.

His pupil duly graduated to the point-to-point scene and rode six winners in his first season. He later had a few rides on the racecourse proper – at low-key courses like Wye, Fontwell and Plumpton – and, although success there eluded him, this did nothing to diminish his fast-growing enthusiasm for the sport. His new-found ambition was to ride in the Grand National.

He was twenty-five when he married Theresa in Chelsea, at St Mary's Church in Cadogan Street. The fact that she was a Catholic and he was a Protestant seemed unimportant, even when the First Queen's Dragoon Guards were posted to Northern Ireland and Swan took his new bride with him. At the time Ulster was a relatively peaceful place and, far from carrying out his duties in daily dread of being shot as his successors were to, the newly promoted captain was able to devote much of his considerable spare time to hunting and point-to-pointing. The only occasion on which he was called upon to raise his rifle in earnest was when he was sent to Aden at the height of the conflict. Needless to say, he was thrilled to be involved in some serious action.

But the seeds of change in the Swan way of life had already been sown before he was posted to Aden. He inherited some money when his father died and, although it was nothing like enough to enable him to fulfil his dream of buying back the family estate at Spilsby, or one like it, he realised it would go a long way in Ireland, particularly in Southern Ireland. And the more he saw of the country, and its easy-going approach to life, the more it appealed to him.

In 1965 he bought Modreeny and its 250 acres for £30,000, and he moved there with his pregnant wife and daughter Natasha the following year. The big Georgian building – it was built in 1760 and expanded during Queen Victoria's reign – is typical of the large houses that were so popular with the Anglo-Irish in the days when the cost of heating, and cleaning them, was only a minor consideration. Cleaning this one, though, was a big job. It had not been lived in for twelve years, at least not by humans. A local farmer had been using it as a barn – sheep on the ground floor and chickens upstairs. The Guards officer decided he would become a farmer himself. He bought some cows, shipped a few horses over from England and, when his tour of duty in Aden was over, resigned his commission and set about converting the surrounding fields from a wilderness of weeds to productive land.

Theresa was somewhat less taken with her new way of life than her husband, who had at last found a task that was to test even his boundless enthusiasm. Modreeny is in a remote spot in County Tipperary and the nearest town, the sleepy hamlet of Cloughjordan, has distinct limitations so far as shopping is concerned. So, as Theresa found out, did towns further afield. She longed for the days when she could go into a supermarket and buy what she wanted. She also had misgivings when she looked out of her kitchen window and saw a vivid reminder of the troubles of earlier times. The huge pile of stones was what was left of Modreeny's predecessor after Cromwell's soldiers had sacked it, and then burned it down.

Those misgivings were shared by her husband when, in 1969, British troops were sent to Northern Ireland to protect the Catholic community from the Protestants, and then stayed on in a vain attempt to stop the emerging conflict between the two sides of the religious divide turning into civil war. In Southern Ireland anti-British feeling, which had never been all that far beneath the surface, flared up angrily. Even worse, the Swans suddenly realised that the seemingly tranquil area in which they had decided to invest their worldly wealth was in the centre of a hotbed of republican sentiment.

'The bubble burst with a bang,' Donald Swan recalls, traces of worry still furrowing his brow as he remembers the anxiety he felt at the time. 'The IRA was particularly strong around Nenagh which is only ten miles away. I felt we were a pretty obvious target. I was English and I'd been in the British army which had become a hated symbol of oppression. I'd also been in the

Guards and had served in the North. People we knew round about, either English or of English descent, had "Brits Out" daubed on their gate-posts. Clearly we were in troubled times.'

It was Donald Swan's enthusiasm that saved him. While many of his British neighbours had adopted a reserved, almost withdrawn, approach when it came to mixing with the local community, the former army captain joined in everything that interested him. Despite all the hard work that confronted him on his farm, he went hunting whenever he could and was soon asked to become Master of the Ormonde. When he heard there was a local dramatic society, he joined that too and at long last he was able to realise some of his thespian ambitions. His pronounced English accent, a giveaway in the eyes of the IRA sympathisers, was positively welcomed by the theatre group. They were rehearsing for My Fair Lady and they needed 'someone who could speak properly' to play Professor Higgins.

The Swans, the locals soon came to appreciate, were as Irish as they were – at least in spirit, and certainly in the things that mattered. Soon nobody even noticed their Brit accents. When they sent their daughters – Melissa arrived almost exactly a year after her sister – to the local school in Cloughjordan, their acceptance was complete. In the meantime the amateur rider had switched to Southern Irish point-to-points and had also taken out a permit to train. One of his best horses proved to be Zimulator, whom he bred himself and rode to win a bumper on his first Irish ride on the racecourse proper at Thurles in April 1971.

Just under three years later Zimulator, by now normally ridden by a professional, finished fourth in the Leopardstown Chase. He was a 100-1 shot and his trainer was of the opinion that fourth place was a cause for celebration. Theresa had stayed at home to look after the children and her cousin, Hugo, over from England for a few days, plus a girlfriend, accompanied Donald to Leopardstown. The pair also accompanied him to a Dublin nightclub where they drank, told stories and sang songs until four in the morning. They were still laughing and singing when they climbed into Donald's sports car. As they hit the open road on the outskirts of the capital, he saw in his rearview-mirror a Garda patrol car looming up with its lights flashing furiously. Most people would have cursed their luck and pulled in to the curb to await their fate. Not Donald Swan. He'd had too many for that.

'I'll show the buggers,' he informed his by now startled passengers. He waved two fingers out of the window and put his foot down. When he saw the flashing lights fading into the distance, he roared with delight. By the time he neared Naas a quarter of an hour later, he had forgotten all about the incident. When he saw a line of hay bales across the road, he was finally convinced he had drunk too much. Closer inspection revealed half a dozen policemen sporting rifles and standing at strategic intervals. He wound down the window, sobering up rapidly.

He was asked to produce his licence and to explain what the hell he thought he was doing. He was still calculating what his chances were of avoiding ending up in prison, when the Garda officer took a closer look and declared: 'I know you. I backed your horse each way. Pity he didn't finish third.' Swan told him Zimulator was going to Cheltenham the following month and he might get his money back. The policeman muttered his thanks, shouted at his colleagues to clear a path through the hay bales and the sports car roared off into the night.

In the Sun Alliance Chase Zimulator again finished fourth so there was no reward for the Garda Siochana. There was no big pay day for Donald Swan either – fourth place was worth only £423 – but four days earlier the gelding gave his intrepid rider one of the thrills of his life by finishing third in the Past and Present Chase at Sandown, a race which also gave him another story with which to regale visitors to Modreeny.

> Zimulator could be a bit of a rogue and, when we came to one of the fences in the back straight, he ran out, almost onto the railway line. I had to pull him up, then turn him round, take him back onto the course and showjump the fence. The rest of the field were miles in front by this stage. But he really got going and began to pass horse after horse. We collared Nick Gaselee on Ashville on the run-in and finished third. John Oaksey, who won the race on Tuscan Prince, was astonished because he had seen me run out and he assumed that was the end of me. He said 'I shouldn't say this but thank God you did run out.'

The following season Donald Swan upped his sights and aimed both himself and the horse at the Grand National.

> I normally rode at 10st 7lb plus, but I managed to get down to 10st to ride Zimulator, who started among the 100-1 others. Lots of people sent me telegrams wishing me good luck and these

were delivered to the weighing room, but I was nervous when I went out for the race and even more so in the parade. Then, when we were down at the start, Junior Partner spread a plate and a blacksmith had to be called. We all got off and I can remember sitting on the rails talking to Mick Cummins, who was riding Spittin Image, and who had ridden Zimulator for me earlier in the season. But my mind wasn't really on our conversation. I was extremely edgy and becoming anxious about the whole thing. We were kept waiting for fifteen minutes, and it felt like an awful lot more.

I'd planned to go straight to the front and try to make the running because Zimulator liked to do that. He took the first three fences well but at the fourth he clipped the top and, as he landed, he began to keel over. I sat tight hoping he might somehow pick himself up. It took him a long time to fall, but eventually he did, and the whole field galloped over me. I was bitterly disappointed to be out of the race so early on but it was still a great thrill and probably my greatest moment in the saddle.

Back at Modreeny Swan's seven-year-old son, watching it all on television with bated breath, was horrified to see his father buried beneath a sea of flailing hooves. He was glad he had decided to become a showjumper and not a jockey.

Donald Swan planned to try again the following year but his hopes – and his left leg – were shattered in a fall at Thurles some five weeks before the race. As Our Baloo came to the second flight in the W.T. O'Grady Memorial Hurdle, he ducked to the right. His rider still had hold of the reins when the gelding galloped the wrong side of the wing and his leg was hammered against a wooden upright at over 30mph. It broke in five places.

Swan was nearly thirty-seven, more than old enough to call it a day. But he refused to do so. At the end of September he had recovered sufficiently to ride Our Baloo in a two mile amateur Flat race at Listowel, and at Limerick Junction a fortnight later he won a hurdle race on the horse. He was still claiming 7lb at this stage because he had ridden less than ten winners. He did not ride many more. Nobody ever called him either good or stylish. His son certainly did not inherit his ability from Donald, but his bravery he undoubtedly did. It takes a special kind of courage to overcome the sort of dreadful fall Donald had had at Thurles and resume race-riding. Donald Swan had that courage, and more. To him, riding again after smashing so many bones in his leg was the sort of challenge that was there to be met. Not meeting it would have been shirking the issue, and that is something he has never been prepared to do.

He also had other preoccupations at the time, the principal one being to earn a decent living. He steadily built up his cattle numbers until he had a herd of 100 dairy cows. He continued with his farming activities until 1988 when he decided to sell the cattle, and lease both the milk quota and much of the land to a nearby farmer.

Some thirteen years earlier he had converted the cellar at Modreeny into a restaurant. In the evenings he exchanged his milking duties for those of mine host and acted as the resident barman while Theresa, struggling to cater for a husband and three children, was roped in as both caterer and chef at The Fox's Den.

'It was hectic,' she recalls with masterly understatement. 'I was frequently exhausted while Donald eventually found it impossible to combine late nights with early mornings, and so we leased it out.'

Leasing the farm as well has enabled her husband to concentrate on what he enjoys most, training racehorses. He has a string of about a dozen, mostly jumpers, and facilities which warrant a whole lot more. He has a horse walker, a well-laid-out schooling ground, some superb uphill gallops – grass as well as all-weather – and the best schooling jockey in Ireland.

He and Theresa have watched their son's path to the top with a mixture of pride, surprise and anxiety. 'I find it difficult to take in that I have a son who is famous,' says Theresa. 'Somehow you don't expect that with your own child.'

> 'His mother is probably not as surprised as I am that Charlie has done so well,' Donald admits. 'When he became champion jockey the first time, I threw a tremendous hooley, and invited all the local people, because I felt this was something we ought to celebrate. Frankly, I thought he would never do it again. Blow me, if he hasn't gone on to do it season after season.
>
> 'Theresa still worries about him becoming injured, but he is bound to from time to time with all the rides he has, and I have long since become conditioned to the risks he runs. I am also conditioned to the fact that one day he will have a really serious fall which will either break him up so badly, or affect his nerve to such an extent, that he will never ride again.'

3

Pony Racing

On 20 January 1968 the local doctor motored slowly down the drive at Modreeny and paused by the gate lodge to check that there was nothing coming in either direction. He smiled to himself as he remembered his parting words – 'I'm not doing any more house deliveries. If you're going to have another baby, you can damn well have it in hospital.' The exhausted but delighted Mrs Swan, sitting up in bed with all 7lb 6oz of the new arrival cradled in her arms, had smilingly nodded her agreement.

The baby who was descended from Bonnie Prince Charlie's surgeon, and who was born of English parents, was christened in Ireland as Charles Francis Thomas. The first two names were in honour of Donald's father and the third was in recognition of the contribution to the turf made by the Chaloner family. Surprisingly, the priest who performed the ceremony was a member of the Protestant Church of Ireland. The Catholic Church likes to make certain of its continued expansion by insisting that the children of mixed marriages are brought up in the Catholic faith. But Donald and Theresa had already decided that their loyalties should be split. Their daughters would be brought up to acknowledge their mother's religion but, when they had a son, he would be a Protestant like his father.

When he was four, Charlie joined his sisters at the national school in Cloughjordan. Natasha, over three years his senior, and Melissa made a point of looking after their small brother, but at home they were not always so kind to him. One of the sisters' favourite games was to pretend that he was a girl. He would be forced to wear a dress, and told that his name was not Charles but Charlotte. The sisters particularly enjoyed playing this game when their parents had friends in for a meal or a drink, and they could show off their captive to an audience.

Natasha, who now has two small daughters of her own, recalls: 'We were horrible to Charlie at times. He hated being dressed up as a girl and, because I was the stronger, I held him while Melissa put our old clothes on him. He would fight like hell as we did it and then, once we were happy with his appearance, we would drag him downstairs – with him struggling all the way – in front of Mum and Dad's guests.'

It was while he was at the Cloughjordan school that his parents realised, to their horror, that their son had serious problems – as Theresa recalls.

> He developed a terrible stutter and he had difficulty learning to read. We thought he was dyslexic, and it was only two or three years later that we discovered he could read. I found him one day engrossed in a newspaper. He was reading the racing page. The stuttering proved to be primarily nerves and he had a terrible time with it, not just at school but afterwards too. I can vividly remember him making his first speech – it was at the jockeys' dance after he had won the championship for the first time – and Dessie Scahill was standing behind him trying to prompt him while I was sitting there saying 'Oh my God, poor Charlie'. The dyslexia, or what we thought was dyslexia, was one of the reasons we decided on Headfort because we knew he would get individual attention.

Headfort, just outside Kells in County Meath, is a preparatory school which gears its pupils towards some of the famous public schools in England, and the more expensive Irish boarding schools. But the emphasis is much more British than Irish. Learning the Irish language, for example, is not compulsory as it is in almost every other school in the country. On the games field, soccer, rugby and cricket predominate. Gaelic football has only recently been introduced into the curriculum but hurling might as well not exist. The boys – and girls – normally go there at eight and leave at thirteen. There are less than 100 of them at any one time and, because of the fees, they tend to be from the country's wealthier families.

The school has a strong racing tradition. Arthur Moore went there and so did Jim Dreaper, Neville Callaghan, James Fanshawe and David O'Brien. Other past pupils include Edmond Mahony (chairman of

Tattersalls), Hubie de Burgh (manager of Derrinstown Stud), Charlie Murless (manager of Punchestown), Alan Cooper (racing manager for the Niarchos family) and former Irish Grand National-winning trainer Guy Williams. Jonah Barrington, who became the world squash champion, is the school's most notable non-racing achiever.

The boy, who was to become by far the most successful jockey the school has ever produced, went there in a state of near fear – 'I can vividly remember hanging out of my seat belt pleading with my parents "I don't want to go". I kept on saying this almost throughout the journey.'

> The school itself is a huge daunting-looking building and, to begin with, I was allowed out only every third weekend. No contact was allowed with my parents other than by letter. I couldn't ring them and they couldn't ring me. I was homesick, and I found it all very strange. I was only seven and a half.
>
> The bedrooms were bitterly cold in winter. There were no such things as radiators at Headfort. And nor were there curtains. The headmaster, Lingard Goulding, used to go round the bedrooms at night to make sure that the big sash windows were all open. If they weren't, he would pull them down so that they were open to the maximum. The cold air would come flooding in. I suppose he thought it was healthy but he allowed us only two or three blankets, not particularly thick ones either. I would be absolutely frozen but, like everybody else, there was little I could do about it except curl up as best I could – and suffer.

The lessons that he learned were not only the ones on the curriculum – 'Headfort, like other boarding schools, had its ups and downs, and it could be rough. There were always people being bullied. I learned to talk my way out of it whenever anybody tried anything.' It was the beginning of the celebrated Swan charm, which was later to leave owners glowing after a race and ensure that he was their number one choice in the future.

For forty-two years the senior master at Headfort was Jack Sweetman, a racing enthusiast whose son, Alan, is a successful tipster with the *Racing Post*. He was fifty-two, and had been at Headfort for twenty-five years when Charlie Swan arrived. He remembers the new boy as 'a little fair-haired fellow with a chirpy, attractive personality. But he was very nervous. I pitied him with his stutter. I could tell it was a tremendous strain on him. As time went on, and when he was with people in whom he had confidence, it wasn't so bad – but it was always there.'

Every school has its own traditions which each new pupil has to follow. Charlie Swan was horrified when he found out what he was going to have to do at Headfort.

> At morning prayers an extract from the Bible was read out by the pupils, a different person every day, starting with the seniors and working all the way through the school as the term progressed to the most junior person there. This was me. I was going to have to stand up in front of the whole school and somehow try to get through it. It was a nerve-wracking prospect.

For weeks he worried and worried as he tried to work out how he was going to manage it, and all the time the nightmare moment was nearing. Eventually he plucked up courage to ask which piece he would be required to read. Once he had studied it, and learned it off by heart, he practised for the dreaded moment – and kept on practising every day until it was his turn.

> Somehow I got through the whole passage. My stutter was quite bad in those days and it's still with me to a certain extent. Sometimes I am very aware of it. When it affects me, and when I am conscious of it, it seems as if it is taking an awful long time before I manage to get the words out. It's particularly bad when I desperately don't want to stutter, when I am in a hurry to say something or when I am nervous about talking to somebody.

Headfort takes a great deal of pride in the academic achievements of its pupils. Those who win awards or scholarships to the great public schools are singled out for special mention, both at the school and in the magazine which is sent to parents. There was never any danger of young Swan going on the roll of honour, although Sweetman refuses to be dismissive of the boy's lack of academic achievement: 'I taught him history and geography. Possibly he found other subjects more difficult but I never had any reason for complaint about his attitude. He was an honest worker, and he was conscientious.'

The pupil realised his limitations – 'I was all right at history and maths, the two subjects that interested me. But I was weak on English, and I wasn't great at either reading or spelling.'

What he was good at was games – 'A courageous wing-forward on the rugby field,' remembers the schoolmaster, with a hint of admiration in his voice. C.F.T. Swan was awarded his colours for cricket, hockey and squash as well as rugby. He also excelled on his pony.

I started riding when I was four. My father spent a lot of time working on the farm and with the cattle, but neither appealed to me. I much preferred the excitement of the horses. To begin with, I used to ride my sisters' ponies. I wanted to be a showjumper and, although I was put off riding a bit when my father had that fall in the Grand National, I was soon badgering him to buy me a pony of my own. Eventually he agreed and, when I was eight and on holiday from Headfort, I went to Myley Cash's place near Birr. He is a dealer and is Walter Swinburn's uncle. Three ponies were produced for me to try. The first one was too big, while the second was small, had no mouth and tried to run away with me. That left Lightning. I noticed he was a bit dirty. We'd just decided to take him when he got down and rolled. He was filthy, and I almost said no. But my father handed over £200 and Myley gave him back £2 for luck.

The next day I fell off the pony ten times. I was trying to get him to jump and he kept refusing. It didn't look as if he was going to do much to help me become another Eddie Macken. But my father and I kept persevering, and eventually we got him going. He became a brilliant showjumper. I won several competitions on him and, when I was ten, a big hunter trial in Abbeyleix.

I also took him to Headfort. Only fifteen ponies were allowed at any one time and so the rule was that, if you took yours, everybody was allowed to ride it. The owner ended up by having only one or two rides a week. Some people didn't like other children riding their ponies but I never complained. I knew all the exercise Lightning was getting meant that he would be fit by the time the holidays came round.

But the would-be showjumper became soured when he was roped in to help with his father's thoroughbreds: 'Because I was so light, I was put up on the ones that were being broken. I got a lot of falls and I didn't enjoy it at all. For a while it put me off riding altogether.'

His mother blames her husband: 'Donald over-horsed him and he nearly put Charlie off for good. He asked him to do too much and for nearly a year Charlie didn't want to know anything about riding.'

It was the local farrier who changed the boy's mind, and who inadvertently launched him on a career that was to bring him lasting fame. Jack Cavanagh shod Donald Swan's horses, and those of a lot of other people in the area, for his living. For his hobby, he raced ponies. Not the neat little ones that appear in the show rings and on the hunting field but the small thoroughbreds on which a whole string of Irish jockeys first experienced the thrills of race-riding.

> I was twelve when Jack first put me up on one of his ponies and, after having a couple of rides, I won on St Chad at a course in County Galway near Ballinasloe. I found the racing tremendously exciting and very soon I was hooked on the idea of becoming a jockey. St Chad was a really good pony and the following year I won seven races on her. She was only 14.2 hands but she was fast. However, she had a few problems with her steering and her brakes weren't that great. Some of the tracks were very tight and if the surface was at all slippery she and I would be in trouble. There were quite a few falls but I didn't mind.

One of those suitably impressed was Michael O'Kennedy, the then Minister for Finance. He wrote a letter to 'Master Charles Swan' congratulating him on the Ballinasloe win and wishing him 'continued success in the future'. The motives of politicians in such circumstances are sometimes questionable – nobody knows to what extent they mean what they say or whether their primary aim is simply to ensure they pick up enough votes at the next election to get in again – but the letter was given an honoured place in the Swan family scrapbook and, for the rest of his political life, O'Kennedy was able to point out that he was one of the very first to spot the future champion.

Theresa Swan, and sometimes Donald too, were called upon to devote their Sundays to ferrying their by now racing-mad son from course to course: 'Lester Piggott became his hero. Charlie worshipped him and used to watch him on television all the time. He copied him even in the way he held his whip and waved it.'

On one notable occasion Jack Cavanagh decided to lighten the pony's load, with disastrous consequences.

> I travelled to the meeting with my parents and Jack took St Chad. When we arrived, he came up and said that the pony had kicked a hole in the horsebox and had cut her leg. My father looked at the cut and said she should be withdrawn, but Jack

didn't agree. He felt that she was sound enough to take part, but not with the 14lb penalty she was carrying for winning her last two races. He said he wouldn't bother with the lead. It wouldn't matter because she wouldn't win.

But I finished second and the rule was that the first three had to weigh in. I didn't know what I was going to do, and I stopped by the car on my way to the scales to ask my father. He produced two big bottles of orangeade and put them under the saddle. But, when I got onto the scales, one of them fell onto the floor and started to fizz all over the place. Needless to say, I was disqualified. But I was not suspended. You had to do something really serious to be given even a minor ban.

The would-be jockey was embarrassed by the incident, even more so when his father began regaling the diners at The Fox's Den with his own highly-embroidered version of events – 'he was telling everyone that I'd burst into tears. I certainly didn't do that. He exaggerates and sometimes you can't believe half what he tells you.'

Another of Swan senior's anecdotes – but one whose accuracy is borne out by his son – concerns a meeting at Whitegate in County Clare. There was a faller on the first circuit of one of the races in which Charlie Swan was riding, and the ambulance drove up to the pony's injured rider. When the field rounded the turn on the second circuit, the ambulance was still there. The riders saw it only when they were seconds away. Miraculously they all avoided it except for one unfortunate pony. It crashed into the back of the ambulance and the rider was smashed against the bodywork. John Egan, who later became a successful lightweight jockey in Ireland and England, was lucky to get away with only a broken arm.

Charlie Swan's arms, which were later to prove his Achilles' heel, survived unscathed from his own frequent falls. So did his other bones and his nerve, while his finances profited. Winning riders were given cash presents: 'A few people only gave me a fiver but usually it was either a tenner or twenty pounds. That was a lot of money to me at the time, and I saved it all.'

He also learned some valuable lessons:

> Probably the most important one was pace. Many of the riders tended to push from a long way out and, as a result, the races were run too fast. I found that I could win by sitting behind and keeping some of my mount's energy in reserve for the final

furlong. This proved particularly telling at Dingle, which was the best pony-racing track in the country. It's the home of the Dingle Derby and I twice rode in the race.

The Dingle Derby is the most important pony-race in the country, and Adrian Maguire is among the big-name jockeys who have won it. He was still an unheard-of schoolboy when he did so but these days neither he nor Charlie Swan can even go and watch. The Dingle Derby meeting is – in the eyes of the Irish Turf Club and the British Jockey Club – a highly illegal flapper fixture and anyone in racing spotted there would be asked some serious questions about what they thought they were doing. If they were suspected of helping out with any of the runners, they could be suspended or even warned off. Mind you, the racing authorities are right to take such a tough stance. Skulduggery knows few limits at the meeting and in 1995 the big race was won by the racehorse Masai Warrior, running under a false name and with brown shoe polish covering up the distinctive white star on his forehead!

But, although Charlie Swan's pony-racing was a big success, school was not. His parents had long since decided that their only son should not follow Donald's footsteps to Gordonstoun. They felt it was too far away and, even more relevant, they could not afford the five-figure fees. Instead they decided to send him to St Columba's College, an Irish public school picturesquely situated at the foot of the Dublin mountains. Their dreams were shattered when Jack Sweetman had a private word with them. The boy would not get through the exam, he told them. What was more, he should not even be allowed to sit it. This would only demoralise him. In any case, there was no point. Failure was certain.

Donald and Theresa desperately searched for somewhere suitable. One of the schools they had heard about was Wilson's Hospital, a large Protestant boarding school at Multyfarnham, a few miles to the north of Mullingar in County Westmeath. The standard of education seemed good, the fees were reasonable and there was no exam to be taken. Charlie Swan went there, together with his pony, when he was thirteen. For the first time in his life, he was able to master the lessons.

Pretty well all of what I was taught in the first year I'd already been through at Headfort. It made life easy but, as a result, I was only half-listening most of the time and it didn't do me much good. I didn't mind history – usually there was a story involved – and maths and French weren't too bad either, although I

31

couldn't spell the French. But I wasn't mad about the other subjects.

One not on the curriculum was the small racing stable of Jimmy Tormey, just down the road from the school. Charlie Swan was allowed to ride out every Saturday morning and the small-time jumping trainer was more than happy to have the pony-racing star helping out.

By the time his son was fourteen, Donald Swan had resumed his earlier practice of putting him up on the youngsters that were being broken. There was no question of over-horsing him now and Charlie was only too pleased to lend a hand. In the autumn of 1982 the centre attention in the yard at Modreeny was Final Assault, a colt by Smooth Stepper and bred by Donald. He was the only yearling Swan had but ten years earlier he had laid out another home-bred, Dirty Harry, for the opening two-year-old race of the season at Phoenix Park and the colt won at 25-1. Despite having only jumpers to work him with, he reckoned Final Assault had what it would take to do the same and he set about preparing him, not for the St Patrick's Day meeting, but for the two-year-old race at Naas two days later. His pony-racing son would ride the colt in as much of his work as possible and would be old enough to be allowed to ride him at Naas.

The bookmakers opened Final Assault at 20-1 on 19 March 1983. They had never had any reason to fear Donald Swan and, since pony racing was a closed book to them, the kid claiming 7lb meant nothing either. They were surprised to find a few takers – a friend of Donald's had been told about the colt's work – and they were soon forced to halve the price. But the kid did not share the punter's confidence:

> I didn't think we could win. I knew that he had been working well, that he could trap fast and that he loved the soft, but none of our other horses was fast enough to give us any idea of how good he was. Also he was badly drawn – and I was nervous. This was a proper race, quite different from the more relaxed atmosphere of the pony races, and there were some top jockeys in it, including Mick Kinane.
>
> I walked the course with my father before racing and, when we got to the five furlong start and walked over to the outside stall where I was drawn, my father pointed down the straight in the direction of the winning post and said that the shortest distance between two points was a straight line. He then said that there

were two more reasons for not crossing over towards the rail with the other runners. Firstly the ground on the inside had been used for hurdle races and was very cut up. Also Final Assault was used to galloping on his own. We agreed that I should keep straight and, to make sure I did, I was to aim to go close to the wings of the two fences on the chase course which was next to the stands side rails.

I was still very nervous when I got changed, weighed out and walked into the parade ring. But I felt better when I was cantering down to the start. Final Assault jumped out very quickly, as I knew he would, and after two furlongs I was in front, even though I was wide of all the others. My instructions had been to push for the first half furlong and then sit still until I got to the two furlong marker. Here I was to start kicking. I was going so well – and I seemed to be two or three lengths clear – that I could hardly bear to wait for the two pole to come up. When I kicked, he quickened and we won by six lengths. I knew I hadn't ridden very well but I was thrilled to bits.

So was his father, whose loud and repeated cries of 'Come on, Charles' echoed through the stands. Most of the papers mentioned the performance of the diminutive fair-haired boy, and by the time he next rode the colt, the bookmakers had taken note. At Navan on 2 May they opened up the Swan family favourite – the colt carried the colours of his grandmother – at 4-1.

If they had stuck to their previous 20-1, though, they would have collected a packet:

When we were walking round the parade ring, I heard an announcement over the public address that there was something wrong with the stalls and, as a result, the race would be started by flag. This didn't suit Final Assault and, when the starter let us go, he whipped round. If I had not been riding so short, I might have been able to do something about it. But I couldn't, and I got left. We were tailed off until halfway and we only beat three home. On the book we should have won because the winner, Acclaimation, ridden by Christy Roche, had been second to us at Naas. I was bitterly disappointed. I'd made what I thought was a dream start to my career and then this happened. It didn't half bring me down to earth. It also made me realise the game was far more difficult than I thought.

4

Prendergast Impressed

Few people, apart from the French, had much reason to remember 1983 Irish 1,000 Guineas day. Two exceptions, however, were Mick Kinane and Charlie Swan. Horses from France occupied the first two places in the classic and Kinane's dreams of Epsom glory began in earnest when he rode Carlingford Castle to win the Gallinule Stakes. The fifteen-year-old, apprenticed to his father, had had only three previous mounts at this stage and this was the first time he had ridden at the headquarters of Irish racing.

The jockeys' changing room at the Curragh is a dark, depressing, old-fashioned and overcrowded affair long overdue for modernisation, but to Charlie Swan it was a veritable hall of fame.

> When I went in I saw Willie Carson, Pat Eddery, Freddie Head and Lester Piggott, all champion jockeys. My jaw was on the ground. I tried to say hello to Lester but all he did was give a sort of grunt. I was on Final Assault in the third race and Lester was drawn next to me. He was also the reason I was riding too short. I was trying to model myself on him and it was a great thrill to be in the same race, never mind that he won it and I finished down the field.

Donald Swan had another runner that day, Sesetta in the two mile handicap. He put his son up and the pair won by eight lengths. They won again at Limerick ten days later. The youngster was fast becoming the golden boy. He had now won on three of his first six rides. Other trainers began putting him up. Victor Bowens, Clem Magnier, John Kiely and Andrew McNamara were among those who gave him rides. Few said anything about him riding too short. Only Swan was conscious of this and it was only later that he came to look upon it as a fault. But he is convinced that his short leathers saved him from death at Killarney in July.

The turn from the back straight into the straight at the County Kerry course is shaped like a hairpin and, although much has been done in recent years to alleviate the tightness, it was in 1983 a tricky course for an inexperienced apprentice.

I'd had twelve rides at this stage and, after partnering Lady In Red for Thomas Walker in a long distance handicap on the first day, I was booked for Andrew McNamara's Martinelli in a race over a mile the following evening. A lot of apprentices don't realise the dangers of letting your mount clip the heels of the horse in front. If he does, he will fall. But I'd already learnt this from pony racing and I took good care not to let it happen. As we went down the back straight, though, I was in the middle of the field when a horse on my outside came in on me. Martinelli was knocked off a straight line and onto the heels of one of those in front. There was absolutely nothing I could do to stop him. His head went down and I was flung up into the air. When I came down again, I was off the horse but my foot was hooked up in the stirrup iron. I was trapped upside down, and being repeatedly thumped by Martinelli's hind legs as he kept galloping. I didn't realise it at the time but he was probably almost as frightened as I was. This is every jockey's nightmare, and normally it's made worse by your head being constantly smacked against the ground. It was firm that day and it could have done me terrible damage, even with a helmet on, but as I was riding so short my head made contact with the ground only every now and again, and it really only brushed the surface. For the best part of 100 yards I was dragged along like this. It was terrifying. Then, just as we were going into the bend, my foot miraculously slipped free. I was very lucky to get away with nothing worse than some slightly pulled shoulder ligaments. When I went out for my next ride at Roscommon a week later, I was nervous that it might happen again. But, when all went well in the race, I was able to put it out of my mind.

He had almost forgotten it altogether by the time he rode at Tramore for the first time in mid-August. This is another tight course – it is hilly too and, when there are showers on firm ground, it can become as slippery as an ice-rink. Indeed some of the senior jockeys give the course a miss, regardless of the weather.

It was desperate that evening. The rain turned it into what I was later to discover is regarded as typical Tramore. A horse had already slipped up in each of the first two races. I made the running on Zimuletta and she slipped a bit, more than five furlongs out. She began to fall back through the field and she was at the back by the time we came to the bottom of the bend. Her legs suddenly went from under her. As I was picking myself up, I saw Christy Roche standing beside the rails. His car was nearby and he had obviously just driven up. He called out, 'Is it very slippery?' and when I replied that it was, he said, 'You didn't see me.' He promptly got back into his car and drove home!

The budding jockey was still at school at this stage, and he spent the two months of his summer holidays living in digs in Newbridge, and working as a stable lad for Dermot Weld.

There was a bit of opposition from some of the apprentices in the first week or so. They seemed to think I was trying to move in and take their rides but, once I'd explained that I was there only to gain experience, they didn't object. Indeed I didn't get any rides from Dermot but I enjoyed my time there. I mucked out three horses each day and I rode them out every day. The only bit I didn't enjoy was cycling to work in the mornings. There was a real killer of a hill going up to Rosewell House and, waking up in the morning knowing I had that to face, seemed like a nightmare repeatedly becoming reality.

However, when the term started again at Wilson's Hospital in September, he found school more of an uphill struggle than the Rosewell hill. The dull monotony of the hours in the classrooms made his days seem like a prison sentence after all the excitement of life in a busy racing stable, and those action-packed days when he was race-riding. He rapidly came to the conclusion that he was wasting his time. Even worse, he was wasting his opportunities. Other apprentices, freed from the strictures of school, were taking his rides. If he waited until he had sat his inter exam the following summer, he might never get going at all – and his parents wanted him to stay put until he had taken his leaving certificate another two years later!

> I'd had lots of rides after those first three winners but none of them finished closer than second. Somebody told me that Willie Carson did not ride a winner in his first three years, but I was disappointed not to get more. The school was good to me in that they gave me the odd day off to ride in races – my mother would come and collect me – but I needed to be in the game full time. I decided to ring my father.

Donald Swan was not ready for this. He felt that his son wasn't either.

> I said, 'Why don't you wait until you have taken your leaving certificate and then decide?' Charlie said no. If he didn't start then, he would miss out. He had to leave that term. I felt this was not something we could discuss over the phone and I said we would go into it when he was next home, which was either that weekend or the following one. We then had a heart-to-heart in the drawing room. I was all set to put the boot in and say that he had to stay at school. I was going to put it to him that, if he got an accident or didn't prove to be any good, he would have nothing to fall back on. But I didn't get a chance.
>
> He said: 'Dad, don't worry about me. I won't let you down. Whatever I do, I will do it well.' This struck me as quite something, particularly coming from a boy who was only fifteen. It made me realise just how level-headed he was. It also convinced me that, even if he didn't make the grade as a jockey, he would be able to make a go of it in some other aspect of the racing business, possibly on the breeding side. Obviously I already knew that he was not at all academic, and that racing and riding were probably what he was going to do best. I told him he could leave at the end of term but he could not stay with me at Modreeny. He would have to go to a big trainer and learn the job properly.

It was not a stipulation that worried his son. Quite the opposite.

I knew I would ride Dad's horses anyway, so I might as well get in somewhere else where I would have a chance of picking up their rides. We discussed where I should go. Having spent two months with Dermot Weld, Rosewell House was an obvious option but I was against it. There were too many apprentices there already. I could see myself not getting many rides. But Dad and I both knew Squibs Curran. His wife, Pauline, used to work in the yard at Modreeny and he was first jockey to Kevin Prendergast. Having the stable jockey for a friend could give me a bit of pull. Squibs would also be able to put me in for rides that he was offered but couldn't take. We agreed that Dad would speak to Squibs and get him to have a word with Kevin.

He did – and so did Donald. 'Kevin told me he would be happy to take him. But I told Charlie he would have to muck in with all the other lads, and fight his corner if he had to. I didn't ask Kevin for any favours. He wouldn't have given them even if I had. Kevin is very nitty, gritty.'

The elder son of the legendary Paddy Prendergast – a tough, ex-jump jockey who recovered from a broken neck to start training with one horse and became one of the most famous Irish trainers of all time – Kevin was born in Australia in 1932. The following year his father and mother brought him home and later, when his father's finances took off, he was sent to Newbridge College and then to Rockwell, the Irish public school just outside Cashel. His father sent him back to Australia to learn what was to become the family business. Younger brother Paddy junior – known as Long Paddy because he is so tall – also took up training. For nearly four years Kevin worked as head lad to Frank Dalton at Randwick on the outskirts of Sydney. He spent another six as assistant to his father before setting up on his own. He had trained six classic winners by the time Donald Swan approached him and he had long since acquired a reputation, not just as a good trainer, but for his outspoken opinions. He was, however, impressed with the new boy.

When an apprentice first comes into the yard, I always put him with an experienced stable lad for a week or so to learn the ropes. Charlie learned very quickly, and from his first day he was a worker. He was very willing and it was obvious he wanted to get on. Soon he didn't have to be told what to do. He would do it on his own initiative. He was a quiet little fellow and you didn't get a lot out of him in the way of conversation. Mind you, he is the same now! But, despite appearances to the contrary, he was a hard, tough boy.

The small fifteen-year-old had a motorbike when he first went to Rossmore Lodge in January 1984. Not a big, shiny high-powered affair, but a modest Honda 100 whose top speed – downhill and with a following wind – was 65 mph. However, Charlie Swan went a lot slower than that – the roads were covered with snow – on the sixty-mile journey to the digs in Kildare that he was to share with another apprentice, Ron Hillis. The following morning it was still dark when he set off for his new job, far from sure of exactly what faced him.

I found it tough, particularly the mucking out. There were no wheelbarrows. Instead they used muck sacks which were simply square bits of sacking material. You had to pile all the manure onto one of these, pick up the four corners so that it didn't spill the contents all over the place, and heft it over your shoulder onto your back. I found it so heavy that I had to get somebody to help me lift it. I then had to carry the load to the muck heap which seemed – to me at any rate – to be between 150 and 200 yards away. I then had to struggle up some steps and throw in the contents without spilling them. Monday mornings were the pits. The horses had not been mucked out on Saturday evening, or all Sunday. It was bloody hard work. I reckoned I lost four or five pounds every Monday.

We mucked out between lots, and we had to be quick because we each had three horses to do. We would start at either 7.00 a.m. or 7.30 a.m., depending on the time of year, but I soon started going in early. I was trying to do everything right, and I did not want to be under so much pressure. I also wanted to be able to take the break that we were allowed for a cup of tea. It was particularly hard in the cold weather. There was no hot breakfast to warm you up, just a sandwich that I'd brought with me from my digs. I used to eat it after we had finished first lot.

In most large yards – Prendergast had ninety horses – it is not the attitude of the trainer that determines the quality of life for the young apprentices but that of the head lad. Tom Fitzgerald was the man in charge at Rossmore Lodge. He had been head lad to Paddy Prendergast for twenty years before he joined Kevin, and he was a stablehand of the old school.

He was hard and strict, and he wouldn't hesitate to shout at you. The one good thing about him, from our point of view, was that he used to whistle all the time so you knew when he was coming. But he didn't get on with Squibs, which was bad news for me. He would come round the yard and say the box was not clean. So I had to do it again. To be fair, he wasn't that bad with me but he really used to pick on Shaunie Fitzpatrick – he came from Mullinavat so we called him Mull – who was a good friend of Squibs.

Fitzgerald may have put the fear of God into the apprentices but he was held in high regard by Kevin Prendergast, and by Kevin's father before him. However, early in 1990 tragedy struck him down. He went home to his house in Kildare one day with David Parnell, who had replaced Squibs Curran as stable jockey. The house was locked and he could not get in. He and Parnell peered through the windows and saw his wife lying on the floor. She was dead. Fitzgerald soon found his grief impossible to bear. He committed suicide, painfully, with weed-killer. Less than a month later Parnell was dead too. One fateful Monday morning, when his newly acquired Mercedes was in for service, he had trouble starting the car he had been lent. His mother, called in to help, had to use a screwdriver on the ignition. The car was found on a narrow stretch of the back road that leads from Newbridge to the Curragh, the same stretch that Charlie Swan used to find such hard going as he cycled to work at Dermot Weld's stables. The car was upside down and Parnell's body was halfway out of the open window on the driver's side.

The 1984 season was nearly six weeks old before Kevin Prendergast gave the new apprentice his first ride. He did not give him another until May and the next not until June. The neglect was deliberate.

You can't bring somebody in from outside and put him above the guys that are already in the yard. If you do that, you cause a lot of animosity – and I had two of the best boys you could get, Eddie Leonard and Kieren Fallon. Eddie was a hell of a good rider but unfortunately he got too heavy. Kieren was bloody good too. Charlie, though, was getting plenty of outside rides and the way I look at it is, if you can help them do that, they have a better chance of making the grade than if they are just riding for the home team. Some trainers don't want their apprentices to ride for other stables because they like to keep their claim for use on their own horses, particularly on those that have just won and have a penalty to carry. But they don't have enough horses to do that and the kids don't get the winners. Letting them out to other trainers gives them many more opportunities to win races. It also gives them the experience they must have.

Kieren Fallon, son of a plasterer in County Clare, was almost three years older than the new arrival and he had been apprenticed to Prendergast for nearly two years. But he had yet to ride a winner, and he soon made clear his resentment of the new boy. Fallon was to move to England four years later to join Jimmy Fitzgerald and was to develop into one of the top Flat race jockeys. In 1996 he finished third on the list with 135 winners, a still-rising reputation and an appointment as first jockey to Henry Cecil. But he also had a reputation for having a fiery temperament which sometimes got him into hot water, most notably at Beverley in September 1994. Fallon, in full view of those in the stands and of the many thousands more watching on SIS in the betting shops, pulled Stuart Webster (who had just won the race) off his mount. There was a further clash between the two in the jockeys' room and, although the witnesses to the latter incident closed ranks and refused to testify, the Jockey Club suspended him for six months. Charlie Swan viewed Fallon's behaviour towards himself with understandable wariness.

> He seemed to regard me as a threat because he thought I was going to take his rides. But I was determined not to rub anybody up the wrong way. I made it clear to him that I was in the yard to get on. What was more, I wanted to get my own rides. Eventually he realised I meant what I said and we ended up becoming good friends.

The dark-haired Fallon is, in view of his volatile history, a surprisingly quiet-spoken man and these days there are traces of a North of England accent in his Irish lilt as he recalls:

> Eddie Leonard and I were both trying to get on and we were more or less sharing the rides that went to the apprentices. With somebody else coming in, it was obviously going to be more difficult.
>
> After a bit, Charlie moved to new digs in Rowanville. Declan

Murphy and John Egan were there too. I was in another set of digs and, as we became friends – my initial opposition to him had long since worn off by this time – we decided to share a flat. It was over a butcher's shop in Kildare town, and we had some great times, even though Charlie was always pretty quiet. I had my ups and downs but I can't recall Charlie ever being in any sort of trouble. He never got into any scrapes and I never saw him fighting, or even arguing, with anybody.

Throughout the sixteen years of his life, the new arrival at Rossmore Lodge had called himself Charles. None of his family had ever referred to him as Charlie. Nor had the boys at either Headfort or Wilson's Hospital. He would have regarded it as an insult if they had. Charlie carried with it unwelcome connotations of being 'a proper Charlie'. But stable lads have an earthy approach to life. Nicknames are the norm. To them, Charles sounded all too grand. If the British army officer's son had not been so friendly, and had not adopted the same way of talking and behaving as the other lads, he might well have been called Prince Charles. Or worse. One day one of them addressed him as Charlie. The others, including Eamon Murphy, who is the elder brother of the mercurial Declan and who was later to become stable jockey to Josh Gifford, followed suit. The name stuck – even with his parents who recall, with wry amusement, their young son instructing them that they were to call him Charlie from that point on.

Kevin Prendergast, who often used to ride out first lot in those days, took a keen interest in the way his apprentices fared when they rode in races. If they were riding for other trainers, he usually did not have an opportunity to talk to the boys until the following morning. It was his practice to discuss the rides, the tactics adopted and any shortcomings, when he was riding alongside the apprentice concerned on the way to the gallops on the Curragh, or when the string was returning to Rossmore Lodge. If there was not time for this, he would make a point of going into the box when the lad was mucking out and talking to him then.

He would tell me what I had done wrong in a race, and what I needed to do to improve my style and method. Initially this included getting lower in the saddle and grabbing hold of the horse's head when I started to ride a finish. He also gave me some videos of Australian jockeys in action. Kevin was mad about

Australian riders; he told me to study them and copy their methods.

His boss recalls lending out a lot of these Australian videos to his apprentices, and getting very few back!

The best exponents of race-riding were the old -time Australians like Bill Williamson and Scobie Breasley. They were real artists, as well as great race-riders. I would impress upon the boys that these jockeys, and fellows like Mick Kinane, are the people to study. Not the ones who jump out of the gate and try to be in front all the way. Indeed they should use these videos in the apprentice school instead of letting them ride too short with their knees under their chins all the time. Years ago, apprentices were allowed to ride with dummy spurs and it's a great shame this was stopped. Unlike whips, they do no damage whatsoever, and they teach apprentices how to ride with hands and heels because you have to ride with a proper length to use them.

Even without the dummy spurs, Prendergast was impressed with his new pupil's progress.

He did everything he was told, and every day he got better. As time went on, I found that I didn't have to tell him how a horse should be ridden. Having already ridden the horse work, he knew. He also became both a good horseman and a good stablehand. This last because he was interested. An awful lot of good jockeys don't make good trainers because they had no real interest in stable work during their apprenticeship, and they didn't bother to look at what was going on. Some of the apprentices take so little notice of what goes on in front of them that they wouldn't even look at what they're eating!

Charlie Swan had ridden only one winner since joining Prendergast – and that was for his father – by the time it came to the two bank holiday meetings on 4 June 1984. He had no ride at either Leopardstown or Tramore that day, and he returned to his digs in Kildare earlier than usual after finishing work at Rossmore Lodge. He was hardly through the door when his landlady told him there was someone on the phone for him. Charlie was surprised to find he was talking to Paddy Mullins, the then sixty-five-year-old County Kilkenny trainer who had won the Champion Hurdle with Dawn Run less than three months earlier. He listened carefully, and wondered what was coming while the quietly spoken man told him, with more than a hint of annoyance in his voice, that he had been trying Kevin Prendergast's number for the best part of an hour and it had been perpetually engaged. When he did get through, Swan was not there. He had also been down the list of jockeys who had ridden winners that year. He had started at the top and had now reached the bottom. None of those any higher up the table was free to ride a five-year-old called Ash Creek in the fourth race at Tramore that afternoon. Could Charlie Swan do so?

The young apprentice gulped, said 'Yes sir', and immediately rang his mother. The long-suffering Theresa agreed to drop everything, drive sixty miles to Kildare to pick up her son and another eighty to take him to Tramore. Ash Creek won by five lengths and Mullins was delighted, even though his customary deadpan expression kept the fact well concealed. He resolved to use the boy again, and he was to provide Swan with five winners that year, as well as two of the most important. The versatile Ash Creek's next race was over hurdles at Navan and he was ridden to a short-head win by Tony Mullins, the youngest of the trainer's four sons. Tony, despite being repeatedly slated by the British press for his lack of style, and repeatedly being jocked off Dawn Run, was good enough to get the better of a photo finish that day with a little-known amateur who appeared in the racecard as Mr R. Dunwoody.

Stephen Craine, who rode quite a few of Mullins's Flat runners in those days, took over when Ash Creek returned to the level at Gowran Park. But he was beaten half a length and Mullins made up his mind to use the boy who had won on the horse at Tramore in the valuable Hennessy Handicap at Leopardstown sixteen days later. The big advantage of young Swan was that he claimed 7lb and so Ash Creek's weight was reduced from 7st 12lb to 7st 5lb.

> I rode Edwin's Edwina for Bert Kerr in the second race and finished fourth. The Hennessy was the next. I was in a good position turning into the straight but I promptly got murdered. Jazz Me Blues, ridden by Declan Gillespie, pushed me on top of Nonno. Ash Creek clipped Nonno's heels and cut his hind legs with his front shoes. I was lucky not to be brought down, but I was only beaten half a length by Declan's mount. The stewards held an inquiry and I was awarded the race. It was the first Listed race I'd won. But Declan was annoyed and Jim Bolger, who trained Jazz Me Blues, appealed against the stewards' decision.

Luckily for me, Nonno was trained by Kevin Prendergast. The horse was only third but Kevin got sixty per cent of my earnings and, if the appeal went against me, he was going to be something like £350 worse off. He took a photograph of the cuts on Nonno's legs and produced them at the hearing. We won and I kept the ride on Ash Creek when he next ran in the McDonogh Handicap at Galway. That was also a Listed race but nearly thirty per cent more valuable. I won again and these two wins really put me on the map. Both were competitive handicaps, and the fact that I won them for a trainer of the calibre of Paddy Mullins was a big help in getting me noticed.

In the autumn I had three good winners for Kevin. I rode Rising in a Listed race at Gowran Park and beat Christy Roche a short head, I won on Picadilly Lord at Leopardstown and then won the Naas November Handicap on the same horse. I finished up the season with fourteen winners and over 170 rides. I felt I was well on the way to making the grade as a Flat race jockey, and I was optimistic that I would stay light enough because I could do seven stone without any problem.

He had even managed to put behind him an embarrassing incident at the Curragh earlier in the year.

I rode a filly for Des McDonogh in a mile and a half handicap. The breeches I was given by the valet were a bit small and tight. But I didn't complain. I should have done because, as we came out of the stalls, the poppers they were done up with burst open. After half a furlong the breeches were down by my knees. I kept trying to pull them up. Christy Roche yelled at me, 'Leave them alone. You'll fall.' But I continued trying. I couldn't bear to think what all the people in the stands were going to say when they saw me with just my underpants on. So I kept struggling. It was impossible with one hand. I had to hold onto the reins with the other. All the jockeys were laughing. Eventually I had to give up and I rode for the line with my breeches hanging loose below my knees, and me feeling a complete fool. I finished a close third and I might well have won if the breeches had not come down. So many people came up to me afterwards to say they had seen my predicament. I didn't half feel embarrassed.

At the Curragh the following April, riding Affitavolo for his boss, Charlie Swan got the better of a driving finish with Quintillion to record his nineteenth success. But this one was special. The runner-up was ridden by Lester Piggott.

> I went to the front with over a furlong and a half still to run. Lester really came at me in the final furlong and threw everything at Quintillion. It was a great thrill to hold him off particularly because, when we were pulling up, he muttered 'Well done'.

The 1985 season saw Charlie Swan ride two less winners than the previous year. They included two Listed races and his first double, at the evening meeting at Phoenix Park on 15 May, and his number of rides went up to 220. But there was nothing to suggest he was going to make anything other than a middle of the road Flat race jockey. Indeed, once he lost the advantage of his claim, the chances were that he would drop right down the order and find it a real struggle to ride winners. Making a living would be equally hard.

5

Too Heavy

When Charlie Swan looks back over his life, he tends to remember 1985 most for two events that happened towards the end of the year. One was a trip to Australia to spend two of the winter months at Randwick with Neville Begg, a friend of Kevin Prendergast's ever since his educational stint with Frank Dalton thirty years earlier.

> I'd never been further than the Channel Islands before. That was on holiday with my parents, and I found the long flight a real killer, despite stopping in Bahrain. But I loved Australia. The atmosphere was a bit like Ireland. Everybody seemed relaxed and friendly. John Egan, who was by this time apprenticed to Mick O'Toole, also went for two months. He arrived a few days after me and we shared a flat.

Charlie Swan rode a winner at Randwick and had a dozen rides at courses like Canterbury, Rosehill and Warwick Farm. He enjoyed himself immensely. Even the stable work seemed light after all the muck sack hauling in the rain in Ireland. The sunshine was not only a big plus. It dominated his way of life.

> All the work was over by 9.30 a.m. because the idea was to get everything done before the sun came up in earnest. We would return in the afternoons but we did little other than let the horses out for a bit of grazing. In the evenings I went to the various discos and met the Australian girls. I would often stay there until

nearly closing time. That was 4.00 a.m. when I was due back at the stables to start work. The idea was to catch up on sleep when I got back to the flat at 9.30 a.m. but often I went straight to the beach to go surfing.

When his two months were up, though, Charlie Swan was anxious to return to Ireland. The reason was his experience at Clonmel the previous November.

My father ran Barna Beauty in a handicap hurdle and we agreed that I should partner the mare. I wanted to see what it would be like to ride in a jump race. Also Kevin had a couple of hurdlers and I felt that, if I did well on my father's mare, he would put me up on them. In addition, my weight was beginning to creep upwards. I had a feeling I was going to be forced out of Flat racing in a year or two.

I found jumping hurdles at speed a great thrill. I held her up, as we had agreed I should, but I began to make progress in the back straight and even more going down the steep hill towards the second last. She made a mistake at that one but she kept going to lead at the last and win by a length and a half. She was due to run at Gowran Park on 13 February, shortly after my return.

Barna Beauty duly won again and, when Charlie Swan went to Limerick on St Patrick's Day to ride her once more, Michael Hourigan asked the eighteen-year-old to partner his Rotomar Melody in a novice chase. For once Swan was hesitant about taking a ride. Not because he had never ridden over fences but because he had won on his first ride on the Flat and on his first over hurdles. He had dreams of completing the treble – and Rotomar Melody had no chance. He stuttered something unintelligible to Hourigan and then said yes. The no-hoper somehow got round to finish seventh of the ten who completed the course, and twelve days later his father agreed that he could ride Zimuletta in a chase at Mallow. This seven-year-old mare was a half-sister to the horse Donald Swan had ridden in the Grand National. But she was just the sort a novice rider should not be put on. At Mallow she fell at the second. At Gowran Park next time she fell again. Charlie insisted on riding her in the Tattersalls Gold Cup at Punchestown and, although she finally managed to get round, she was totally outclassed and finished tailed off.

Kevin Prendergast, watching with an increasing sense of annoyance his good apprentice dicing with death, resolved to speak to Donald Swan at the first available opportunity: 'I told him bluntly that, if he wanted to get his son killed, he was going the right way about it. But he didn't take the slightest bit of notice!'

C. Swan's name was to appear on the racecard in several jump races as the year wore on and he even rode in both the Galway Plate – in which he was fourth – and in the Galway Hurdle.

On the Flat he went from strength to strength. Five days before he partnered Zimuletta at Punchestown, he rode his first Group winner on The Bean Sidhe in the North Ridge Farm 1,000 Guineas Trial at Phoenix Park. This filly was trained by John Hayden, a tall and slightly eccentric farmer from Kilcullen in County Kildare. Hayden once went to Royal Ascot with an ill-fitting top hat which he hung up among a row of others when invited to one of the boxes. His friends were amused to see him later that same afternoon sporting a topper that was a perfect fit! When The Bean Sidhe, owned and bred by his school-teacher wife, won at Phoenix Park, the filly was the only horse Hayden trained. Later Tony O'Reilly, the Heinz president whose Castlemartin Stud borders the Hayden farm, gave his training ambitions a considerable boost by sending him some of his horses.

Charlie Swan was not allowed to claim his allowance in the Group Three race and so The Bean Sidhe was effectively carrying 5lb overweight, but Hayden seemed happy to put him up, even when he ran her in the Hungerford Stakes at Newbury in August. It was the apprentice's first ride in England. He finished down the field, but at Punchestown less than two months later he rode his fiftieth winner in a Flat handicap, and half-an-hour later he won a hurdle race. The double brought him rave reviews in the following day's papers and he finished the season with seventeen Flat winners and second place in the apprentices' table. He also finished his Flat career.

> With just under a week of the season still to go, I thought I had a real chance of becoming champion apprentice. I was only two behind John Egan, and Kevin had some decent horses running on the final day. Out on the Curragh at the beginning of that final week, there were a couple who needed schooling. I got up on one of them and another lad went on the second horse. Kevin told us to go a circuit and a half of the schooling hurdles, and he pointed to where we should finish. When we got near that point neither of us could remember whether we were to jump the flight or not.

We both stood off a long way and, although my horse jumped it perfectly, the other horse fell sideways and knocked my mount's legs from under him. I landed on my feet and I was actually running when I felt an agonising pain in my shin. I slumped to the ground. I'd never broken anything before but I knew I had this time. I went back with Kevin in the car and the X-rays showed that I had chipped the bone. I was out of action for six weeks and I spent a lot of it at home. I'd been struggling to do 8st 7lb in the second half of the season and, when I weighed myself after the plaster was removed, I found to my horror that I'd put on a stone. I knew in my heart of hearts that, while I would be able to lose a few pounds when I started riding again, I would be struggling to ride at nine stone, and that was too heavy for the Flat.

I'd been putting myself through hell all year trying to keep my weight at a reasonable level. I had been living mainly on fruit because I knew that could not put weight on, and I chewed gum throughout the day to take away the hunger. I also took up smoking in a desperate bid to prevent the pounds going on. But I hated it, and I had to stop. I found the wasting hardest of all on Sundays. While everybody else was tucking into their Sunday lunch, I would go to the apprentices' school in Kildare to sweat in the sauna. Derek Byrne, who was in the same boat, would often come with me but we had to go back in the evening for another session to really do any good. I knew I could not continue like that for another year, not after putting on so much weight.

I rang Kevin and asked him if I could go and see him. I'd bought my first car a few months earlier, a Fiat Ritmo, and I drove over to his house at Friarstown. We discussed the weight situation and, when he asked me if I wanted to go jumping, I hardly had to tell him the answer. He was sitting in his armchair and he started reeling off the names of one jump trainer after another. When he got as far as Dessie Hughes, he stopped and said, 'What about him?' I wasn't sure. I simply said 'Whatever you think.' Kevin picked up the phone and arranged for me to go and see him there and then.

As Prendergast watched the little Fiat go down the drive that Friday, and turn left up the road towards the Curragh and Osborne Lodge, he wondered how Charlie Swan would make out in his new way of life.

I knew he had the makings of a jump jockey and he seemed to have plenty of bottle. But I also knew that there were many before him who had much the same qualities but who'd failed to make the grade. Being a jump jockey is all about courage. Nobody really knows what is going to go on in other people's minds until the challenge is put to them. Only then do you find out if they have the necessary courage. I hoped Charlie would have. But I wasn't sure.

The man Prendergast sent him to certainly had. Dessie Hughes had been a tough and highly successful jump jockey with a string of Cheltenham winners to his name, including the 1977 Gold Cup on Davy Lad and the 1979 Champion Hurdle on Monksfield. Tall for a jump jockey, his 5ft 10in frame carried little spare flesh and he never weighed much more than ten stone. Lean, like a gunfighter, and just as deadly, was how one writer eloquently, and accurately, described him.

He had climbed up the racing ladder the hard way, and for a long time looked destined to reach no further than the lowest rungs. Brought up in a Dublin suburb, he had no family connection with racing when he joined Dan Kirwan in County Kilkenny after leaving school. He was only seventeen, and still without a winner, when Kirwan died. He found work with Willie O'Grady and eventually managed one success on the Flat and another over fences. But that was all. In desperation he answered an advertisement and found himself in Scotland not far from the fateful spot which in December 1988 was to go down in history as the scene of the Lockerbie air disaster. For the first time in his racing life Hughes clicked. He rode four winners inside two months for his new boss, the little known Eugene Ferris, who lived at the Lockerbie House Hotel. The far better known Reg Akehurst was impressed with the latest Irish jockey to hit the racing scene and he invited Hughes to move south. The switch promised much – Hughes began 1966 as stable jockey to the Baydon trainer – but the job turned into a personal disaster. Hughes went almost a year without adding to his still single figure score, and at the end of it he had a terrible fall at Wolverhampton. For almost three months he lay in St Margaret's Hospital in Swindon trying to recover from a badly damaged chest and a pair of punctured lungs.

He was all set to give up, and start looking for a less dangerous way of earning a living, when he bumped into Mick O'Toole, an irrepressible optimist then training both horses and greyhounds in the Phoenix Park. O'Toole and Hughes became a formidable partnership with the stable jockey spending long hours working in the yard whenever he was not away riding. All the experience he gained began to pay dividends when, in 1979, he bought the famous Osborne Lodge stables, next door to the bungalow that Mick Kinane was to make his home a decade later.

When Charlie Swan walked into the yard just before Christmas 1986, the forty-three-year-old trainer was well established with a string of nearly seventy horses, two-thirds of them jumpers. He was still almost as lean as in his riding days and still impeccably turned out, even when working in the stables.

Hughes told him he could not promise him an awful lot. The wages would be £85 a week, after tax and social insurance, and he would do his three horses like all the other lads in the yard. But he would get rides. Maybe not that many. But a few. After that it would be a matter of how things went. Swan was happy to accept. Even in the days when he first joined Kevin Prendergast, he had been self-sufficient. His net wage was £50 and his digs £30. The wages had gone up each year. But it was the rides that the real money came from. In any case, he was not that interested in money. So long as he could make ends meet, it was infinitely more important to get rides. Mounts in races meant opportunities of winning, and winners meant progress, recognition and more progress. They agreed that he would start work the following Monday.

Hughes went into the house and mentioned to his wife, Eileen, that he had taken on Charlie Swan even though his first impressions, gained just over three years earlier, had been far from favourable.

> I well remember the first time he rode for me. It was at Naas in November 1983. I'd booked Jimmy Coogan for a two-year-old called Another Tale. But for some reason I can't remember, he had to cry off. It was the first race of the day and I walked into the jockeys' room trying to find somebody. Charlie Swan was sitting there, so he got the ride. But I was not impressed. Quite the opposite. He sat on the horse as if he was riding a motorbike. He'd improved a lot, though, by December 1986. I was on the look-out for somebody who seemed as if he might be on the way up. I'd watched Charlie a few times to see if he might be suitable and I was actually thinking of him when Kevin Prendergast rang.

Prendergast had picked out Hughes because he had a large string and would obviously be in a position to offer rides to other than his stable jockey. But it was the stable jockey himself who was to provide a heaven-sent opportunity for the aspiring jump jockey by producing one of those 'being in the right place at the right time' moments that Charlie Swan is convinced has been the key to his phenomenal success.

Tom Morgan was twenty-three and only days away from dead-heating with Frank Berry in the race for the jump jockeys' title. The younger brother of Ken Morgan, for many years stable jockey to Jim Dreaper, Tom had enjoyed a meteoric rise since joining Hughes nearly six years earlier. Although a pony racing champion when still at school, he had ridden only one winner during the three years he had been apprenticed to Michael Kauntze. But it was a different and infinitely more successful story when he switched to National Hunt racing. He won the Supreme Novices Hurdle on the Hughes-trained Miller Hill, on his first ride at the Cheltenham Festival, and he was to go on to even greater glory when he moved to England, where he quickly gained a reputation for being both an outstanding horseman and a really top-flight jockey. In 1988 he won the Queen Mother Champion Chase and on Yahoo the following year he nearly beat Desert Orchid in the Cheltenham Gold Cup.

However, he had a lot of trouble with his weight. It was to soar after it eventually forced him to hang up his boots and it was already a source of dissension at Osborne Lodge. Earlier in 1986 he returned from holiday far heavier than when he left, and too heavy to ride many of the stable's horses. His boss told him to go home and not to come back until he was a lot lighter. When he did return to work, his attendance was not as punctual as an employer has the right to expect. Morgan's behaviour, and his weight problems, were the talk of the yard in Charlie Swan's first few weeks at Osborne Lodge.

> I found Tom in some ways a hard man but in others a nice, genuine person. He enjoyed the game for its own sake, rather than as a means of making money. He certainly did not seem to regard me as any sort of a threat. But why should he? He'd been leading jockey virtually all year and I was only an apprentice. But he was going through a funny stage. The weight problems made him depressed and on occasion he was late for work. I suspect he'd already had an offer to join John Edwards and was making up his mind whether or not to take it.

When the string was forced to pull out without the stable jockey one Monday morning in January 1987, Dessie Hughes decided it was time to teach Tom Morgan a lesson. He took him off the strongly fancied Black Monkey at Navan that afternoon. He replaced him with the ex-Kevin Prendergast apprentice, who had only been with the stable five weeks and who had had only one previous ride for his new yard. But Black Monkey was beaten and, if Morgan felt any remorse, he quickly shrugged it aside to win the main race, the Proudstown Handicap Hurdle, for an outside stable. Swan rode a Hughes no-hoper in the same race and finished down the field.

Relations between Hughes and Morgan deteriorated rapidly from then on and nine days later their six-year partnership came to an acrimonious end. The master of Osborne Lodge informed both Morgan and the press that he was taking him off his three booked rides at Naas that afternoon. He put up Frank Berry on two of them and Charlie Swan on the third. The following day he announced that Swan would get the bulk of the stable's rides in future. Morgan accepted the job with John Edwards and Dessie Hughes set about instilling the art of riding over jumps into his replacement.

> I had a lot to teach him. He hadn't even ridden a winner over fences and in his early chase rides for me, he didn't see a stride like he should. By this I mean he wasn't measuring the strides of his mount as the horse went into a fence, and he didn't know what to do when the horse was meeting a fence wrong. I found from my own experience that the most important thing of the lot over fences is to sit still when this happens. You have to allow the horse to shorten his stride so that he is right, or nearly right, by the time he actually jumps the fence. You sometimes see a jockey praised for his bravery when he gets his horse to take off outside the wings. This is all very well if he is a good jumper and he is meeting the fence right. But far too many jump jockeys seem to kick into every fence. If they do that when the horse is wrong at it, he will put in an extra stride and take it by the roots. You watch the good jockeys on television. You will see how they simply sit still when the horse is wrong. They don't make ground going into a fence like this. But they don't lose all that much – and they don't end up on the floor.

Charlie Swan had been at Osborne Lodge for more than two months before he succeeded in riding a winner for his new boss, and he was promptly given a rollocking!

I thought I'd given Arabian Sands a great ride to win the second division of the mares maiden hurdle at Tipperary that day but Dessie really gave out to me. All the time I was riding on the Flat, I felt people were criticising me for having my leathers too short, so I decided I should take them down a fair bit if I was to succeed over jumps. Dessie, though, used to ride quite short and he thought I looked silly. He didn't hesitate to tell me, and to bring me down to earth with a painful bump.

Two and a half weeks later Charlie had his first taste of the Cheltenham Festival. It was a taste that turned sour. He went to the Mecca of National Hunt racing buoyed up with hope and excitement. He left it in pain, and in an ambulance.

I'd never been there before, not even as a spectator. In fact I hadn't been to England all that much, and The Bean Sidhe at Newbury the previous August was still the only ride I'd had there. I travelled over with my parents, and we stayed with Ranulph and Hope Middleton. They are friends of ours and they have an art gallery in the town. I have stayed with them for every Cheltenham meeting since. The atmosphere at the course was fantastic. The place was packed and the racing was incredibly exciting. But, to be honest, I found it all rather daunting, particularly with the crowds being so big. My only ride was on Irish Dream in the Daily Express Triumph Hurdle. Dessie had a couple of runners but he had made it up with Tom Morgan sufficiently to put him back on them.

Irish Dream was trained by my father and I'd won on her at Thurles three weeks earlier. She was one of the rank outsiders and she was a long way back early on. But we stayed on well after the second last and I felt I was going to finish about fifth or sixth. But, at the last, Nos Na Gaoithe fell some way in front of me. He was just picking himself up when I was jumping the flight. Irish Dream swerved to avoid him and I went the other way. As I was flying through the air, I put out my left arm to try and save myself. As I hit the ground, I felt something snap. I knew immediately that I had broken a bone below my elbow. I'd also hurt my hip but this proved to be only bruising. The first aid people helped me into the ambulance and they said they would drive me to the weighing room where the doctor was based.

The driver cut through the car park and suddenly there was an almighty crash. I was shot forward out of my seat. As I desperately tried to protect my left arm, I saw that we had driven straight into a car. We'd given it a real belt too. The doctor sent me on to Cheltenham General Hospital. After X-rays had been taken, I was told I had to have a plate inserted to help the bone to heal. This meant an operation and I immediately made up my mind to go back to Ireland. I decided to go to Fred Kenny at Navan. He is a brilliant surgeon and almost all the Irish jockeys prefer to be treated by him when they break anything. He understands the sort of injuries you suffer, and what needs to be done to get you back into the saddle in the shortest time possible. The doctor at Cheltenham General agreed to let Fred do the operation but he insisted that I stayed put overnight. He gave me painkillers to deaden the agony in my arm.

Donald Swan, who initially thought the injury was simply a broken collar-bone, wrote off the fall as an occupational hazard. But his wife was horrified. She was also more than a little surprised when her only son handed her a packet of cigarettes, and asked her to stop off in Kildare town on her way from the airport to Modreeny. She was to go to the small supermarket on the Maryville housing estate and give the cigarettes to the dark-haired girl at the check-out desk. Mrs Swan was to tell the girl that Charlie would be in touch as soon as he could.

6

Jumping Lessons

Tina Daly had never met either of her boyfriend's parents when he flew off to Cheltenham for the first time. She had been going out with him for less than five weeks and, until somebody walked into the supermarket a couple of hours after the Triumph Hurdle and told her that Charlie had broken his arm, she had given little thought to the dangers of a jump jockey's life. Indeed, even though her grandfather had been a jockey, she had never been to the races before she started dating Charlie.

Michael Barrett rode for Senator Jim Parkinson, whose powerful Maddenstown Lodge stable was the largest, and one of the most successful, in Ireland in the first thirty years of this century. Michael Barrett had two brothers who were also jockeys, Anthony and Willie. The last-named was the best of the three. He was the leading professional in 1914, he won the following year's Irish Derby and he repeated the feat two years later.

Christina, one of Michael's daughters, married Ben Daly, who served for twenty-five years in the Irish Army, all of them as a private. They brought up ten children at Maryville. Their small house is part of a block of four. It is at the opposite end of the estate from the supermarket where Tina worked for eight years, and is just across the road from the Kildare-Dublin railway line. Tina was the second of their six daughters to be romantically involved with Charlie. For the best part of six months, he went out with the dark-haired Paula, who bears a striking resemblance to her two years older sister. She is slightly lighter in build than Tina but she has similar facial features, and has the same tendency to speak her words quickly. Like Tina, she also confesses to being a nervous sort.

Paula, who did not get married until March 1996 (to one of John Muldoon's stable lads) and now lives on an estate adjoining Maryville, was working on the assembly line at the Oral B toothbrush factory at the time she met Charlie.

> I can't remember exactly where it was we met but it was in Kildare town, probably in one of the pubs. We mainly went to cinemas and pubs. Only now and again did we go to a disco. Charlie is a quiet sort of person, and he didn't like discos much, whereas I loved them and I wanted to go every weekend. I thought he was a nice boy but very soft-hearted.

This particular romance was over when Charlie first invited Tina out but, according to Valerie, who is a year older than Tina, the next one might have started a bit earlier than it did if some of the sisters had not looked so alike.

Valerie, a pretty and lively blonde, is more outgoing than most of the family (Paula: 'We all tend to be rather nervous and to be worriers. Except Valerie, and she's mad!') and she recalls one particular evening in a Kildare disco.

> We would go to the discos in a group, and Charlie would ask nearly all of us to dance in turn. I remember thinking he was terribly nice but I am convinced that he got mixed up. He thought Bernadette was Tina, he went up to her and invited her to join him on the dance floor. I said to Bernadette that she should go out with him. I told her that he had a lovely little car. But she didn't. The one who did was Tina. She went out with other fellows before Charlie, but none of them lasted very long. She used to do a lot of reading and she was always working on a crossword.

The brown-eyed Tina was twenty-two, and slightly more than three years older than Charlie, when she first went out with him. She admits that she fell for him immediately.

> Our first date was on St Valentine's Day in 1987 and he took me to the disco at Mondello. I knew straightaway that this was the man for me. I can't pinpoint exactly why except that he was a real gentleman, and by far the nicest fellow I had ever been out with.

Perhaps Paula read the signs wrongly. Charlie had had no hesitation in going to discos when he wanted to meet girls in Australia. He went to plenty in Kildare for the same reason, and it is significant that the place he chose to take Tina on their first date was also a disco. The lovely little car that so appealed to Valerie was his Fiat Ritmo. It was the best part of two years before he upgraded it to a Mazda, and it was in the Fiat that Charlie took his new girlfriend to Modreeny to meet his parents. Tina might have been excused for being over-awed by the size of the house – huge by comparison with the one at Maryville – but she was struck more by how friendly Donald and Theresa were towards her. They told her she was welcome to go there whenever she wanted, and they promptly showed this was no empty gesture by inviting her for a succession of weekend stays.

However, Charlie could hardly wait to get back to work and to Osborne Lodge. When he did, there were more lessons to be learned. Dessie Hughes would sometimes take a few minutes off when working in the yard to impress upon his new jockey what he should do and, just as important, what he shouldn't. But, more often, he would give Charlie Swan the benefit of his considerable experience when they were driving to the races.

I stressed to him that one of the most important things in a race is to start in the right position, and that means on the inside or as near to it as you can get. If you're on a horse that has to be up there, you line him up at the front. By and large, those in the front rank will be the fastest away. If, on the other hand, you are riding one that has to be waited with, you will obviously start a little bit behind the first few, otherwise he will already be running too freely by the time he gets to the first.

That type of horse apart, though, I told Charlie he should aim to jump the first hurdle in front. He could then tuck into a good position and let those who wanted to go on, do so. The top jump jockeys have always gone round the inside. It's the shortest way and it normally means that they run into the least trouble. You will usually find them about third or fourth, tracking the leaders. If you're on the rails, you can only suffer interference from the one side. Of course, you have to accept the risk of one of those in front falling, but there are only going to be one or two of them, and horses tend to fall away from the rails rather than into them.

I also did my best to ram home the message that he should

endeavour to switch his horse off during the race, and then bring him with a smooth run at the right time. But there must only be one run, and the horse's energy must be conserved for it. You will often see jockeys driving their mounts to get to the front, and then asking them to race all over again in order to try and win. This is no good. You can't ask a horse to win more than once in the same race.

In addition, I talked to him about how to make ground at the fences, as opposed to simply seeing a stride and putting a horse right when he is meeting it wrong. I found that, when a horse is meeting his fences well, you can gain a length at each of them by giving him a kick as he is going into the obstacle. In the course of a race, that can add up to a fair amount of ground.

You then get to the second last and you're in with a chance. The horse is meeting it wrong, or at least he is not meeting it spot-on. It's no good simply sitting still now. You've got to go for it, and that means getting him to throw a big one. It's what I call all duck or no dinner!

But my lessons were about race-riding. I can't claim to have spent hours on the schooling ground teaching him how to get it right. He had to learn that himself. My priority in schooling sessions was always the horse, never the jockey. However, he was extremely conscientious and he kept learning, often from his own mistakes.

Charlie Swan finished up his first year as a jump jockey with twenty-six winners. He also had four on the Flat but they did not count in the total that put him into fifth place in the jump jockeys' table. Frank Berry, champion for the tenth time, rode just over twice as many and the tenth in the table was separated from Swan by just two winners. In short, it was a middle-of-the-road performance from a jockey who seemed surprisingly content to remain at that level.

I know it's meant to be every jockey's ambition to be champion but I hardly gave it a thought. Frankly, I didn't think I could reach the top and, if I had stayed on about the same level as I was that first year, I would have been satisfied. I was trying to improve myself, trying to be successful and trying to ride as many winners as I could, but my main aim was simply to make the grade.

He was still in single figures in 1988 when his hopes for a better score suffered a painful setback at Gowran Park on 1 May.

> I rode Saracen for my father in a two mile handicap hurdle, and I thought I had a good chance of winning. The horse started second favourite and, as we went into the final turn, I was travelling really well on the inner just behind the leaders. I'd ridden just the sort of race that Dessie Hughes had taught me to ride, and I was waiting until we got into the straight before I started to make my move. But suddenly a horse on my outside came in on me. It wasn't much but it was enough to force Saracen's front hooves onto the heels of the horse in front. He dropped like a stone and I was badly kicked as Lornaaron was brought down. Peter Kavanagh, who rode her, was injured far worse than I was. His jaw was badly broken. I was kicked on my forehead – I still have a scar from the gash – and I broke my right arm. We were both taken by ambulance to Kilkenny Hospital, but Peter was in such a bad way that he had to be transferred to St James's Hospital in Dublin the following day. I was attended to by a doctor who got his right and left mixed up. When I was taken into the X-ray area, with my right arm in a sling, the nurses told me that they had been instructed to X-ray the other arm!

Charlie Swan was out of action for ten weeks and it was August before he returned to the winner's enclosure. At this stage the vast majority of his jumping winners were over the minor obstacles and he found that he had earned a reputation he did not want.

> People kept saying that I was not as good over fences as I was over hurdles. I suspect they were talking through their pockets because I sometimes hear this said even today. Certainly it took me a while to get used to riding over fences. There is quite a difference. Apart from the actual obstacles, you really have to concentrate on getting the stride right going into a fence, and you have to learn to sit a bit further back when you land. But by this stage I was just as happy during a chase as I was during a hurdle race. The one that seemed to get me going over fences, at least in the eyes of those trainers who might have been a bit wary of putting me up in a chase, was a mare called Bean Alainn who won the Troytown Chase at Navan in November. In those days the Troytown was still quite an important race, and it was my

> biggest success over fences. Mind you, I had a few awkward
> moments as we turned towards the second last in the lead. The
> ambulance was too close to the course, and the mare saw it. She
> cocked her jaw and tried to run out.

However, at Naas at the end of that month, Charlie Swan found himself in big trouble with the stewards for taking too much notice of some uncalled-for advice from one of the other jockeys. He had led from the start on Lucky Baloo and he felt he was going to stay in front when Tommy Carmody, a supremely talented rider who had for three years been first jockey to the powerful Dickinson stable and who was heading for his second Irish title, challenged Swan on his inner. There is an unwritten law among jump jockeys that you do not try to go up somebody's inside. If you do, he is entitled to slam the door in your face. This is a dangerous manoeuvre – the challenger has been known to end up in hospital – and the stewards stamp down hard on offenders. But it is the punishment that may be dished out by the leader which is the one feared most. However, Carmody, up against an inexperienced opponent, reckoned he could get away with it. Tony Mullins, on Derrymore Boy, was incensed to see Carmody taking such liberties – primarily because he himself was travelling strongly and had a big chance of winning.

> Tony shouted at me to close the gate and, being a bit green, I
> did so. Tommy was forced to snatch up as I moved my mount
> over towards the rails, squeezing him out. He finished eight
> lengths back third, and I held on to beat Derrymore Boy by a
> head. The stewards had me in, told me what they thought of
> my riding and awarded the race to Tony Mullins. What was
> worse, they banned me for seven days, which meant I couldn't
> ride Lucky Baloo in the Mercury Communications Hurdle at
> Cheltenham.

Donald Swan lodged an appeal against the disqualification of Lucky Baloo and the suspension imposed on his son. He was privately hoping that the hearing would be deferred until after the Cheltenham race. This would mean that the suspension, due to start the day before it, would not begin until after the senior stewards had ruled on the appeal. The stewards of the Irish National Hunt Steeplechase Committee initially dashed his hopes by deciding to stage the hearing five days before Cheltenham. But they then raised them sky-high with an incredible display of bias that, had it happened today, would have brought them columns of condemnation on the racing pages. They dismissed the appeal so far as it concerned Lucky Baloo – she was to remain disqualified – but they reduced her rider's ban to five days, stating that this was because he had a good record. Amazingly, though, they said that the ban would not start until the Monday after the Cheltenham race!

Charlie Swan picked up rides in two of the other races on the day of the Mercury Communications Hurdle, St Coleman's Well for John Crowley in the A.F. Budge Novices Hurdle and Condor Pan in the Charles Heidsieck Champagne Bula Hurdle. His lucky streak ran out with St Coleman's Well – the 20-1 chance finished down the field – and Lucky Baloo belied her name by managing only fifth. Condor Pan, though, despite not having raced for over fifteen months, ran out a convincing winner.

> This was the first winner I'd ridden for Jim Bolger and it was the most valuable jump race I had ever won. The fact that it was at Cheltenham was another plus, and I regarded it as an important break. I am sure it helped to get me noticed by trainers in England and to get me more rides in Ireland. The Saracen injury had cost me a lot. When you're out of action for a long time like that, other jockeys take over your mounts. By the end of the year my Irish jumps total was three less than it had been in 1987, and I dropped to ninth in the table.

The Grand National meeting the following April brought Charlie Swan more recognition. It also brought him a major disappointment. On the eve of the big race, he rode Boreen Belle in the White Satin Novices Hurdle. He had already won two good races that year on Bill Harney's mare, and she scored in good style from a high class field that included future Grand National winner Royal Athlete and Cahervillahow who, although Swan had no inkling of it at the time, was to play a major role in his progress up the ladder.

Harney, a vet based at Templemore in County Tipperary, also trained Monanore who had finished third in the previous year's Grand National and who was to try again the following day. He had booked Graham McCourt but the horse had only 10st 3lb, and Harney was concerned about the amount of overweight McCourt had told him he might have to put up.

Bill said that, if Graham was 3lb or more too heavy, he would take him off the horse and give me the mount. It had been one of my ambitions to ride in the National ever since I started winning pony races, and I'd taped every running since Ben Nevis won when I was twelve. I set off round the course on foot. I looked closely at every fence and tried to work out how I would jump each of the famous ones. That night I prayed that Graham McCourt wouldn't be able to do the weight. When I got to the course the next morning, I tried to find out how much he had sweated off. But, before I did, I met Bill Harney. He told me Graham looked like getting near enough and he felt it would be wrong to replace him at this stage. I was very disappointed. In a way, I had reason to be. Graham rode at 10st 6lb.

One of those who took note of the way Swan rode Boreen Belle was Nicky Henderson, who trained a powerful seventy-strong team of jumpers at Lambourn. Henderson, thirty-eight at the time, was the Eton-educated son of a wealthy stockbroker who lived near Newbury. Johnny Henderson was keen that the boy should join the family's firm in the City, but Nicky hated it, even though he came to an arrangement with a street-corner newspaper seller to wrap up *The Sporting Life* inside his copy of the *Financial Times*! He had already started riding as an amateur – he was to ride seventy-five winners, including the 1977 Imperial Cup Handicap Hurdle on Acquaint and that year's Aintree Foxhunters Chase on Happy Warrior – and he turned his back on stockbroking to become assistant to Fred Winter.

He set up on his own in 1978, shortly after marrying Diana Thorne whose father, John, went so close to winning the 1981 Grand National on Spartan Missile. Nicky Henderson is a cheerful, likeable character who frequently confesses to being a dreadful worrier. But training is a worrying, stressful occupation with constant in-built tensions created by the proneness to injury of racehorses whose legs – because of generations of in-breeding – are not strong enough for their heavy frames. The stress is aggravated by the fact that owners invariably have higher expectations than is merited by the ability of their horses. As a result, almost all trainers are worriers. The difference with Henderson is that he constantly admits to it. The fact that he gets it off his chest probably has a lot to do with his cheerful disposition.

Nicky Henderson was due to visit Ireland in May 1989 to look at a number of prospective purchases with Johnny Harrington of the Curragh Bloodstock Agency. Before he left Lambourn, he spoke to the

CBA man about Charlie Swan. Harrington was bullish about both the young jockey's ability and his potential. He agreed to contact him and set up a meeting. Henderson recalls:

> Johnny told me that Charlie was a rising star, and the three of us met in the Keadeen Hotel at the Newbridge end of the Curragh. My idea was to get Charlie to come to me initially for a year because I believe it takes a jockey new to the country that long to get to know all the courses. I already had John White, who was a super back-up to Richard Dunwoody. But I wasn't sure what Richard was going to do. He was also stable jockey to David Nicholson. But I was in no position to offer Charlie a first jockey job at that stage.

Few Irish jump jockeys say no when they are given the chance of a job in Britain. There is far more racing there, and far more opportunities than in Ireland, where all bar the top half-dozen struggle to make a worthwhile living. Nicky Henderson's was a top stable, and most would have regarded the chance to even get a toe in the door as the opportunity of a lifetime. Charlie Swan was not in that first half-dozen but he was far from enthusiastic about Henderson's offer, and a few days later he telephoned him to say he was turning it down.

> Richard Dunwoody seemed to have the pick of the rides. John White was well established there and so I would have had to take my place in the queue. I wasn't at all sure how things would work out for me in such circumstances.

Four weeks later he went to the Derby Sale at Fairyhouse. This two-day affair is the most important sale of prospective jumpers in either Britain or Ireland. Swan was neither buying nor selling. He was there purely to have a look, and to enjoy the social occasion. Among the trainers he bumped into was Mouse Morris. The County Tipperary trainer took him to one side and quietly asked him if he would like to become his stable jockey. There was no lack of enthusiasm this time.

> I had ridden for him very little but he had some good horses, real chasing types like Lastofthebrownies who had finished fourth in that year's Grand National, while Trapper John had been second in the Sun Alliance Hurdle. Mouse mentioned the possibility of a

retainer, although it never actually materialised in my first season with him. He also told me that I would ride everything except Lastofthebrownies, who was to remain Tommy Carmody's ride, and Granville Hotel, who was regarded as Conor O'Dwyer's mount. I was a bit sorry about Lastofthebrownies but not about the other one. He was a horrible ride.

The Honourable Michael Morris is a son of Lord Killanin, the former Olympic Games supremo who was also a steward of the Turf Club and the author of what is widely known as the Killanin Report. This was published in 1986 and was a report produced by a Government-appointed commission on the Irish racing industry. Killanin was the chairman of the commission and its well-researched analysis is widely regarded as a benchmark in the evolution of racing in Ireland. Its recommendations were seen as a blueprint for the future.

Killanin sent Michael to Ampleforth, the famous Catholic public school in Yorkshire, but the boy was more of a rebel than an aristocrat, and at the tender age of fifteen he dug in his toes. He insisted that he hated the school and, in any case, he was no good at the lessons. His father engaged a private tutor but, a year later, he gave in to the boy's wish to be sent to the only school he regarded as of any use, the celebrated apprentice academy run by Frenchie Nicholson. He spent two and a half years with the former jockey-turned-trainer at Cheltenham – Pat Eddery and Tony Murray were apprenticed to Nicholson at the time, and Michael Dickinson was also learning the ropes in the small stable. Nicholson then arranged for Morris to return to Ireland to Willie O'Grady. When the Ballynonty trainer died in January 1972 his son, Edward, took over. Morris stayed on and Timmy Jones, the stable amateur, began to refer to the then twenty-year-old firstly as Mickey, then as Mickey Mouse and eventually as Mouse. The nickname quickly caught on with the other lads. It's a long time since anyone outside his immediate family circle has referred to him as anything else.

Morris turned professional after winning the 1974 National Hunt Chase on O'Grady's Mr Midland. Two years later he won the Queen Mother Champion Chase on Skymas. He repeated the performance on the same horse the following season and promptly won the Irish Grand National on Billycan. A succession of accidents then transformed a rising star into a candidate for the racing scrapheap. He broke his leg riding in the Colonial Cup in America. He was out of action for almost a year. When he returned, he broke his hip. No sooner was he back in the saddle than he broke his arm. Three separate falls each fractured collar-bones. Morris also broke his nose. As soon as it was mended, he had another fall – this time out hunting – and broke it again. By this stage owners and trainers regarded him as yesterday's man and, with no other prospect of making a living, he started training at the farmhouse he had bought at Everardsgrange near Fethard. The luck which had forsaken him as a jockey returned with a vengeance. Within three years he had sent out a Cheltenham winner – Buck House in the Supreme Novices Hurdle – and that horse went on to win the 1986 Queen Mother Champion Chase.

Tommy Carmody rode Buck House in both those races, and indeed he had been riding the bulk of Morris's runners. However, he was becoming increasingly required by John Mulhern for his horses and Morris disliked being relegated to the role of second fiddle: 'Tommy was a serious jockey, but the way I looked at it was that you were either part of the team or you were not. If you were, you should ride the lot and I'd had my eye on Charlie for some time.'

Swan immediately went to see Dessie Hughes, not to tell him he was leaving but to try to come to some sort of an arrangement with him. Charlie wanted to have his cake and eat it. What is more, he succeeded – as he was to again several seasons later when he managed to get himself into the enviable position of being able to pick and choose his mounts from the bulk of the country's jumpers. He proposed, and Hughes agreed, that he would continue to ride out for the Osborne Lodge stable, and that he would ride the horses in their races when not required by Morris. Hughes was not surprised to see the jockey he had taught so much move on to better things.

> Mouse Morris had a good string and he seemed to be on the upgrade, whereas I was going downhill. I had plenty of ordinary horses but no real big name ones. Charlie had improved a fair bit since he joined me two and a half years earlier. He was totally dedicated to race-riding. All the time he wanted to learn, and to improve his jockeyship.
>
> When he started with me at the end of 1986, he had been much the same as any other jockey at a similar stage in his career, except for two things. The first was all the riding he'd done on the Flat. This meant that his mounts would want for nothing after jumping the last. The second plus was that he was light enough to ride the bottom weights, and this gave him more opportunities than most young jockeys get.

But Hughes admits to a fair degree of amazement at Swan's later progress.

> At no point in the time he spent with me did I think he was a future champion, or that he was going to be anywhere near as good as he has become. He has never minded work – if somebody asked him to get up at 5.00 a.m. to school a horse, he would be quite happy to do so – and he has remained the same polite, unassuming, almost-shy person he has always been. But to begin with, he was no better than any up-and-coming young rider. He was no better in his two subsequent seasons either. Frankly, I never thought he was that special – or likely to be.

7

Champion

Charlie Swan's number one priority was to get on with his new boss. Mouse Morris is not the easiest person to talk to. He is a man of few words and he does not make much noticeable effort to put others at their ease.

> I found him quiet, but laid back and easy going. People who don't know Mouse that well will say he is a bit funny and that he can be abrupt. But I discovered that this is just the way he carries on. When you get to know him, he is not at all abrupt and, underneath that difficult exterior, he is quite soft.
>
> I was a bit surprised to find that he only wanted me to go down to Everardsgrange to ride out, or ride schooling, about once a fortnight. I discovered later that a number of trainers adopt this approach with their stable jockeys. I suspect they don't want the jockey to find out too much about some of the horses, particularly the bad ones; otherwise he will want to get off them to ride somebody else's! It suited me because I was able to ride out for Dessie Hughes, and make sure I kept his rides in the process, and it also gave me time to ride schooling for other trainers who might give me mounts.

On 7 November 1989 Charlie and Tina were married in St Brigid's Church in Kildare despite some opposition from Donald Swan – 'I was twenty-five when I married Theresa and my father said I was too young. Charlie was only twenty-one and I felt that this was far too early in life to make such a commitment.'

James Collins, who was with Dessie Hughes and was riding the stable's runners when Swan was claimed by Morris, acted as best man in conjuction with Pat Healy. The latter, a racecourse photographer, did not share Donald Swan's reservations.

> Tina is shy, quiet and nervous but she was good for Charlie. He would never have had the success he has if it hadn't been for her. Indeed it was lucky for him that he was going out with her when he was. If he hadn't been attached to her like that, he would have done the same as most other young men of that age – gone out drinking and chasing girls night after night. Instead, he had few late nights and was able to concentrate on his riding.

There was no honeymoon, and the young couple moved into a semi-detached house in Beechgrove in Kildare town. When Kieren Fallon decided to leave the flat over the butcher's shop early in 1988, and go to Yorkshire to try his luck with Jimmy Fitzgerald, Charlie had moved to Beechgrove to share a house with James Collins and Paul Coyle who also rode for Dessie Hughes, but on the Flat. Swan had bought his own house in the same road ten months before his marriage.

In June 1989 the Irish jumps season was changed from a calendar year basis to bring it almost into line with the one in Britain which begins and ends in early summer. Charlie Swan had twenty-five winners on the board by the time of his marriage and he was heading the table for the first time in his career. Four days after the wedding, he and Bean Alainn won the Troytown for the second successive year. When the Cheltenham Festival came round the following March, he had ridden fifty-two. Just as importantly he had, for the first time, a mount at the meeting which he knew had a winning chance. The horse was Trapper John, owned by Jill Fanning, the daughter of Mrs Miles Valentine of Pennsylvania and a trainer of note in America. Her big race triumphs have included no less than four winners of the Maryland Hunt Cup, which has long been one of America's most sought-after jump races.

Trapper John had been slammed twelve lengths by Mrs Muck when he was sent to Haydock for the Premier Long Distance Hurdle in January 1990 but he subsequently handed out a similar beating to Galmoy in the Boyne Hurdle at Navan. This race, then run over two and three-quarter miles, is a recognised trial for the Stayers' Hurdle and Galmoy had won Cheltenham's famous test of stamina in both 1987 and 1988. He was the only Irish horse to win at the Festival in either of those two years and in 1989 the huge Irish contingent, invariably noisy and enthusiastic, had returned home dispirited without a single winner to call their own.

Mouse Morris reckoned that in Trapper John he had what it would take to rekindle Irish spirits, but first he had to educate his jockey into how he believed Cheltenham should be ridden. The education was done in private, firstly in discussions in Ireland and then when the pair walked the course on their own on the morning of the race.

> I never had to teach Charlie much about race-riding. When he came to me he was pretty experienced, although I felt he was much better over hurdles than he was over fences. However, he had done a lot of hunting when he was younger and that made him a natural as regards schooling horses. Cheltenham, though, is a law unto itself. There are certain parts of the course where I like to see a horse make ground, and other parts where he must not be asked to do so. By following this method, I have succeeded in getting several relatively moderate horses to do well.

Morris was reluctant to expand on this when I interviewed him – 'I don't want to give my secrets away to everybody else' – but he had no such reservations as he took his stable jockey round the course. Charlie Swan recalls what he was told as if it happened yesterday.

> Cheltenham, as I had already found out, is a hard course to ride, particularly when there are big fields. People often seem to think that it is a galloping track. But it's not. It's quite tight and you need plenty of luck if you are to get a clear run. Races like the Triumph Hurdle and the County Hurdle can turn into nightmares. You are on the turn most of the way – down the back straight it seems as if you are always on a slight curve – and the hills make it even tighter.
>
> What Mouse impressed on me most was that I should not go down the inside. If I did, I would be pushed about and I would run the risk of being knocked back. You can get away with going down the inner on this course if you are on a horse that can lie handy just behind the leaders. But, if you are going to be any further back, you must be towards the outer. You will lose ground at the turns but nothing like as much as you would if you were interfered with, as you surely would be on the

inside or in the middle of the field. I found that the only other time you can afford to go round the rails was if you are plumb last. Then you will often get a clear run and, if horses in front of you get knocked back, you have time to pick a path round them. Mouse also told me that, as I passed the stands, I should move in a bit to avoid losing too much ground at the next turn. I was also to make sure I gave the horse a clear view of the hurdles as we swept down the hill towards the straight.

I was a bit conscious that people watching on television would be criticising me for going wide in that 1990 Stayers' Hurdle, but I found that following Mouse's instructions, and keeping Trapper John towards the outside of the field, paid off. He was not one of the best jumpers, and it had taken him a long time to get the hang of jumping hurdles, but he was a really tough, genuine horse. Richard Dunwoody, who had made the early running on Bluff Cove, went on again at the third last. But I caught and passed him after jumping the final flight. Tom Taaffe on Naevog promptly came at us, but Trapper John galloped all the way to the line. When I pulled him up, though, he was lame and I had to lead him back to the winner's enclosure. I was a bit upset about this. Ever since I had first ridden at the Festival on Irish Dream three years earlier, I had thought about how I might one day ride into the winner's enclosure in triumph. I knew it would be one of the most exciting and satisfying feelings in the world. And there I was returning on foot. I had other problems too. People were grabbing at me in their excitement. Don't forget, there hadn't been an Irish winner at the meeting for two years. I was worried that somebody would take the saddle off me, or part of it, and I would be disqualified. After what seemed like an age, I made it into the winner's enclosure. The tears were pouring down Mouse's face.

After I had weighed in – thankfully nothing was missing – I was told that the stewards wanted me. They said I was guilty of excessive use of the whip, and that they were suspending me for two days. But I was too thrilled to give a damn. I'd ridden a Cheltenham winner. That was all that mattered.

Just over three weeks later Trapper John was sent to Aintree for the Oddbins Handicap Hurdle but he had top weight and was beaten half a length. Again Charlie Swan was called before the stewards, and they suspended him for another two days. But this time the jockey did care.

I was annoyed. Trapper John needed plenty of driving and I'd taken the trouble to use a padded whip so that I wouldn't either hurt him or mark him. The stewards said I had hit him too many times after the last. I can remember replying that, if they had moved the hurdle a bit nearer the winning post, there wouldn't have been any need to suspend me. Normally the stewards are deadly serious, and the chairman of the acting stewards reads out the sentence as if he is pronouncing the death penalty. But this time they laughed. The suspension, however, still stood. I thought it was most unfair.

He didn't reflect on it all that long, though. What occupied his mind was his first ride in the Grand National two days later. Again Mouse Morris walked the course with him on the morning of the race.

He was laughing and joking most of the way round and so, unlike Cheltenham, it wasn't a serious lesson in how the course should be ridden. But he did stress that I should jump off with the leaders and then simply hunt round until after I jumped the water at the end of the first circuit. Then I was to try to get into it. In other words, I was to ride a traditional Grand National race.

Lastofthebrownies had finished fourth the previous year when the ground had been really testing. This time it was fast which I knew wouldn't suit him, but it was great to be on a horse with a chance in my first National. I had terrible butterflies in my stomach before we went out into the paddock. I was excited but I was affected by nerves too. I felt even worse in the parade – it seemed to take an awful long time – although I was sure I would feel better once we turned to canter down to the start. But, when we rounded the turn and went on to the first fence to have a look at it, Lastofthebrownies tried to take off with me. He had always been a bit of a runaway at home, and I had a terrible job trying to get him under control. I had visions of him carting me over the first few fences and me looking a complete idiot on television all round the world. I stood up in the irons and gave him a real yank as he careered towards the first fence. We were pretty close to it by this time and, just as I was convinced he was going to jump it, he got the message and slowed up.

I cantered him slowly back, breathing several sighs of relief. But, as I circled round with all the others, the nerves came flooding back. I could tell a lot of the jockeys were in the same boat. Several of them were trying to crack jokes. Others were very obviously attempting to put a brave face on the whole thing. Then we were called in. I got my horse into a good position, and I thought it would be a go. But the starter shouted at us to get back off the tape. I had to turn and come in again. Eventually we were off. Although Mouse had told me to hunt, I found I had to start pushing very early on. I was much too far behind the leaders, basically because both the ground and the pace were too fast for Lastofthebrownies. From then on I was flat to the boards and, even though he hardly made a mistake, I never got into the race. We began to pass a few horses after jumping the one after Becher's second time round – the one they call the Foinavon fence – but the leaders were miles ahead of me. We kept on to finish fifth, but Mr Frisk was almost out of sight. Still, it was a big thrill. And it was every bit as exciting as I had imagined it would be.

At Cheltenham, Charlie Swan had also been engaged by Jim Bolger for Vestris Abu in the Daily Express Triumph Hurdle. Bolger, for whom Swan had won the Bula Hurdle on Condor Pan fifteen months earlier, had few National Hunt runners but he had established himself as one of the dominant forces among the Irish Flat trainers. One of eight children of a County Wexford farmer, Bolger was an accountant for a Ford dealer in Dublin when he took out a permit to train in 1975. The following year, at the age of thirty-four, he left his job to start training full-time. In 1982 he bought Glebe House and its 180 surrounding acres at Coolcullen, a tiny and remote village in the hills of County Carlow. There he built some of the most effective gallops racing has ever known. The main section is a mile long and rises 150 feet. Up until this it was rare for trainers to prepare their horses up such a searching climb but Bolger is no respecter of tradition, and he had worked out that this was the best way to get his horses fit. He has enjoyed phenomenal success.

Bolger is also no respecter of tradition when it comes to the way racing is run and for a long time he was one of the Turf Club's biggest critics. He also has a reputation for working his staff hard. He certainly does not spare himself and he seldom takes a holiday. Charlie Swan admired Bolger's professionalism but he was not quite sure what to make of the man. He had heard stories from fellow jockeys that Bolger could be difficult to ride for, and highly critical if things went wrong.

Jim can be strange enough at times but I found that I got on well with him. I built up a good strike rate on his horses and I never had reason for any complaints about him. Furthermore his horses invariably ran well, and Vestris Abu gave me a tremendous ride in the Triumph. I was well up there the whole way and I hit the front approaching the last which was probably a bit too soon. Vestris Abu dived at it and nearly came down. I was pitched on to his neck and almost came off. Brendan Sheridan was virtually upsides me at the final flight on Rare Holiday. His mount interfered with me on the run-in and, although it wasn't that much, the stewards called an inquiry. Vestris Abu would not have won even with a clear run and I was able to help Brendan by telling the stewards that the interference was minimal. I didn't do that solely out of friendship. I would have done it for any fellow Irishman.

Vestris Abu was one of Swan's four winners at the big Punchestown meeting the following month, but his seemingly relentless progress towards his first championship suffered a setback when he was given a four-day suspension after winning a chase on Forgestown for Paddy Mullins at Roscommon in May.

I made all the running and at the second last my horse jumped a bit to the left. Mickey Flynn on American Lady tried to poke his way up my inside. There was no running rail at this point but, even so, he was taking a liberty. I promptly moved back onto my original line. I maintain that, when you are making the running, you are entitled to move back in such circumstances, and I told the stewards this in the inquiry. They said they didn't agree and they informed me I was guilty of improper riding.

Swan lodged an appeal, primarily to see if he could get the sentence reduced. The last of the four days coincided with the Prix La Barka at Auteuil, and he had been approached by Arthur Moore to ride Joyful Noise in the French race. Once again the Irish stewards were in an amazingly benevolent, and co-operative, frame of mind. They reduced the suspension to three days! Charlie Swan, though, found jump racing in France very different to what he had been used to.

I'd had only one previous ride in France, at Longchamp in October 1986 on The Bean Sidhe who finished last in the Group

One Prix de la Foret. Arthur Moore had never had a runner in France before but I think he had a better idea than I did of what to expect. The crowd was huge and the actual hurdles were different, and I had problems down at the start. The starter said everything in French which was, I suppose, understandable because the other jockeys were French but I found it very hard to make out what he was saying. All the French I had learned at school, or rather tried to learn, wasn't much help. But Joyful Noise finished second and the following month we went back for the Champion Hurdle, the Grande Course de Haies. The distance, though, was an extended three miles and the horse didn't get the trip.

By this time Charlie Swan had already been crowned champion with seventy-three winners. This was the highest total achieved by a jump jockey in Ireland since the legendary Martin Molony had become champion for the fifth successive time with ninety-two winners forty years earlier.

We had great celebrations at the party my parents held at Modreeny and several people were thrown into the swimming pool! Privately, I was extremely happy to be champion – every jockey wants that – but I didn't really feel that I had reached the top. Nor did I feel that I was going to go on being champion in the seasons to come. I said to myself that I was simply going to keep trying to ride as many winners as I could. My real aim was to win one or two of the big races.

He had only five winners under his belt in the new season when disaster struck on the fourth day of the Galway festival at the beginning of August.

I was riding Chamois Boy for Arthur Moore in a three mile hurdle race. He had ten stone and I'd deliberately gone easy on the liquid to make sure I did the weight on a comfortable saddle. He fell at the fourth and, somehow, in the course of the fall, his hoof came down hard on my right arm between the elbow and the wrist. It took about ten seconds for the pain to register. When it did, it was horrific. I managed to stagger to my feet clutching my arm. When I looked at it, it was frightening. The bone had broken in two. All that was holding it together was the skin. My wrist was dangling like a horse with a broken leg. It was a sickening sight.

When they put me into the ambulance, they placed my arm on a special cast which they blew up like an inflatable pillow. Even so, they had to lift the arm to get it onto the pillow. It hurt like hell until the painkillers they gave me began to take effect. Once the pain was reduced to bearable proportions, I tried to flex my fingers. I found I was able to move them. Maybe the damage wasn't quite as bad as it seemed. I hoped, desperately, that it wasn't. It sounds ridiculous to say this now, but what started to go through my mind was how I was going to persuade the racecourse doctor to let me ride The Musical Priest in the next. He was sure to be odds-on and I knew he was a certainty.

But the doctor sent me straight to Galway Hospital. By the time I got there, I felt I was dying of thirst. I pleaded with the staff to give me a drink. They said no. They were going to have to operate. But they must have seen how desperate I looked because they said they would put me on a drip and give me liquid that way. I couldn't see what good that was going to do. It was in my throat that I needed it.

Amazingly, though, the thirst began to ease almost as soon as the liquid started to flow into my veins. There was a particularly nice nurse who was looking after me and, when she had put in the drip, she said she would give me an injection to take away the pain, which was starting to come back. Within minutes, I was as high as a kite! But I wasn't happy about the operation being done there. I wanted Fred Kenny to do it. I'd seen him at the races earlier in the week and he'd said he was on holiday. Then Brendan Sheridan came in to see me. We managed to contact Fred on his mobile, and he said he would go back to Navan that night and do the operation there. Could I get somebody to drive me to Navan? It was the other side of the country but Brendan volunteered. We stopped in Kildare on the way to tell Tina what was happening. Naturally she was upset, but particularly so this time because the broken arm meant that our plans were thrown into total confusion. I'd been picked for the Irish jump jockeys' team which was to fly out to Australia only three days later. Tina had stayed in Kildare, rather than go racing, so that she could buy clothes and suitcases for the trip. We reached Navan at midnight. Fred put two plates into the arm and I had to stay in Navan Hospital the following night as well. It was ten weeks before the break had healed well enough for the plaster to be taken off. A year later one of the plates was removed. It had begun to move and Fred decided that the wisest course of action was to take it out. The other was to stay put for nearly six years.

Charlie Swan's long spell on the sidelines was viewed with mixed feelings at Everardsgrange where the trainer was no stranger to broken bones, and their consequences.

I was sorry to see him breaking his arm, and breaking it so badly, particularly so soon after he had become champion. We'd had a very good first season together and, although he won the title through his own efforts, his association with me had certainly not done him any harm. The opposite in fact. But most of my horses don't normally reappear until November, so the fact that Charlie was not there to ride them didn't put me out all that much.

One of Mouse Morris's main hopes was a six-year-old named Cahervillahow by his owner, Mrs Miles Valentine, after the house she owned in County Tipperary. This elderly lady – she was born in 1904 – has been an ardent supporter of National Hunt racing for most of her life, and she revealed much about her considerable sense of humour when choosing for her racing colours cerise hearts on a pink background. But they did not bring Cahervillahow much luck. He confirmed his considerable early promise by winning the valuable Black and White Whisky Champion Chase at the 1990 Leopardstown Christmas meeting, but that was one of the last things to go right for this unfortunate horse. Morris decided to aim him at the Cheltenham Gold Cup but, when he went on trial for it in the Hennessy Cognac Irish Gold Cup, he fell. Even worse was to follow. At the first forfeit stage for the big Cheltenham race, he was scratched as a result of a clerical error by one of Morris's staff. The trainer appealed directly to the Jockey Club for the horse to be reinstated, but they turned him down. Morris, whose hopes of receiving a reprieve in Portman Square were never all that high, decided to run him in the Ritz Club National Hunt Handicap Chase, a valuable race run immediately after the Gold Cup. But disaster struck again, and Charlie Swan was left feeling thankful he did not get the blame.

Cahervillahow had long been a bit kinky at home, and he used to have a pony in his stable to keep him company. It was the same pony who had shared Buck House's stable. At Cheltenham we were called into line but, just as the starter shouted go and released the tape, Cahervillahow whipped round. I got him going as quickly as I could but we lost a good fifteen lengths. He had 11st 10lb, so he didn't have much chance of making up the leeway. We were beaten five lengths by Seagram. It was a fair performance considering we were giving him virtually a stone and that next time out he won the Grand National. But, of course, nobody knew that was going to happen, and I came in expecting to get a lot of flak for losing so much ground at the start. Not from Mouse – he knew that the horse was quite capable of doing something like that – but from those who had backed him, and in the papers the next day.

But I was lucky. Just when we were being called in, the television coverage was switched over for a news flash. The Birmingham Six had just been released and by the time the programme went back to Cheltenham the race was almost over. I was as relieved as the Birmingham Six!

Victory in the Jameson Irish Grand National would have been fitting compensation for the Ritz defeat, and for the disastrous blunder that had ruled the horse out of the Cheltenham Gold Cup. But the fates had it in for Cahervillahow. He was beaten a short head by Omerta, ridden by a certain Mr A. Maguire. At that stage Adrian Maguire was only nineteen and claiming 5lb. Because of the value of the Irish National, he was unable to use his allowance, but he had already been a star on the pony racing circuit and then in point-to-points. He had an ice-cool temperament and a brilliant tactical brain. His biggest worry had come the previous week when he had spent three days in traction in hospital – following a point-to-point fall – and he feared he might lose the ride.

Cahervillahow, though, had revealed to his rider at Fairyhouse what was to prove an ominous portent of worse to come – and for once this was not directly related to bad luck.

Adrian took it up a long way out in the Irish National and he was in front from the sixth last. I knew he was the one to beat so I never let him out of my sights. At the second last, he was the only one in front of me. But Cahervillahow then started to hang to the right and, as a result, I had to switch him to the inside of Omerta at the final fence when I was only a length behind. If he hadn't hung so badly, we would have won.

Mouse Morris sent him to Sandown for the Whitbread Gold Cup. He made a couple of mistakes, including one at the third last, but he jumped pretty well and he really responded when I asked him to quicken rounding the final turn. At the last, I was fractionally in front of Docklands Express, ridden by Anthony Tory. I knew he was my only danger. We had already passed Seagram, who was having his first race since winning the Grand National. I had to keep after Cahervillahow but he kept responding, and we succeeded in holding off Docklands Express all the way to the line. But my horse was hanging to the right again. It wasn't much and, although I possibly did interfere a little with Anthony Tory's mount, I was quite sure it was not enough for the placings to be affected. Indeed, I eased Cahervillahow going to the line when I knew we had the race won. The official margin was three-quarters of a length. It would have been nearer twice that if I had kept riding to the line. And, if I'd felt there was the slightest doubt, I would have done so. The further you win, the less likely you are to have the race taken off you.

Normally if you have interfered with somebody, you hear plenty about it from the jockey concerned when you pull up. Significantly, Anthony Tory said nothing at all to me about any interference. Then I heard the announcement of a stewards' inquiry, but it was quite a time after we had pulled up. If it had really been anything to worry about, they would have announced it a lot quicker. Or so I thought.

I still wasn't worried when I was told that Anthony had lodged an objection. In England, jockeys have a tendency to object. It's as if they are trying to get things going, and make the whole thing more dramatic. It was only when the actual inquiry started that I realised I was in trouble.

I got the impression, before the stewards even asked me to explain what had happened, that they had made up their minds – and that they were going to take the race off me. I explained, carefully, that I had gone over a bit onto Docklands Express between the last fence and the winning post, but there was no way that I had caused the second horse interference of any significance. I also explained that the interference, such as it was, could not have affected the placings. The film showed that Anthony never stopped riding on Docklands Express. I pointed this out and that we had beaten him fair and square. We would have beaten him by just as far even if Cahervillahow had not hung in. But the stewards didn't want to know.

The way they directed their questions at me conveyed all too clearly that they were gunning for me. This was the only chase of the day and they treated the way Cahervillahow had been hanging as if he had come across one of the other runners in a five furlong sprint. They took no account of the fact that this happened at the end of three miles and five furlongs over fences. Although by this stage I knew what was coming, I was still sickened by the verdict. I was also sickened by the attitude of the stewards. I was simply not given a fair hearing.

Charlie Swan was not the only one to feel sick. In Kildare the events at Sandown, relayed on Channel 4, were viewed with emotions that reached the heights of joy and plummeted to the depths of despair. Valerie and her mother had decided to spend the afternoon with Tina at the house in Beechgrove. But Valerie was the only one who remained glued to the television.

Mammy and Tina couldn't bear to watch. They flew upstairs before the race started but, when Charlie went past the post in front, I screamed to them to come down. It was fantastic to see him winning such a big race, and we were all thrilled. We were still all terribly excited when we heard the announcement of an inquiry. The hearing seemed to go on for ages. As it dragged on, we became more and more concerned. Then we heard that Charlie had been disqualified. It was terrible. I didn't know what to say to Tina.

Mouse Morris was stunned: 'I'd watched the race from the lawn but I saw no interference and I couldn't believe there was any danger of Cahervillahow losing the race in the stewards' room. In Ireland trainers are allowed to go into the inquiry but in England they don't normally do so. I had to wait outside. When I heard the verdict I was amazed, and to this day I still can't understand it. I then had to decide whether to appeal to the stewards of the Jockey Club. I felt I should and I was able to get a copy of the transcript of the Sandown inquiry. We went to Portman Square but it proved to be a waste of time. It was all over even before we went into the hearing.'

Swan agrees: 'It was Sandown all over again. After the first minute, I knew we had no chance. The senior stewards already had their minds made up. They listened to all the evidence we presented, but it was abundantly clear to me from the vibes I was getting that the stewards were not being swayed by any of it. They just didn't want to know. We were just as hard done by as we were on the day of the race.'

8

Trouble Down Under

That broken arm at Galway, and the resultant ten weeks of inactivity, made Charlie Swan's second championship a real struggle – and it was not until the end of February that he finally caught up with Tom Taaffe. He had just nine in hand at the end of the season and his hopes of making it three in a row in the 1991/92 season met with a costly reverse at Fairyhouse in October.

I was riding Slaney Sam for Dessie Hughes in a handicap chase. There were only six runners and, when we were circling round down at the start, somebody asked who was going to make the running. Kevin O'Brien said he wasn't. So did Anthony Powell and the other three jockeys. Slaney Sam was a bit funny. He was quite capable of trying to go through the wing of a fence. But he wouldn't have much chance if the race was run at a crawl, so I called out 'All right, I'll make it. But I'm not going down the inner in case he runs out, and I don't want anybody trying to come up my inside.'

I was still in front when I jumped the second last but, as I warned I would be, I was well away from the wing. However, almost as soon as I picked him up and headed towards the last, I saw a horse's head making ground up my inside. I was livid and I headed straight for the marker doll which signalled the start of the running rail twenty yards before the fence. I wanted to teach whoever it was a lesson. Just before I reached the doll, I pulled Slaney Sam to the left so that the other horse could get back onto the course and jump the fence. But the horse – I knew by this stage that it was Reffono, ridden by Pat Malone – had made up his mind he wasn't going to jump it.

I glanced back and saw Pat fall off as his horse went one way and he went the other. I was collared inside the final furlong by Niall Byrne on Golden See and, before I had even returned to weigh in, the stewards called an inquiry. The scout film, the one that takes the pictures from behind, showed quite clearly what had happened. I explained about Slaney Sam's tendency to run out and what I had said down at the start. Pat very decently backed me up. But the stewards weren't having any of it. They banned me for a fortnight and suspended Pat for three days for giving misleading evidence!

When the press quizzed me about lodging an appeal, I said I had no faith in the appeals system, and that my previous appeals had proved to be a complete waste of time. But the only reason I said this was because I was feeling so hot under the collar. I knew deep down I was in the wrong, and that I deserved every single one of the fourteen days. But I wasn't going to admit it. In fact I'd done pretty well out of appeals in the past. However, having got the sentence reduced for doing much the same thing to Mickey Flynn at Roscommon the previous year, I knew my chances of succeeding this time were nil.

The following week, though, I had a real shock. I opened the post to find a letter from a solicitor. It said he was acting for the owner of Reffono. He also said that Reffono would have won if I had not run him off the course. He pointed out that the stewards had ruled I was guilty and he said I was to send the solicitor a cheque for the £3,105 prize money. If I didn't, he would institute legal proceedings to recover the money. It was the first time anything like this had ever happened to me.

Charlie Swan did not know which way to turn. The solicitor's letter frightened him. He found it difficult to argue with the reasoning but it was not as if he had won the £3,105. All he had got out of it was two weeks with no income at all. Eventually he decided he would have to take legal advice. He consulted Fergus Taaffe, a Dublin solicitor, who had horses in training with Paddy Mullins. Taaffe sent a reply to Reffono's owner. He did not tell Swan what was in it but the jockey never heard another word about the matter. It was a long time, though, before he dared to carve up anybody else!

He faced problems of a different sort at Cheltenham the following

March when Trapper John attempted to repeat his Stayers' Hurdle victory of two years earlier. He started favourite but was beaten three and a half lengths by Nomadic Way. It was just as well he was. When Charlie Swan weighed in, he found to his horror that he was 3lb light and he was automatically disqualified. If he had won, and then lost the race, Cheltenham would have erupted in fury. Most of the huge Irish contingent had backed Trapper John. Defeat on the course they could take, but not defeat in the stewards' room. As it was, there was considerable speculation about how Swan could have lost three pounds in the course of the race. The rules allow a jockey to be one pound light but it is rare for this to happen. It is far more common for the jockey to be heavier when he returns to the scales. He may have had a cup of tea and a sandwich after weighing out, but usually the extra weight is caused by the pad under the saddle soaking up the horse's sweat. The story that went round the pressroom, and many of the bars, was that Swan had taken a pound of lead out of the weight cloth after weighing out and before he handed over the saddle to Morris and that the trainer, unaware of what his jockey had done, removed a further pound before saddling up the horse! When he heard this, Morris burst out laughing.

'No way,' he insisted. 'I took the saddle from Charlie at the scales the minute he had weighed out. He had no opportunity to take out any lead and I certainly did not do so. I took the saddle and the weight cloth straight to the saddling boxes and put them on the horse. I was careful with the way I carried them, and there is no possibility that a piece of lead could even have fallen out. I think I know what happened, although I have to be careful how I put it. I believe that there was a mistake made at the scales when Charlie was weighed out.'

However, Geoffrey Hopkins, the clerk of the scales, was adamant that he weighed out Trapper John's jockey at the correct weight and Swan backs this up.

I always check the weight myself when I pass the scales. I am quite sure I did so on this occasion, and that it was right. The story that was doing the rounds is rubbish. At Cheltenham you hand over the saddle to the trainer in full view of the clerk of the scales. If you try to tamper with either the saddle or the weight cloth, you would be spotted immediately. My own theory, and I have given this a lot of thought, is that a piece of lead somehow slipped out of the weight cloth and that this happened during the race. The jockey uses his own saddle but the weight cloths – in fact they are more like satchels and have pockets to contain the bits of lead – are provided by the valets. The one I was given on this occasion was not in great nick and it's possible that the lining became unstitched, allowing some of the lead to fall out. After the inquiry, I went back into the jockeys' room to look for the weight cloth and examine it. When I had come in after the race, I'd put it down on the table with all the others. But the one I had used was missing. Whether or not one of the valets had found it, guessed what had happened and hidden it, I just don't know.

It was a bad Cheltenham for C.F. Swan. Far from returning to the roar of two years earlier, he didn't even make the frame on any of his other rides and he went on to Aintree without a mount in the Grand National. And when he got one, he didn't want it!

In the 1991 National I had ridden Mick's Star, and I had a nose-bleed for much of the race. We went into the first fence far too fast. He jumped it very big and landed steeply. As he came up, his head smashed into my face and damaged my nose. We were always a long way behind and we finished tailed off. He was out of contention for the 1992 race after disappointing in the Thyestes. Lastofthebrownies was dead – he'd had a heart attack after doing a gallop with Cahervillahow at Fairyhouse the previous December – and Kevin O'Brien was on Mouse's only remaining National runner, Rawhide.

At Aintree on the day before the 1992 race, I won the Oddbins Hurdle for Arthur Moore on Ninepins but, in the next, Brendan Sheridan had a bad fall which ruled him out of the National. He was to have ridden Roc De Prince for Ted Walsh and I hadn't envied him the mount. Roc De Prince was a pain at the start, always backing away from the tape and digging his toes in. The last thing you want in the National is a horse like that. He wasn't the best of leppers either. Then Ted came into the jockeys' room. I somehow knew he was looking for me. I also knew why. I felt I couldn't turn him down, much as I wanted to. The only good thing was that the owners gave me a good few quid for the ride. There is a long tradition in the Grand National that you get a special fee – sometimes £500, sometimes more – for the risk involved. You don't always get it, though. Some owners won't pay and, if you are riding for your own stable, I feel it's cheeky to ask. You also wouldn't ask if you were ringing up for the ride on one of the favourites. The best owners are the ones who give you the money before the race. Otherwise, if you fall at the first, you feel guilty about asking for it! But I felt the fee was more than justified with Roc De Prince. He got round but he scrambled to do so.

Charlie Swan continued to ride work for Dessie Hughes and one morning the trainer's nineteen-year-old son, Richard, decided to take advantage of the Irish champion's presence at Osborne Lodge. Hughes junior is nearly five feet nine inches tall – a physical characteristic that meant he towered over many of the Flat jockeys, and which was later to lead to Willie Carson referring to him as 'the window cleaner'. Richard had been intent on becoming a jockey since he was a small boy, and he had had his first ride in a pony race when he was only eight. Although his father then decided this was too dangerous a sport for a boy who weighed only four stone, Dessie relented when his son was thirteen and Richard rode more than seventy winners. He was Leinster champion in 1986 and 1987.

He was an instant hit when he started on the racecourse proper too, and in 1991 he finished runner-up for the apprentices' title. The following year he rode for Noel Meade but, even though he had his own car, he still lived at home where his father, concerned that his son's lively approach to life might see him led astray by the twin delights of girls and drink, was determined to keep a close eye on him. The night before this particular morning, Richard had decided it would be unsafe to drive home and risk the unwanted attentions of the Garda Siochana. He had therefore left his car parked outside a shop in Kildare and had taken a lift back to Osborne Lodge.

But his father, going out into the yard before the lads arrived, immediately noticed that his son's car was missing. When Richard walked over to the nearest row of boxes, a few minutes later, he was asked where the car was. He explained that it was in Kildare; he had had a puncture and left it there. He would go back later, change the wheel and bring it home. Whereabouts in Kildare, his father wanted to know. Richard told him and immediately started trying to work out how he was going to get there before his father did. He could hardly ask his father to drive him into the town. Nor could he ask one of the lads to do so. The lad would have to ask for time off. Hughes senior might decide this would involve too much disruption in the stable's routine, and get his wife to go instead.

When Charlie Swan drove into the yard, Richard realised he had found salvation. As the horses moved out and started across the Curragh, he trotted his horse up to Swan's mount, and quietly explained his predicament. He then told Swan what he wanted him to do. Swan refused point blank. It would be wrong to deceive Dessie. In any case, somebody might see him. Nonsense, said Richard. Anyhow, how was he to get away? Charlie pleaded. He had promised Dessie he would ride out all three lots.

On one of the horses immediately behind the pair was Pat Healy, who had for once swapped his camera for a saddle. He listened to the exchanges with growing amusement throughout the next half hour. All Charlie had to do, Richard insisted, was to tell his father he had promised to ride a bit of schooling for another trainer. He could be back in fifteen minutes. Eventually Charlie, much against his better judgement, relented.

He drove cautiously up to Richard's car. It was parked where he had said it would be: on the main road, outside a small shop and opposite a garage. He parked his car alongside Richard's, but on the garage side. The danger was that somebody would come out of the shop. He peered through the door. It was empty. Nor was there anybody walking along the pavement. He slipped between the two cars, undid the valve cap on the front wheel, pressed the point of a biro into the valve and, despite going scarlet with embarrassment, held it there while the air hissed out. He stood up and glanced across at the garage. Somebody, surely, must have heard the noise? But no, thank goodness. There was still not a soul about. He drove off in his own car and was back at Osborne Lodge five minutes later.

An hour afterwards, Dessie Hughes drove into Kildare to where his son had said the car was parked. When he saw it, with the front wheel flat, he smiled to himself. The boy had told him the truth. Really, he should never have doubted him. The phantom puncturer, meanwhile, was back on the Curragh riding out and making it quite plain to Hughes junior that never again was he going to do anything like that for him. It was only several months later, when Pat Healy went into a busy newsagent's in the town, that he discovered that his dark deeds were no longer a secret. Healy heard two women talking about the town's champion jump jockey. Seemingly they both lived near him in Beechgrove. The first said what a charming young man he was, he always said hello to her and gave her a cheerful smile. 'Yes,' replied the other, 'but he is not always like that. My Sean works in the garage on the main road, and do you know what he saw him doing?. . .

In August 1992 Charlie Swan finally made it to Australia with the Irish jump jockeys' team. He had been meant to go the previous year – twelve months after the Galway fall – but Natasha was getting married and her brother felt family commitments should take precedence over what was primarily a fun fortnight. However, for the now three-times Irish champion the enjoyment ran out in Melbourne. He rode King Taros in a chase at Sandown and, to the horror of the crowd, particularly all those who had backed the horse, the 11-8 favourite took the wrong course. Swan was hauled before the stewards and banned for five weeks. In Ireland or England a fortnight's suspension would be considered stiff but in Australia suspensions can last for months. The stewards informed Swan of this, and told him they were letting him off lightly because he had never before ridden in a chase on this course.

Everything had seemed very relaxed about the competition against the Australian jump jockeys, and our minibus was late arriving at the course. To save time, and because it was lashing with rain, we went round the course in the minibus rather than walk it. There was a motor racing track around it but, for some reason best known to himself, the driver took us the opposite way round to the way we would be racing. This made it all a bit confusing. We were told that, on the final circuit, we were to jump two fences in the straight and then there would be a gap in the rails to take us onto the Flat course and the winning post.

In the race I turned for home in front and I jumped the first two fences. Suddenly I couldn't remember whether it was two or three fences we were to jump before switching courses. There were no dolls or cones to be seen. That convinced me the gap in the rails had to be after the next fence. But, as I was nearing it, I saw out of the corner of my eye a horse behind me veering across. I tried to turn my mount to go after him. But I was too late. I was out of the race. I felt awful. I wished I could have just galloped off into the blue, never to be heard or seen again. The crowds were bound to be booing when I neared them. Fortunately, though, it was such a dreadful day that there were only about 500 people there.

However, that was just about the only saving grace. What happened in the stewards' room was horrific. I pointed out that there were no dolls. I said I'd ridden in Ireland, England and France. In all three countries there were always dolls when you were required to switch to a different course. But the Australian stewards said they didn't use dolls, and I should have known they didn't. They asked if I had walked the course. I explained about the rain and the minibus going the wrong way round. They seemed unbelievably strict, particularly one called Pat Lalor. I had already been warned about him by the Australian jockeys. I thought I was sure to get a fine, possibly even a two-day suspension. When they said five weeks, I just couldn't believe it. Five weeks, just for making a simple mistake which wasn't even all my fault. I thought about all the rides in Ireland, and the festival meetings at Tralee and Listowel. I would miss the lot. I would also miss a lot of winners.

On the television news that night, his blunder was shown to most of Australia. The following day's papers simply rubbed salt into the wound. Swan was horrified to find himself sharing one front page with the Duchess of York. Fergie was having her toes sucked and Ireland's champion jockey was looking as unhappy as if he had somehow become involved in the royal scandal himself!

He decided to lodge an appeal, not against being suspended but against the severity of the sentence. Then he had a stroke of luck. One of the people taking the visiting jockeys from course to course was employed by a company that made videos of races. He went through the old videos. He found one that showed a chase at Sandown. In the straight there were dolls directing the runners onto the Flat course.

Swan asked for the video to be shown at the appeal hearing. He pointed out the dolls, and said that the Sandown stewards had told him dolls were never used. Why weren't they in use when he took the wrong course? If they had been, he would have known where to go. His argument was accepted, at least to a great extent. The suspension was lifted and replaced with an A$500 fine. Swan went over to Pat Lalor and held out his hand to show there were no hard feelings. But Lalor declined to shake it.

However, there was soon trouble brewing back in Ireland even though, on the surface, everything seemed to be going better than ever. Tommy Carmody, who by coincidence had been suspended for a month when he had gone on the 1988 Australian trip, had torn ligaments in his left arm in a bad fall in a novice chase at Naas at the beginning of the year. He was unable to recover full power in the arm and was eventually forced to retire. One of his principal employers was Noel Meade, who trained more than sixty horses not far from Navan in County Meath. Meade turned to Swan for some of his runners.

Other trainers did the same. When the 1991/92 season ended at the end of May, he had ridden seventy-nine winners, his best total so far. He was also stepping up the tempo – forty-seven of them had come in the first five months of the year. He was frequently finding himself in the enviable position of having several rides offered to him in the same race. Since he usually went for the one who had the best chance, his winner-rate increased still further. But Mouse Morris maintained he still had first call on the champion's services, and he did not like it when Swan started getting off his horses to ride more fancied runners.

> It was proving much the same sort of situation that I had been in with Tommy Carmody over three years earlier. So far as I was concerned, you are either in or you are out. I had no official hold on him for the 1992/93 season – just a gentleman's agreement – but I made it plain to Charlie that, if he was to ride the good ones, he was also to ride the bad ones. They are the horses for which you need a good jockey. Anybody can ride the good ones.

Charlie Swan considered the ultimatum carefully, and looked up the records. Morris had sent out just ten winners in Ireland in each of the two previous seasons. He had some good horses, admittedly, but so did some of the other trainers who were just as keen to secure Swan's services. Charlie decided to take his chance. Morris promptly engaged Liam Cusack for Cahervillahow and many of his other runners. Noel Meade decided this was too good an opportunity to miss.

> Noel approached me one day and asked me if I would ride all his horses. I explained that I had a few commitments, basically to Dessie Hughes. But, of all the trainers I have ridden for, Noel proved to be the one who has been the most understanding about letting me off if I wanted to ride another horse in the same race. At the time I thought this surprising because he hadn't been a jockey himself, and so he might not appreciate how you sometimes want to opt out of riding the stable's runners. In fact, I have subsequently found that trainers who used to be jockeys are the most awkward of the lot about letting you off. Furthermore, unlike some of those, Noel never held a grudge against me when I didn't ride one of his.

Noel Meade was forty-one at this stage and had been training for twenty years. The son of a prosperous farmer, he inherited half of a considerable amount of land when his father died. His father had wanted him to follow in his own footsteps, and in those of younger brother Ben (who got the rest of the land), but Meade was hooked on racing. His early ambition was to become a jockey, even though he is over six feet tall. He succeeded in riding one winner as an amateur but he freely admits that he was a terrible jockey. He decided to concentrate on training and, when he married Carmel when he was twenty-three, his new wife added her enthusiastic support by becoming her husband's assistant. But the marriage did not work. Meade later struck up a relationship that did, with Gillian O'Brien, a daughter of Phonsie O'Brien, who is a brother of Vincent's and was a highly successful amateur before turning to training.

Meade, slim and hard-working, has an enviably cheerful disposition. Few trainers manage to shrug off defeat as easily as he does but he is supremely professional in his job and invariably sends out plenty of winners. He also had some useful horses.

At Fairyhouse on 29 November 1992 Charlie Swan beat Martin Molony's 1950 record of ninety-two National Hunt winners in a calendar year when winning the opening maiden hurdle on Atone. At Navan thirteen days later he rode a double for Noel Meade to reach his century and he finished up the year with a total of 109 plus a further two in Britain. It was a staggering achievement, and a cause for celebration. But for Swan it was more a moment for reflection.

> I looked back over my career to the time I had started with that first winner at Naas, and I thought how lucky I had been. And how lucky I had been to be in the right place at the right time. For instance, joining Dessie Hughes when Tom Morgan was about to leave, and coming in for the rides on Noel Meade's horses when Tommy Carmody retired. There are several other jockeys who are just as good as I am, but they haven't had the breaks that I have. I looked at some of them in the jockeys' room. In a way I felt a bit sorry for them. If circumstances had been different, one of them would have ridden into the record books in my place.
>
> I certainly never expected to break any records and I was flattered when Martin Molony rang me after I had drawn level. He said he wanted to congratulate me, and I had never even met him. At Clonmel shortly afterwards, I was presented with a sketch of the two of us together. That sketch now has an

honoured place in my sitting room. So does the clock that Navan presented to me when I rode that 100th winner. But I was determined not to let any trace of cockiness creep in. The minute you do that in jump racing, you find yourself on your back with a bad fall. Indeed, you never know what fate awaits you from one day to the next. Being full of yourself is, in my book anyway, a sure way of tempting that fate.

Charlie Swan travelled to the 1993 Cheltenham Festival knowing that, for the first time at the meeting, he had a strong book of rides. He was in incredible demand with Irish trainers, thanks in no small part to having clocked up eighty-eight winners with the season little more than three-quarters of the way through. He was even back on Cahervillahow (much to the chagrin of Liam Cusack, who was to lose the bulk of Mouse Morris's rides the following month) and the luckless chaser had finally made it to the Cheltenham Gold Cup. Nicky Henderson, still an admirer of the Irish champion despite having been turned down by him nearly five years earlier, also booked him for two of his runners.

Swan's best chance appeared to be on Noel Meade's Heist in the Festival Bumper, but there were other possibles he had his eye on in the days leading up to the big meeting, including Montelado, who had won the first running of the Festival Bumper twelve months earlier. Richard Dunwoody rode him that day, and he travelled to Ireland to partner the big gelding in his first two outings over hurdles. But Dunwoody was retained by David Nicholson who had Dreamers Delight in the Supreme Novices' Hurdle, Montelado's objective. Pat Flynn, who trained the Irish hope, held on as long as he dared in the hope that either Dunwoody would be able to persuade Nicholson to let him off or that Dreamers Delight would not run. In fact, it was Montelado who was almost withdrawn.

Flynn would have been a worrier even if he had not chosen to train horses for a living. Fair-haired and stocky, he was twenty-four when he first took out a licence in 1981 on his father's farm in the hills behind Carrick-on-Suir. He had only one horse, one box and a broken-down farmhouse. He had been a Munster junior boxing champion when he was seventeen, winning three-quarters of his forty fights, and despite having back problems caused by a horse falling on top of him three years earlier. But he attacked his new profession with the same fighting spirit that he had shown in the ring, and he soon built up his stables to a more economic level. He was also able to build a house for his wife and their rapidly growing family.

He could not, though, overcome his in-built tendency to worry. Frequently he could not sleep. The more horses he trained, the more he had to worry about, or so it seemed when he was tossing and turning at three o'clock in the morning. But few in his stable caused him as many sleepless nights as Montelado whose legs were simply not strong enough for his near seventeen hands, 525 kilo frame.

> 'Montelado developed problems with sore shins and a tendon after his first hurdles run at Limerick in October 1992,' Flynn recalls. 'As he was approaching the final flight, a loose horse cannoned into him. Richard Dunwoody was shouting at the riderless horse, trying to make it stay clear of him, and Montelado lost his concentration. He stumbled over the hurdle and struck into one of his front legs. The problems were bad in the build-up to Cheltenham, and the night before the race we had to put his front legs in ice packs to keep down the inflammation.'

Charlie Swan had no inkling that the horse had any sort of problem until he rode him for the first time on the morning of the race.

> He did not seem to be moving at all well. I was concerned. But when I told Pat Flynn about it, he said: 'Don't worry. By the time we get to the race, he will be grand.' They packed ice round his legs when he returned to the racecourse stables and, going down to the start, it felt as if I was on a different horse altogether. He moved quite brilliantly.
>
> Because he'd had so little experience – this was only his third race over hurdles – Pat told me to give him plenty of daylight at each flight, and I decided to keep him to the outside for much the same reason. I felt I could afford to – he was the best horse in the race. He was some machine that day and he hardly put a foot wrong. He was always travelling well, and I was pretty hopeful as I moved him up into fourth place on the downhill run to the third last. At the next, we joined Boro Eight in the lead and Richard Dunwoody on Dreamers Delight fell. Turning for home, I asked Montelado to go on. He surged into another gear, pinged the last and strode home to win by twelve lengths in record time. I was thrilled and I punched the air in triumph as I passed the post.

Three hours later the famous Festival roar again erupted for Swan when he brought Fissure Seal home in front in the American Express Gold Card Final, to delight the group of dentists who owned the horse, and Harry de Bromhead who trained him. On the final day of the meeting, he rode two more winners – on Shawiya and Shuil Ar Aghaidh – to win the Ritz Club Trophy for the first time.

Shawiya, like Montelado, had problems which nearly caused her withdrawal. She bruised a foot and there was so much doubt about her running that she could not leave Ireland until the morning of the Daily Express Triumph Hurdle. Her trainer stayed at home. He had already decided that Cheltenham's milling crowds were no place for a man in a wheelchair, which is what Michael O'Brien had been ever since he was kicked with such force in a fall in the Carolina Cup in March 1974 that he was paralysed from the chest downwards. The paralysis was not the only thing he suffered. When a blood-clot moved from one of his legs to his lungs, he came close to death. Two months later, when depression set in, the thirty-one-year-old former champion jump jockey of America wished he was dead. He was given an immense amount of counselling, and somehow he managed to perform miracles to overcome his considerable handicap and build up a new career as a trainer in Ireland. He later had to perform them all over again to rebuild his stable after he threw everything away with a disastrous decision to move back to America. He had not been feeling well for a long time and he thought the Florida climate would help. It did, but it did not suit his wife, who had sacrificed so much of her own life to nurse her husband to recovery – mental as much as physical. Shawiya's Triumph Hurdle victory was the sort of example that doctors look for when explaining to others, struck down with paralysis, just what can be achieved if you try hard enough.

For Swan, though, Shuil Ar Aghaidh's victory in the Stayers' Hurdle brought with it sentiments every bit as feeling.

> She was trained by Paddy Kiely and owned by his wife, Marie. Paddy used to be a jockey – he won the 1980 Galway Plate on Sir Barry and finished third on General Symons in the 1972 Grand National. His brother, John, had given me rides since my first year as an apprentice, and I felt that winning on Paddy's horse was a way of repaying the family's faith in me. Also I had ridden Shuil Ar Aghaidh from early in her hurdling career, and I had been impressing on Paddy for quite some time that she would have a right chance in the Stayers' Hurdle. But he is a conservative individual and he wasn't at all keen on going to Cheltenham.

The one that got away, though, rankled. Heist was beaten in the Festival Bumper and his rider flew back to Ireland convinced he should have won.

> Heist started favourite, and I thought he was my banker. But I never got him into the position I wanted and, partly as a result, I got checked a few times including, crucially, at the top of the hill. Then he didn't come down it that well. He stayed on strongly in the final furlong but we couldn't quite peg back Paul Carberry on Rhythm Section. I came in for a fair bit of stick for getting beaten.

Noel Meade had double reason for disappointment. In the Festival Bumper the previous year he had also sent out the runner-up – the potentially brilliant but injury-prone Tiananmen Square – and Paul Carberry was attached to his stable. Furthermore, he too had been convinced that Heist was a good thing, and he was among those who put defeat down to pilot error.

> Charlie Swan is the most calculating professional jump jockey I have ever come across. You never have to tell him whether a horse stays, how he goes in the ground or whether or not he jumps well. By the time he comes up to you in the parade ring, he has already looked up who rode the horse in his previous races, where the horse ran and how he ran. He has also worked out what ground and distance the horse likes, and how he should be ridden.
>
> I would therefore be a bit hesitant about blaming him for getting beaten on Heist but, even though the going was a bit fast for the horse, I think he should have won – and the reason he didn't was because he was over-confident. Shortly before Cheltenham, he rode Heist in a piece of work at Fairyhouse with some very good horses and my fellow absolutely annihilated them. When he got off Heist, Charlie said: 'This horse won't just win the Festival Bumper; he will win it by a furlong.'

9

The Pipe Job

The 1993 Grand National has gone down in history. The National-that-never-was has had all sorts of descriptions applied to it, and most of them are derogatory. It turned into a shambles largely because two of the key officials blundered, but also because some of the equipment turned out to be totally inadequate.

For John White, who rode the 'winner', what he believed to be the greatest moment of his life was transformed in a few horrendous seconds into a nightmare that was made all the worse for being viewed by millions all over the world. It was a nightmare that will live with the poor man for the rest of his days, and that will be relived on innumerable sporting flashbacks for as long as there is steeplechasing. For Charlie Swan the agonies will also never be forgotten, and for the unfortunate Cahervillahow it was one more chapter in the horse's hard luck story that ended every bit as unhappily when he shattered his shoulder in a schooling accident after racing at Leopardstown eleven months later.

It was my fourth ride in the Grand National and the weather was horrible. The one saving grace was that I had a brilliant pair of goggles that were guaranteed not to mist up. They were called Uvex goggles and the company that made them also did skiing equipment. I was sponsored to wear them. They had a special coating on the inside and it was this that stopped them fogging up. But the problem with them was that the coating was apt to wash off. On really wet days you pick up a lot of mud on your goggles, and you have to wash them to get it off. This virtually destroyed these Uvex ones.

But I was thankful that I had them as we circled round down at the start in the wind and rain. For some reason we were sent to the start ten minutes early. I am always pretty nervous before the National and the delay made things worse. I was alongside Carl Llewellyn on Party Politics as we circled. Carl had won the previous year's race on this giant of a horse, and he was favourite to win again. Cahervillahow had never been a brilliant jumper and he had a tendency to land steeply – just what you don't want in the National. I said to Carl that I would be lucky if I got as far as the third!

When we were called in, I lined my horse up near the outside. I thought my only chance was to give him as much space as I could to see the fences. But Cahervillahow was on his toes and edging back. He could be funny at the start. The 1991 Ritz was no one-off. I had to turn him and come in again. But I couldn't find a gap in the line to slot him into. I yelled at the starter to wait. Fortunately, or so I thought at the time, the starter decided we should all take a turn and then come in again. This gave me a chance to get where I wanted.

But this time I could see the police dragging somebody off the course about 200 yards in front of us. There seemed to be a lot of animal rights protesters there. Several jockeys stood up in their irons and peered through the rain, trying to make out what on earth was going on. It was a good five minutes before the starter, Captain Keith Brown, called us in again. This time I lined up in the middle. The starter yelled at a grey horse – he didn't give the jockey's name, presumably he didn't know it – to get back off the tapes, and some of the crowd seemed to be shouting at the starter. They could have been more of the protesters. I could see Party Politics backing away, and Royle Speedmaster, who was ridden by John Durkan, doing the same.

Then the starter let us go. But I could see a man waving a flag some way up the course. I knew it was a false start. I also knew why. Some of the horses were carrying the starting tape along with them. Everybody was pulling up, and I cantered along with some of the others towards the first fence. I let Cahervillahow have a look at it. There were more protesters by the rails, and they were shouting at us. As I turned to head back to the start, I caught a glimpse of their flags and banners.

It was annoying – and upsetting – to have to go back and do it all over again. Everybody seemed to be getting very tense. I lined up towards the middle. The shouting from the crowd was louder this time. Chatam was reluctant to line up, and Royle Speedmaster was backing away again. This time Gerry Scott, the assistant starter, who had ridden Merryman II to win the race thirty-three years earlier, took hold of Royle Speedmaster and led him in. Then we were off. I got away well. I could hear a lot of shouting and I realised that somebody had got tangled up in the tape. I looked questioningly at some of the other jockeys as we galloped fast towards the first. I sensed that there was some doubt in their minds too. But, unlike a few minutes earlier, there was no sign of anyone waving a flag. That convinced me, and the others, that the race was on.

It was not until I saw the re-run on television much later that I found out that the tape had been caught under the neck of Formula One, ridden by Judy Davies, and round Richard Dunwoody's body. But I had put all the earlier problems out of my mind long before we reached Becher's where I got a bit squeezed on landing. Cahervillahow could be a bit lazy at times and I had to niggle at him to get him back onto the bridle. But, by the time we got to the open ditch two after Valentine's, I was travelling really well. Andy Orkney was in the lead on the grey Howe Street, a horse I knew because I had ridden him in the days when he was trained in Ireland, and I was not far behind.

As we headed towards the Chair, I could see that some of it was dolled off. There were people waving flags. I thought the protesters must have set fire to part of the fence and that the dolls were to steer us to the rest of it. Alan obviously thought that too because he jumped it on the left hand side, and the rest of us followed him. Just before the water, the next fence, I caught a glimpse of somebody else waving a flag but there were so many protesters around that it was impossible to tell what was happening. In any case, we were past them all in a flash and I was more concerned about concentrating on the race.

It was only when I watched the re-run that I realised the crowd were booing. But in the race itself all I could make out was a lot of noise, and you always get that going past the stands in the Grand National. I also realised that some of what I thought were protesters were in fact officials and some of the trainers of horses still in the race.

Mouse Morris was not one of them: 'I was watching the race on television in Vincent Daly's box in the stands, so I was in no position to run out onto the course and shout at Charlie to pull up. My impression was that the jockeys were enjoying themselves. Indeed, I'm convinced they knew it wasn't a proper race. Certainly Charlie didn't want it to be a non-race, he was having a great ride on a horse that a lot of people had said would not get round.' Charlie Swan shared the latter sentiment.

> I was convinced beforehand that Cahervillahow would fall, or at least make so many mistakes that he would have to be pulled up. The reason Liam Cusack got the chop was because the horse hadn't jumped well for him. But Cahervillahow, like some other dicey jumpers before him, quickly developed a respect for the unusual Aintree fences.
>
> Two before Becher's on the second circuit, Howe Street and Sure Metal both fell. Fortunately they were well clear at the time and I was able to avoid them. I felt I had a real chance of winning. I was going well and I knew my horse would get the trip. I took Becher's towards the outside, just to be on the safe side, and he jumped it cleanly.
>
> On the BBC commentary Jim McGrath said at this point that the jockeys were realising it was no race and were slowing up. That's nonsense. The pace was strong the whole way. That's borne out by the time, which was then the second fastest in the history of the race. None of those I could see were showing any sign of slowing, and I certainly wasn't. Mrs Valentine had told me beforehand that she would give me half the prize money if I won. That would have been over £50,000, and I was really going for it.
>
> At the Canal Turn, I had my only really anxious moment. Cahervillahow tried to bank the top of the fence. He paddled over it but somehow he landed all right and I got him going again. At the next, Valentine's, I was third but I had to start riding him after crossing the Melling Road. Cahervillahow had plenty left but he had a bad habit of switching himself off at the wrong time. He went through the top of the second last, and he did same at the final fence. Esha Ness was only just in front of me and I thought I would win because Cahervillahow tends to fly at the end. I gave him a right few belts and, as we neared the line only a length and a half behind, I was worried that I would get done for the stick.

Then I saw all the people waving their arms as if to say 'It's all over'. Somebody shouted 'It's void'. I felt sick. I'd got round on a dodgy jumper to finish second and now it was going to be taken away from me. I heard people saying that the race would be started all over again. That was madness. There was no way Cahervillahow, or any of the other six who had finished, could be asked to go round again.

I went back to the weighing room but, before I got there, I was grabbed for a television interview with Desmond Lynam. I was confused and flustered – the race and its repercussions were still buzzing through my mind – and I got the impression that he seemed to be blaming the jockeys. I still had the saddle in my hands and, although I didn't realise it, mud on my face. I was annoyed at what he said, and I did my best to make it clear that it would be totally wrong to pin the blame on any of us. I pointed out that in Ireland there is always a white flagman to signal a false start, and that there had been no sign of any flag here. He asked if the jockeys had said anything to each other during the race. I was annoyed about this too. It was very windy and it was difficult to hear anything, particularly with the crowd making so much noise. I guess I didn't come across that well. But I was upset, and the questioning didn't help.

The Jockey Club set up a committee of inquiry into what had gone wrong and the report, which was not published until more than two months had elapsed, effectively blamed the advance flagman for not doing his job properly. Other critics were not so sure. Captain Keith Brown, who never started another Grand National, came in for plenty of stick. It was part of his job to alert the advance flagman that he had called a false start by waving his own flag. But he had his hand round the flag when he waved it. As a result it did not unfurl, and the flagman would have had difficulty in making out the signal.

The Grey Gate starting system was also criticised for being too antiquated for the task. Indeed, after the 1991 Grand National the starter had recommended that the width of the course at the start should be reduced. He pointed out that the seventy-five-yard span resulted in the tape sagging in the middle. As a result it was slow to rise, particularly in the sort of wet and windy weather that was to prevail in 1993. But the width was not reduced, and the tape failed to rise in time, with devastating consequences. Charlie Swan, though, does not agree that this was the root cause.

The tape had been this width for years and had worked without that many problems, so it's difficult to say that this was what was wrong in 1993. But, when the starter shouts out 'OK jockeys. Go on', you naturally kick your mount forward to get a good start. If the starter is not quick enough to raise the tape – and he didn't seem to be in 1993 – it's all too easy for horses to get their chins caught up in it. However, what was principally to blame, in my view, was the confusion between the starter and the flagman.

The Jockey Club's committee of inquiry felt there should be a more effective way of warning jockeys that there has been a false start. It considered a complicated system of flashing lights but these might well not be seen if the race is run in bright sunlight. John White, who suffered more than anyone from the chaos and now trains in County Wexford, believes that the officials should have shown a lot more common sense. If they had, the race could have been brought to a halt quite easily.

The Chair was the obvious place to stop the race. It was close to the enclosures and there were enough people in authority to get officials out onto the course. There was also enough time. There was nearly five minutes between the race actually starting and the runners reaching the Chair. What they should have done was to have a line of people standing in front of the fence with their arms linked. It would not have taken too much intelligence to work that one out. But all they had was one man waving his arms.

At Ascot, just four days after the Aintree fiasco, Peter Scudamore plunged the racing press into a fever of speculation by announcing his immediate retirement. Then thirty-four, Scudamore had been champion seven years on the trot and he hung up his boots with three impressive British jumping records to his credit – the most championships (eight), the most winners in a season (221) and the highest total of winners (1,678). The press immediately started trying to work out who would succeed him as stable jockey to Martin Pipe. This job appeared at the time to virtually guarantee the championship because the Somerset trainer was sending out far more winners than any of his rivals, and he had topped the 200-mark in each of the previous four seasons. Charlie Swan, a record-breaker in his own right as well as on the way to his fourth successive title, was widely assumed to be on the shortlist.

Less than a month earlier he had received a second offer to join Nicky Henderson who, even though he had little inkling that Peter Scudamore was shortly to set into motion a high-profile game of musical chairs, was again concerned about which way Richard Dunwoody would move. He was still effectively sharing the supreme stylist with David Nicholson, whose stable was becoming an increasingly powerful force, and he still had his eyes on the Irish champion. When he booked him for those two months at the Cheltenham Festival, Henderson resolved to try to persuade Swan again.

> Frankly, I did not expect him to say yes because he had established himself to such an extent that he had the cream of the Irish horses to choose from. I certainly knew I was a lot less likely to be able to tempt him over than I was in 1989. But I tried, primarily for two reasons. In the first place he had become a supremely effective jockey, and secondly because he is a seriously nice guy. When you choose a stable jockey, you have got to pick somebody who you yourself are going to get on with – and be able to work with, and somebody whom the owners will enjoy having on their horses and being in their company.
>
> But, sorry to relate, he turned me down again. I got the impression that he was not all that interested in leaving Ireland. If anything was going to tempt him, it was the horses rather than the job. But the horses, seemingly, were not a sufficient pull. Subsequent events have proved that he was right to stay put. He has cornered the market like Bunker Hunt cornered the silver market!

Not much goes on in racing that is not somehow picked up by the news-hungry journalists who make their living from writing about the game's small, but rumour-filled, world and on the Thursday evening, only a few hours after the last race at the Cheltenham Festival had been run, word somehow got out that Henderson had made an approach to Swan. Possibly it was a case of putting two and two together, and equating the offer of a couple of rides with something more meaningful. Whatever the reason, two reporters rang Swan the next day. He gave the same reply to each. There had been no job offer, and things were going so well in Ireland that it would take something exceptional to make him even consider a move.

I said this because Nicky Henderson had asked me not to say anything to anybody about our discussions. It certainly dampened the press circulation but, of course, the Martin Pipe situation sparked it all off again and to a far greater extent.

The son of a bookmaker, Martin Pipe had some early success as a permit holder but he did not take out a licence until he was in his early thirties – he was forty-seven when Scudamore retired – but he steadily expanded his operation and within ten years he was sending out over 100 winners a season. He paid extraordinary attention to the medical and scientific side of training – he found he was able to tell far more about the well-being of his horses from blood-tests than more traditional trainers were from all their years of experience. He was also able to run his horses more often than most of his rivals, and make them keep their form in the process.

However, Pipe also found that he had to contend with all sorts of rumours and stories about how he had achieved his phenomenal results. Most of these were inspired, and fuelled, by the jealousy of his less successful rivals. The rumours came to a head in May 1991 when Pipe was the subject of a particularly unpleasant investigative television programme in the Cook Report series. In fact this proved to be something of a turning point in that it brought the allegations into the open. They were shown not to amount to much and, after many people in racing rallied to the trainer's defence, the stories died down and were replaced by a widespread acceptance that those brought up to follow the training methods of their ancestors had something to learn from the man from Somerset.

Part of the Pipe method was to keep detailed dossiers on each horse, and those riding for him were expected to fax him a report on their observations each evening. Some jockeys, accustomed to driving away from the races with nothing more pressing on their minds than the thought of a good meal and a pretty girl to share it with, considered this an almost intolerable burden. It was widely regarded as one of the drawbacks to the best job in racing.

Richard Dunwoody, a serious character and a total professional for whom such paperwork would be no bother at all, was the obvious favourite. But there was also the ultra-determined, winner-hungry Adrian Maguire, who was a rapidly rising star and who had already ridden some important winners for Pipe. The bookmakers fuelled the media speculation by opening a book on the outcome. Maguire and Dunwoody were the favourites but there was also significant support for the Irish champion.

Charlie Swan gave his prospects a boost five days after Scudamore's retirement by winning the Irish National for Francis Flood on Ebony Jane although this race, for a few agonising moments, had ominous shades of 1991 about it.

> I went clear soon after jumping the third from home but in the last fifty yards, just when I thought I had it in the bag, I suddenly heard the crowd. It wasn't the normal noise you hear when you near the stands at the end of a race. There was a subtle change in pitch as if they somehow sensed a surprise. I knew immediately what it meant – something was coming up fast. I thought, 'No. Please, no. Surely I am not going to get beaten in this race again?' Then I could see who it was, Rust Never Sleeps, a 66-1 shot, ridden by Tony O'Brien. I asked for more, and Ebony Jane produced it. We won by a length, but the gap was closing uncomfortably fast.

Soon afterwards Swan answered his phone to find Martin Pipe at the other end.

> He asked me if I would be interested. He did not go into a lot of detail but he said he would come back to me. I wasn't at all sure what I should do. In a way I was rather hoping that he wouldn't pick me. If he did, I wouldn't be able to say no. It was too good a job to turn down but, unlike most Irish jump jockeys, I never had any real ambition to move to England. What was preying on my mind was that Tina and I had just moved into the house we had built at the top end of the Modreeny estate, and named The Cobs. It has a magnificent situation, with superb views of my father's gallops and of the surrounding countryside. It was where I had long wanted to live, and the last thing I needed for either of us was the upheaval of a move and a new way of life.

Martin Pipe promptly added to the media frenzy by asking Swan to make a flying visit to Britain to partner three of his runners at a minor Cheltenham meeting in the week after the Irish National. Charlie had never ridden for Pipe before and it was patently obvious that the trainer was giving the Irish jockey a trial run. But Pipe, a canny character, denied this and even that he had asked Swan if he was interested in taking the job.

I simply asked him if he wanted to come to England and those three rides were not to try him out. I had seen him riding quite a bit, so I knew how good he was. He finished fifth on Dagobertin in the handicap hurdle that day at Cheltenham, and he then won the four-year-old hurdle on Her Honour while Saraville fell in the handicap chase. He is a good jockey, confident and very competent. He has all the qualities a jockey needs, including having the right build and being the right weight. Also he gave me a good report on how each horse travelled, and I was able to learn a lot about the horses from him.

The fact that one of the three won seemed sure to put him right into the reckoning and further proof, if any were needed, that Charlie Swan had a foot in the door emerged when it became known that he had been booked by Pipe for Cyphrate at the following week's Punchestown festival.

Pipe told Swan they would speak again at Punchestown. He did not go into any details, and indeed at the big Irish meeting he seemed to enjoy keeping the speculation on the boil. Although he gave Swan the leg up on Cyphrate on the first day of the three-day meeting, and indeed spoke to him at length in the parade ring beforehand, he made no mention of the job. Nor did Swan. He felt it would look as if he was being too pushy. In any case he was still not sure that he wanted it.

But the Pipe-induced suspense seemed to grate with both David Nicholson and Richard Dunwoody. The latter remained the newspapers' favourite for the job and, even though he won two big races for David Nicholson on Viking Flagship, many of the journalists wrote about him as if he was only days away from signing on Pipe's dotted line. Nicholson seemed to think the same way. He told Dunwoody he wanted to know by the end of the week what he planned to do for the following season. There was also a press report that he had already spoken to Adrian Maguire about him replacing Dunwoody as his stable jockey. Nicholson denied this but stressed that he was determined not to be left in the lurch.

Pipe's response was to say, in the middle of a packed press room, 'I am afraid Mr Nicholson is trying to force the issue.' He added that he had not offered the job to anybody, and nor was he in any hurry to do so. But he then stoked the fire by saying that he had been hoping to speak to Adrian Maguire, but that he was not at the meeting. He also said that he was looking for a Dublin bookmaker who, he had heard, was offering 4-1 against Dunwoody getting the job!

Pipe's obvious good humour was in marked contrast to his disgust over Milford Quay's controversial disqualification after winning at the same meeting twelve months earlier. Pipe had never before had a runner at Punchestown. Milford Quay led from pillar to post in the hands of Peter Scudamore in the Goffs Silver Gavel Novice Chase. But the victory turned sour little more than a fortnight later when it was discovered that the nine-year-old appeared to have carried the wrong weight.

As the winner of two chases, Milford Quay's correct weight was 12st, and this was the figure shown in the racecard. The officials work off a bigger card – it is primarily for use by the press and has a wide margin for note-taking. The large card, as it is known, is printed by the same printers and is run off at much the same time as the ordinary cards sold to the public. For some reason which has never been satisfactorily explained, the large card on this occasion gave Milford Quay's weight as 11st 10lb.

The stewards of the Irish National Hunt Steeplechase Committee held an inquiry at the Turf Club's registry office six weeks after the race. Martin Pipe, away in America, was represented by his father, David. Peter Scudamore attended the hearing, as did Jimmy Rodgers, one of the part-owners of Milford Quay. It was confirmed at the inquiry that George Walsh, the clerk of the scales, had relied on the large card. But neither jockeys, trainers nor their representatives have access to these cards. They invariably used the normal cards and Scudamore, apparently, was adamant that he had weighed out at the correct weight.

> 'Peter's evidence was that he had weighed out, firstly on the trial scales in the jockeys' room and then on the real ones, at 12st,' relates Rodgers who adds, 'this was confirmed by the two valets concerned, Dave Fox and Adrian Heffernan. There was also a signed statement by Eddie Buckley, Martin Pipe's assistant, saying he was at both sets of scales, that both read 12st and that he went with Peter from the trial scales to the actual ones. Peter, Eddie and the valets all relied on the official racecard. They also referred to that day's *Sporting Life*. Both the card and the *Life* gave the weight as 12st. Eddie's statement was quickly dismissed, seemingly because he was not present to be questioned about it. It developed into a matter of the stewards either taking the word of Peter, Eddie and the valets, or that of the clerk of the scales – four against one. Amazingly, the stewards refused to believe our team.'

The stewards disqualified Milford Quay but little more than a week later the boot was on the other foot. It was discovered that, through an almost unbelievable oversight, the Punchestown prize money had been credited to the accounts that Jimmy Rodgers and the other two owners, Alan Jones and Pat McDonald, maintained with Weatherbys. The accounts of Martin Pipe and Peter Scudamore had also been credited with their percentages. The money had somehow been remitted from the Turf Club to Weatherbys. Needless to say the owners refused to pay it back!

The affair rumbled on and in February 1993 Jimmy Rodgers revealed that the Turf Club had finally conceded that the owners could keep their money but, so he claimed, it was not prepared to extend this concession to Pipe and Scudamore. Chester Barnes, the former star table-tennis player who was Pipe's assistant, added that his boss was so furious about the whole thing that he had vowed not to enter horses for Irish races in future unless the owners insisted. The Turf Club, far from attempting to douse the flames, poured petrol on them when Cahir O'Sullivan, the Keeper of the Match Book, hit back saying: 'Martin Pipe is under no illusions as to what happened with Milford Quay. The matter has been explained to him through his lawyers on numerous occasions. It is just that he does not accept our explanations. So far as the stewards are concerned, the horse was disqualified for carrying the wrong weight. They are not prepared to pay over money simply to entice people to enter their horses in Ireland. I am sorry that all this has happened. It is a pity, not least because we have paid out almost double.'

The last two words were a reference to the percentages of Pipe and Scudamore. The Turf Club had been able to recover these by debiting their accounts.

The Punchestown committee, alarmed at the prospect of losing one of jump racing's biggest attractions at its April festival, stepped in and offered to pay Pipe what he had lost. He promptly accepted the gesture in the spirit it was intended, gave the money to charity and declared an end to any further talk of a boycott. The only people unhappy about the outcome of this torrid affair were those who had presided over the original decision to disqualify Milford Quay and Jimmy Barry, the senior steward of the Irish National Hunt Steeplechase Committee, complained: 'The stewards found against Martin Pipe and Peter Scudamore – and all the people involved in racing should accept this ruling.'

Shortly after the 1993 Punchestown festival Pipe and Richard

Dunwoody agreed terms, Adrian Maguire was signed up by David Nicholson and later Nicky Henderson appointed Mick Fitzgerald, the season's top claiming rider, as his stable jockey. The only person left without a seat when the music stopped was Charlie Swan. He was relieved.

The following season, though, Dunwoody was made to fight to the last day to hold off Maguire, and twelve months later he put an end to his own personal rat race. He announced that he was cutting down on his commitments and that he intended to enjoy life once more. Martin Pipe, forced to look for a new stable jockey, rang up Charlie Swan again. This time there was no ambiguity about the offer. Nor was there any hesitation on the part of the Irish champion. He explained that he had major commitments in Ireland and that therefore he had to decline. Pipe gave the job to David Bridgwater.

In mid-June, on the only one of Royal Ascot's four days on which there was no racing in Ireland, Charlie Swan flew over to ride at the meeting for the first time. John Mulhern had asked him to partner Approach The Bench in the Royal Hunt Cup. The five-year-old had 9st 10lb, Swan could do the weight and, even though the horse was a 33-1 shot, he was thrilled to accept.

> I had never been to Royal Ascot and I had expected the atmosphere to be something like Cheltenham. But it wasn't. It was more tense and far more serious. I thought everybody treats the Cheltenham Festival pretty seriously, but they don't in comparison with what happens at Ascot. I suppose it's because there is so much money involved, not just prize money, but with the future stallion values of the horses.
>
> Approach The Bench never really got into contention and what I remember most about that day is what happened when we arrived at the course. I flew over on the morning of the race with Johnny Murtagh, who was riding Salmon Eile for Pat Flynn in the Hunt Cup, and Dessie Scahill, who was the course commentator in Ireland. Tina decided to stay at home. On the same plane was Dermot Weld, who was running Goodnight Kiss in the Jersey Stakes. At Heathrow he asked us if he could join us in the taxi to the racecourse. When we got there, he said he would pay. We all thought that was generous of him but he then said, 'Mind you, I shouldn't. Charlie cost me a lot of money at Fairyhouse one day.' He was referring to me getting beaten on

one of his that he obviously thought should have won. I wasn't best pleased.

It was lashing with rain. Someone pointed to a shop just outside the entrance. It sold cheap umbrellas. We each bought one. I tested mine and it worked perfectly. We then went to the office to get our vouchers to get into the course. It was still bucketing down when we got in. Dermot was in a hurry and he went ahead. I put up my umbrella and it collapsed. It had somehow got mixed up with someone else's dud one. By the time I reached the weighing room, I was soaked to the skin.

10

Danoli

In the summer of 1993, when all the press speculation surrounding the Martin Pipe job had been confined to the files, Charlie Swan received approaches from two Irish trainers whose characters, and whose horses, were to dominate his life for the next two years.

The trainers were totally different, not least because their backgrounds were poles apart. The first, and at the time far better known, of the pair was Edward O'Grady, who had been born into racing. His mother, Mary, is the sister of Pat Hogan, a legendary figure in the Irish point-to-point and hunter chase circuit which he dominated for several decades, first as a rider and then as a brilliantly successful trainer.

Willie O'Grady, Edward's father, was a jump jockey and was Ireland's champion jockey – for Flat and jumps combined – in 1934 and again in 1935. His big race winners included the Galway Plate and the Grand Sefton, in those days the second most important chase run over the Grand National fences. In 1940 he started training. His Cheltenham wins included the 1969 Cathcart. He had a tough constitution, and was quite capable of playing cards all night and then going straight off for a day's hunting. He also had some tough philosophies which he instilled into his only child. Edward wanted to become a trainer too and would like to have gone straight from school into the yard at Ballynonty in County Tipperary, just off the road that leads from Littleton to Killenaule. But his father told him, bluntly, 'This place is not big enough for both of us. You will have to go.'

Edward went to veterinary college in Dublin determined to resume his training ambitions when he had qualified. In the meantime, he rode as an amateur and managed some fifty rides and ten winners, despite his father taking the view that owners paying good money to have their horses in his stable deserved something better than an unfit amateur away at college all week.

In the summer of 1971 there was a massive upheaval in the O'Grady family. Willie developed pneumonia, and complications set in. His son dropped everything, part way through his exams, and returned home to keep the family business on the road. In January 1972 Willie O'Grady died and Edward took over the licence. His ambitions had been realised a lot quicker than he had any right to expect. But within six months they came close to being destroyed.

The twenty-two-year-old part-qualified vet kept the owners happy with eleven winners in his first twelve weeks, but then a virus struck and the initial run of success was brought to an agonising, and frustrating, halt. At the end of the season, most of the owners decided that their horses would fare better in the care of a more experienced trainer. Just when everything seemed lost, Edward O'Grady remembered something else that his father had tried to drill into him. 'Boy,' he had said, 'you were not born with a silver spoon in your mouth. Go out and bloody work.'

He and his young wife, Judy, did just that and they began by scouring the country for owners. Wherever they were likely to meet any, they went. When they made contact, they impressed upon them what the yard at Ballynonty had to offer. The salesmanship worked and soon they were able to build the numbers back up to an economic level, at least economic enough for their business to survive. But money remained tight for years. What they made went on the horses and the stables, not on luxuries for themselves or their house. They took the eminently practical view that, if things went well with the business, in due course it would generate cash for them.

The new O'Grady rapidly made a name for himself and in 1974 he had his first Cheltenham Festival winner when Mr Midland won the National Hunt Chase. For a man so young, and who had been training for little more than two years, it was quite an achievement. Later that year he hit the headlines for his part in the Gay Future affair, a brilliantly conceived betting coup that came unstuck only when many of the bookmakers refused to pay out. Eddie O'Grady, as he was then known – it was some years before he was to ask everybody to call him Edward – did not enjoy most of the publicity but, since it was he who had got the horse ready, his reputation soared. He rapidly became one of the kings of National Hunt racing and between 1976 and 1984 there was only one Cheltenham Festival from which he failed to return home with a winner.

With jumping owners queuing at the door he could, seemingly, have stayed at the top for years. But O'Grady wanted more. This was the era of Flat racehorses turning into stallions worth not just millions but tens of millions. It was also the era of the new Phoenix Park, with glamorous celebrities attracted to the rebuilt course, and every race boosted in value by sponsorship. The boss of Ballynonty looked at the example set by Vincent O'Brien, whose Ballydoyle base was not much more than twelve miles away, and who had turned his back on a brilliantly successful career as a jumping trainer to become one of the greatest trainers of Flat horses, and stallion prospects, that the world has ever known.

O'Grady carefully analysed his own position, and his prospects. He had been steadily building up his Flat team. He had more than proved his ability, he knew he could make the contacts with wealthy owners and, in all probability, get them to send him some of their horses. What was more, he was still young enough to change direction. After all, he was only in his mid-thirties, and a few years younger than Vincent O'Brien when he made the switch.

Some of the rich owners duly sent Flat horses to Ballynonty – including Robert Sangster and Lady Clague. Even the President of Ireland had horses with the stable. But making the breakthrough proved far more difficult than O'Grady had envisaged. Despite the big-name owners, he did not have horses sufficiently well bred, or good enough, to compete at anywhere near the top level. As his numbers dropped, and his hopes of realising his Flat ambitions receded far into what was looking an increasingly uncertain future, he decided to take in more jumpers. However, the National Hunt scene had moved on. New names had taken over the ground on which O'Grady once strode like a colossus. For a time he found it almost as hard to come up with a top National Hunt horse as he had to produce a good one on the Flat. But in the summer of 1993 he felt that the wind of change was at last blowing back in his direction.

> I believed I had got together some nice horses for the coming season, and it was the first time that I could say to myself that I was really back training jumpers. I didn't like to think it was going to be exactly a make-or-break season, but I knew it was going to be a vitally important one so far as my future career was

concerned. If I could make it a successful one, I would be able to build on that success.

But my numbers were quite small and I had been around long enough – and had experienced enough of the ups and downs of racing – to realise that, when you have only a few horses, you are under pressure all the way. You are under pressure from the risks of injury and viruses, from whether or not they will train on from the previous season, from whether or not they will graduate from hurdles to fences, and from whether or not you will have luck on the day. All these are variables but, if you can get the outstanding jockey of the period on your horses, you have a few per cent in your favour when the dice is being rolled. Without that advantage, I would be relying on luck going my way. Luck is important, but it doesn't do to rely on it.

I had another reason for wanting Charlie Swan, and it was every bit as important. J.P. McManus was my main owner and he always likes to have one of the top jockeys on his horses. For a time I had Tommy Carmody riding Blitzkreig for him and, because of this, I was able to use Tommy on many of my other horses. However, I was conscious that he was coming towards the end of his career, and that it was time to investigate new pastures. However, when your horses are not top class, the best jockeys are not always as available as you would like. I had wanted to use Charlie for some time but he was not that free to ride for me. He seemed to be keen to remain freelance and to have no wish to be tied down. But I needed him, and I resolved to try and get him.

Swan was asked to drive over to Ballynonty for a chat. He had a fair idea of what it was about, and he was not as reluctant to enter into an agreement as O'Grady had supposed.

By this stage I had been champion jockey for four seasons on the trot [the most recent with a record 104 winners] and I was keen to win some of the big races. Edward had a tremendous record at Cheltenham and Galway, and so I knew he was capable of delivering the goods. He also had a stable with some real prospects in it – horses like Sound Man, Time For A Run and High Peak – and I felt this was my chance, even though I was a bit reluctant to enter into anything that could disrupt my easy agreement with Noel Meade. Frankly, I liked being able to pick and choose my rides.

Charlie Swan was not quite sure what sort of man he was going to talk to. O'Grady is invariably polite and he can be good company. But, on occasion, he is capable of letting fly with his tongue, and many jockeys are a little in awe of him. Some of the press have also had reason to treat him with a certain degree of caution. At Punchestown in April 1996 one reporter had openly questioned the resolution of Ventana Canyon, and this horse appeared to have been edged out of it in a photo finish with Double Symphony. When the judge eventually announced, to almost universal surprise, that Ventana Canyon was the winner, O'Grady immediately started shouting for the unfortunate journalist to come forward!

He and Swan, though, came to an agreement. But the exact terms were a source of some confusion, and this almost led to an early end to the association with the other man who was to have such a bearing on the jockey's life in the next two seasons. O'Grady recalls what was agreed as follows: 'It was a gentleman's agreement and, because I only had a relatively small number of horses, it was fluid. If there was a better horse available on the day, I would have no problem with Charlie taking the ride.'

However, Swan has a significantly different recollection: 'Edward made it clear to me that, in return for me coming in for the rides on his best horses, I would have to ride for him whenever he had a runner.'

Tom Foley is nearly three years older than Edward O'Grady. He looks more like ten years older. He has had a hard life, and it shows. Willie O'Grady might have pointed out to his son that he was not born with a silver spoon in his mouth, but Foley had no spoon at all. Until Danoli transformed his life, he had to struggle to scratch a living out of sixty acres on the side of a hill in a remote part of County Carlow. The European Union has transformed the lot of Ireland's farmers but sixty acres is not enough to provide a decent income, not when you have a wife and four children to support.

Foley built up the numbers of his beef herd to thirty-five – and on sixty acres that is a lot – but it was still only a bread and butter existence. For the jam, he decided to turn to racehorses and at Tramore in January 1988 he had his first winner, in an upside down handicap hurdle. It was just about the lowest class of race, and at the lowest class of course, and hardly anybody noticed that there was a new figure on the racing scene.

Nor did they for several years. Whenever Foley came up with a half-decent horse, it was sold as soon as it showed any sign of promise. This was the only way his owners could afford to pay the training fees. One who could afford them, although he was far from being flush with funds, was Danny O'Neill, who lived only a few miles from Foley and was a bone-setter by profession. The white-haired O'Neill treated horses as well as humans – if something was out of place, he would click it back in again – but he had no interest in racing. Indeed, he confesses that he thought the owners of his equine patients were mad to pay out all the money it cost to keep them.

Somehow he was persuaded – Foley is as talkative as the most voluble of his fellow countrymen, and that is saying a lot – to accompany the trainer-cum-farmer to Goffs Sales in June 1991 to look for a filly that might make a racehorse. It was not an expensive sale, and fillies were cheaper than colts and geldings. But Foley did not like the fillies he saw. What he did like was a bay horse by The Parson. Each time Foley walked past the horse's box, he looked over the door. The horse was always asleep. Foley was hooked and, when the gelding was led round the ring and the bidding failed to make what seemed to be a 10,000 guineas reserve, he and O'Neill decided to try and buy him. They went to see the vendor – a breeder, farmer and small-time trainer called Willie Austin.

Austin, although Foley had no inkling of the coincidence at the time, lives just up the road from Modreeny. He was disappointed to see his bay being led out unsold, but not so disappointed that he was going to accept the first offer that came along. He could take the horse home and train him himself. It would be a gamble but, if the gelding proved to be any good, he would sell him for a lot more than ten grand. He told the would-be buyers that he was not prepared to accept the 7,000 guineas they were offering.

'Listen,' said Foley in that persuasive tone that was to make him such a big hit with the press and on the television screens, 'the big Derby Sale at Fairyhouse starts in two days' time. I can go there and buy what I want – and buy it for seven. I will give you forty-eight hours to think about it.'

Foley, not for the first time, and certainly not for the last, was exaggerating. The prices at Fairyhouse were a lot higher than Goffs and there were a lot of horses there who made more than 7,000 guineas. Austin knew this too, of course, but after going home and thinking about it, he decided that seven grand in the hand should not be sniffed at. He rang Foley and told him the horse was his.

Danny O'Neill named his first horse by using a combination of his own Christian name and that of his daughter, Olivia. When Danoli made his debut in a bumper at Naas, the bone-setter travelled to the course with the trainer. Foley was agitated. He knew Danoli was smart, so much so that he intended to have one of his rare bets. It was only when he heard that Arthur Moore fancied Atours that he chickened out. But he was concerned about what O'Neill was going to do with the horse if he ran up to expectations and somebody made an offer for him. Was he going to sell? Foley demanded. If so, he should name his price there and then.

O'Neill was hesitant. Having never owned a horse before, he wasn't sure. It was only when his 16-1 shot came home a length in front of Atours that he knew – 'Seeing my horse win gave me such a thrill that it changed my whole outlook on racing. Indeed, Danoli was to change my life. No amount of money – and we were later offered a lot – could buy the excitement that this horse was to give me.'

Danoli went on to prove himself something special by winning his two remaining bumper starts. If Willie Austin had taken the gamble and held on to him, he would have been able to sell the horse at this stage for at least ten times what O'Neill had paid him.

Foley had no regular jockey, other than Padraig English, the blond-haired amateur who had ridden Danoli to his three victories, and if Charlie Swan had not been pushed into the picture, the County Carlow trainer would probably have given the mount to Tommy Treacy when the time came for the horse to go hurdling.

Treacy is the son of Jim Treacy, who used to be Paddy Mullins's head lad. Foley had got to know him well when Treacy was working for the late Denny Cordell-Laverack whose gallops Foley sometimes used. Danoli's trainer admired young Tommy's riding but the boy was still a 5lb claimer and, when Pat Healy started to press Charlie Swan's case one day at Limerick, Foley found the argument almost unanswerable. He found it completely so when Swan came up, as the trainer and the photographer were still in conversation, and was introduced as 'This is the man who should ride your horse, Tom'.

Charlie Swan partnered Danoli in a spin on the Curragh before teaming up with him in a maiden hurdle at Fairyhouse in November 1993. To have the champion jockey on your horse would be a considerable boost for most small trainers but Foley went home from Fairyhouse wondering if he should not have ignored Pat Healy's advice.

> Naturally I felt it was nice to have Danoli ridden by somebody with Charlie's experience but, even though I knew Edward O'Grady had first claim on him, I thought he would want to stick

with the horse. I knew he might not be all that impressed because Danoli had to make all his own running, and he only does what he has to when he is in front. But, when Charlie came in, he simply said he wouldn't mind riding him again if he was free. There was not a word about wanting to keep the ride.

Swan's assessment backs up Foley's misgivings: 'Danoli felt like a fairly decent horse that day but there was no suggestion that he could be a future champion. By no means all horses that are top class in bumpers prove to be as good when they go over hurdles. Danoli was obviously going to win more races, but there was nothing about his performance that day at Fairyhouse to make me think he was going to be anywhere near as good as he turned out to be.'

In any case, Swan had other things on his mind, and they were far more disturbing than one novice hurdle winner. The Irish crowds, or rather some of the noisier element, had surprisingly turned against him. The same ones who had been shouting so enthusiastically 'Come on, Charlie' for the past four seasons, were openly questioning both his ability and his nerve. The problem was that he had not ridden a chase winner for three weeks, and the more vociferous of the punters were convinced that he should have done so on at least two occasions. Their taunts began to get to the champion.

I could hear people in the crowd shouting at me and criticising me when I came in after riding in a chase. It started with Belvederian when he was odds-on at Leopardstown. He didn't jump well and he managed only a well-beaten third. The crowds also gave me stick over Lady Olein at Clonmel five days later. She started favourite but she ran below form, and those who backed her didn't like it. They blamed me. In fact there was a reason for her poor run. The Turf Club vet examined her after the race and she was found to be in respiratory distress.

But the punters didn't know this, of course. They thought I hadn't given her a proper ride. I did my best not to let the shouting bother me. I tried to tell myself that it was one of those things that happen to jump jockeys periodically, and that I should not let it worry me. But it did. Also word started to get back to me that certain owners and trainers were saying things behind my back. I have had to contend with people saying I am a better hurdles jockey than a chase jockey for much of my career. It might have been true in my first season's jumping but not from then on. I can, and do, give horses just as effective a ride in a chase as in a hurdle race. It hurts a bit when people don't think I can.

The shouting stopped when Swan followed up a chase win at Tipperary with a third Troytown success at Navan two days later in a purple spell that saw him win on nine out of nineteen rides. One of those nine was Sound Man in a novice hurdle. He won by eight lengths – almost twice Danoli's winning margin – and Edward O'Grady promptly started talking in terms of taking on Tom Foley's unbeaten star at Punchestown. Charlie Swan knew he had a decision to make.

Edward expected me to partner Sound Man. He is a person with an awful lot of confidence in himself and, if you do something wrong, he does not hesitate to tell you – and I knew he wouldn't like it if I said I wanted to get off his horse. I reluctantly told Tom Foley I was sorry but I would not be free to ride Danoli in his next race.

Foley – 'I knew then that Swan was not that interested in riding Danoli anymore' – has always had the utmost belief in Danoli's ability. Sometimes this belief transcends the horse's capabilities, but he tends to be dismissive of those who do not share his faith. So far as he was concerned, the champion had joined this misguided group of disbelievers. He promptly dismissed any further thought of Swan ever riding Danoli again, and told Tommy Treacy that the ride was his.

Treacy looked like keeping it when Danoli scored convincingly at Punchestown on 5 December 1993 to give his young jockey the twenty-fifth, and most significant, win of his career. Ironically for Charlie Swan, Sound Man did not run. He had developed a muscle problem that was to keep him out of action for more than two months – and Swan was forced to watch a winner that could have been his from a remote fourth place on the back of Legal Profession.

Two separate, but not unconnected, incidents in the next three weeks were to destroy Treacy's dreams and swing an important pendulum back in Charlie Swan's favour. Tom Foley, now more than ever convinced that he was training a superstar, resolved to run Danoli in the following month's AIG Europe-sponsored Irish Champion Hurdle. For a novice hurdler, it was shooting at stars but the voluble, small-time County Carlow trainer decided he must first convince himself, and Danny O'Neill, that his aim was straight.

He elected to run Danoli in a schooling hurdle at Punchestown. These educational affairs normally take place on a day when there is no racing, and almost no audience. They are usually run at a pretty ordinary gallop. This one, though, was different. Tom Foley also ran a useful bumper horse in it called Ambitious Fellow and he arranged for Tom Taaffe to ride him. The son of the legendary Pat Taaffe was instructed to set 'a Cheltenham pace'. Taaffe did as he was told and he could scarcely believe it when Tommy Treacy's mount swept past him in the closing stages with, in Foley's words, 'his mouth open and running away'.

Charlie Swan, who finished a long way back on Shawiya, was impressed. So too was Ciaran O'Toole. Early the previous year Mick O'Toole's son had set up the first jockeys' agency in Ireland. The champion was one of his clients and he was on the look-out for rides for him. An agent gets ten per cent of what his jockey is paid. It's a small figure in most races, so big race success is particularly important. O'Toole believed he had seen a suitable candidate for his biggest earner. When he judged the moment to be suitable – a day or two later – he rang Foley and suggested that Swan should ride the horse if he was to go for the Irish Champion Hurdle.

Foley was noncommittal. Frankly, he preferred Treacy. But at the Leopardstown Christmas meeting the unthinkable happened. Danoli was beaten. It was the first time this had happened, and his trainer was vulnerable. There were, in fact, valid reasons for that defeat. The horsebox broke down on the way to Leopardstown and Jessica Harrington, seeing Foley's plight, stopped to offer Danoli a lift in her lorry. But Danoli stubbornly refused to be loaded into it. When he eventually succumbed to all the pushing and shoving, and allowed himself to be taken up the ramp, he panicked. He had to be held by two people all the way to the racecourse, and he was caked in sweat long before he got there. He was still in an over-excited state before the race, and he sweated up again. Then there was no pace and Treacy, even though he knew this would not suit his mount, was forced to make the running. But he set a poor gallop, and Danoli's last lingering chances were swept aside as he made mistakes at the final two flights.

Again Ciaran O'Toole pressed his case. This time Foley discussed what he had said with Danny O'Neill. 'We now knew that we were out of our depth in the Irish Champion Hurdle – although the horse was not – and we decided we had to get the best jockey in the country. If Danoli had not been beaten, though, Tommy Treacy would have kept the ride.'

Foley's unwavering belief in his horse's ability was not shared by either the bookmakers or their customers. Only two of the seven runners in the AIG Europe Irish Champion Hurdle at Leopardstown on 23 January 1994 started at a longer price than Danoli, who was widely expected to be outclassed. Charlie Swan agreed with the consensus.

> In the parade ring before the race, Tom impressed on me that what Danoli wanted was a fast pace. If I felt I had to make the running to get that fast pace, I was to do so. But he also said that the horse was better getting a lead. Tom talks a lot and he went through it all more than once. He stressed how tough Danoli was, that I was to keep after him when the tap was turned on, and that he would keep responding for me. He said that Danoli could go close, even though he was up against good horses like Fortune And Fame and Granville Again, who had won the Champion Hurdle the previous March. Shawiya was also in the field, as was Destriero, who was thought to be on his way back to the sort of form that saw him win the Supreme Novices in 1991.
>
> Danoli was very inexperienced by comparison and I was astonished by how well he ran. I had him handy all the way and, when Adrian Maguire took it up on Fortune And Fame at the second last, it looked over. But, just as Tom had said he would, Danoli battled back bravely when I asked him. His lack of experience made him make a mistake at the last and, even though Fortune And Fame probably won with a bit in hand, we were only beaten a length and a half. The third horse, Shawiya, was ten lengths away.

Swan promptly won the Leopardstown Chase for Edward O'Grady on High Peak. Less than two hours earlier he had also won the Triumph Hurdle trial on O'Grady's Balawhar. The big race aspirations that had prompted the decision to join the County Tipperary trainer were starting to be realised and, when Tom Foley asked him if he would be free for Danoli at Cheltenham, he did his best to fit Danoli into his Festival jigsaw. Sound Man, he said, seemed certain to run in the two mile Supreme Novices on the opening day. Would Foley run his horse in the Sun Alliance Hurdle? If so, he would ride him.

Foley was hesitant. Danoli had shown by running so well against Fortune And Fame over two miles that he had the necessary speed for the Supreme Novices. He did not need the extra five furlongs of the Sun Alliance. Early the following month, though, Swan put the pressure on. He would definitely be free to take the mount in the longer race. If, however, Foley was going to go for the Supreme Novices, he could not have the services of the champion – and, added Swan, Danoli had a better chance of winning the Sun Alliance. He had proved his stamina by winning those three bumpers.

Tom Foley reluctantly conceded. But first Danoli faced a further test in a two and a quarter mile conditions hurdle at Leopardstown on the day of the Hennessy Cognac Irish Gold Cup; his trainer, still tortured by what had happened at the Christmas meeting, decided that he had to do something special to ensure there was a good gallop. The normal practice is to run another horse from your own stable and instruct the jockey to go off in front. This breaks one of the most fundamental rules – that each horse must run on its own merits – but the stewards invariably turn a blind eye.

However, the small County Carlow stable had no suitable pacemaker. Foley's solution was unconventional, too much so for those he approached for help with his self-appointed task. He spoke to two of the other trainers with horses in the race, pointed out that they were all going on to Cheltenham and that therefore they should make it a true test with a searching pace. Then, like Foley, they would find out whether their horses were good enough to run at the Festival. When Michael Hourigan (Court Melody) and Aidan O'Brien (Idiots Venture) both said no, he was disgusted.

> They turned me down flat. They said I could make the running with my horse if I wanted but there was no way they were going to. Their horses would run their own races. I knew then that nobody was going to do me any favours, so I told Charlie not just to make the pace, but to make it a good one. Danoli grabbed the bit, said 'I'm racing' and he won by ten lengths.

Swan was impressed, even more than he had been in the Irish Champion Hurdle, and he promptly informed the press that this was the best prospect of winning at Cheltenham that he had ever had. The more he was asked about Danoli in the next four weeks, the more enthusiastic he became about the horse. It was only in the last few days before Cheltenham that the doubts began to set in.

Half the country seemed to be talking about Danoli, and all the papers were writing about him being a good thing. It dawned on me that just about every Irishman going to the meeting planned to use Danoli as a banker. People were saying that even the Pope was going to back him! During the weekend before the meeting the pressure on me became unreal. Suppose I had over-estimated him or, even worse, if I made a mistake and got him beaten? This was a horse I was meant to be looking forward to riding. Instead, I was beginning to dread it.

11

Balls of Steel

At Nottingham a fortnight before the start of the 1994 Cheltenham Festival, disaster struck for Richard Dunwoody. Riding in a selling hurdle, just about the most minor event in jump racing, he suddenly saw red when his arch-rival Adrian Maguire tried to come up his inside at the second last. The champion took rapid action to stop the challenger, who went out through the wing. Dunwoody, already regretting this uncharacteristic moment of madness, was hauled before the stewards. They showed him no mercy and suspended him for a fortnight. It was the maximum ban they were empowered to impose. It covered the entire Cheltenham meeting. For a man to whom the Festival is as important as Mecca to a Moslem, it was a savage punishment. Jump jockeys, forced to miss the meeting in similar circumstances, can sometimes be seen walking miserably in and out of the weighing room, unable to bear to admit to themselves that they have no part to play. Not Dunwoody. He knew he could not stomach even watching on television what should have been his. He took himself off to Val d'Isere for a skiing holiday. He knew he wouldn't really enjoy it. But in the French Alps there would be no television programmes, or newspaper reports, ramming home the misery of what he was missing.

Among those Martin Pipe called upon to deputise for the British champion was his Irish counterpart, and Charlie Swan's rides at Chepstow on 12 March included a winning one on So Proud in a handicap hurdle. Pipe, a perfectionist himself, was impressed at the precision with which the jockey carried out his instructions.

I told him not to win by too far – So Proud was due to run again at Cheltenham only four days later – and Charlie gave the horse a terrific ride. He won very easily but he managed to keep the winning margin down to a length and a half.

A total of forty-six Irish horses ran at the 1994 Cheltenham Festival. It was the second highest figure for ten years and Edward O'Grady trained five of them. He, like Charlie Swan, was feeling the pressure.

> I had not had a winner at this meeting since Northern Game in the Triumph Hurdle ten years earlier, and the Cheltenham Festival is a tremendously important cog in the racing wheel. If I was to be back where I wanted to be, namely at the top, I had to make a serious impact. Things had to go right for me to do that. Don't forget, I was training a relatively small number of horses, compared to the big stables, and this increased the pressure. With so few arrows in my quiver, I had to look for the bull's-eye every time – and I knew that this was going to prove extremely difficult.

It turned out to be rather more than extremely difficult. The opening day was a disaster for the Irish, for Charlie Swan and, in particular, for O'Grady. He fired three of those five arrows. Two of them were well-backed favourites and none of the three was even remotely near the target. Indeed the closest any of them finished was tenth. O'Grady and his wife Judy took themselves back to the house they had rented in Bishop's Cleeve and attempted to pick up the pieces of their shattered dreams. The O'Gradys rent that house, little more than a mile from the racecourse, to avoid the hubbub that Cheltenham's hotels become for this three days each March. They knew, from painful experience, just how important it is for a trainer to have his wits about him, and not to leave them behind in the riotous late-night atmosphere where sleep – at least before four in the morning – is considered to be only for wimps.

O'Grady, his thick mop of brown hair streaked with grey, ruefully reflected on his day – and on what had caused it to go so horribly wrong.

> I had given Charlie no riding instructions for either Sound Man or Gimme Five. With champion jockeys, it's not normal to do so. I had rather taken it for granted that he had my horses, the opposition and their jockeys critically assessed in his normal way. In Ireland he is a long way superior to the other jockeys and

he knows all the horses. He does this by sheer hard work, and by riding gallops and schooling for every Tom, Dick and Harry who asks him. He realises that, apart from anything else, it helps him to weigh up the horses he is going to meet. Not only does he know how to win on your horse, he knows how to ride the race in such a way that he can expose the weaknesses of the others. But this was a different league and he was up against the best jump jockeys in the world.

Sadly, it was something that I had overlooked. I came to the conclusion that the day might have been different if I had stressed certain things to him, or if I had given him some helpful instructions. I also felt that it had not been one of his cleverer days either. Possibly it was due to over-confidence.

Sound Man made a bad mistake at the second hurdle in the Supreme Novices and Charlie got him straight back into the race. With a lot of horses this would have been the right thing to do. But it wasn't with Sound Man. Knowing this horse as I do, if I had told Charlie to take his time after something like that, the outcome might well have been different. The horse would have had a chance to come back onto the bridle and run the sort of race we had expected him to.

In the Hamlet Cigar Gold Card Final, I ran both Beau Babillard and Gimme Five, but it was the latter who was fancied and whom Charlie rode. There were thirty-two runners which was a huge field and, although the course was wide enough to accommodate them all at the start, it wasn't when they met the track proper. I'd put blinkers on Gimme Five to wake him up but, when the tape was raised, he took a step backwards. Charlie always likes to line up on the inner and he was so keen to maintain his place, and not be cut off when he met the first curve in the rail, that he slapped Gimme Five down the shoulder. It was a natural reaction but for this horse, particularly wearing blinkers, it was a total disaster. He took off, and for much of the three and a quarter miles he was trying to run away. He was burnt out well before the end and finished only twentieth. Beau Babillard was even further behind.

Tom Foley had just as disturbed a night as Edward O'Grady. He could hardly sleep and the more he tossed and turned, the more convinced he became that he would be shown up as a small man with aspirations and expectations totally out of touch with reality. Back in Ireland he had thrived on the pressure. As the Cheltenham meeting had drawn closer, he had taken to sleeping with a gun beside his bed. Danny O'Neill had turned down an offer of £250,000 for Danoli the previous November and, because the horse was hot favourite, he would be worth even more to an unscrupulous bookmaker if he knew he could not win. Foley had heard all about dopers, and he reckoned he knew how to deal with them. Each night he locked all the gates around his stable yard and turned his dogs loose. He was fond of saying that, if he heard anybody trying to get into the yard, he would shoot first and ask questions afterwards!

But he had deliberately given up all personal comfort for the sake of his horse. On the Sunday before the meeting, he had actually travelled with Danoli on the plane from Dublin to Bristol. He had never flown before and, as he expected, he found it a traumatic experience. He also raised a good few eyebrows by announcing that he would stay in the stable lads' hostel. There is a strict social hierarchy in racing, and for a trainer to spend Cheltenham week in the building reserved for the stable staff was almost unheard of. Not even the humblest, and most hard-up, Irish trainers did this. Foley, though, wanted to be near his horse. In addition, like O'Grady, although for slightly different reasons, he did not fancy the idea of a crowded hotel.

In fact the hostel at Cheltenham provides accommodation far superior to that on most of the other English courses. Jim Treacy, who travelled with Foley and who seventeen years earlier had led up Counsel Cottage when he won the race Danoli was going for, described it as 'like a Grade A hotel' with each person having their own room. But the privacy was no help to Tom Foley as he struggled to sleep.

> Sound Man getting beaten so comprehensively troubled me. He had been beating similar horses to those Danoli had been winning against. Just as relevantly, Winter Belle had finished only eighth. It was this horse who had won the race in which Danoli had lost his unbeaten record at Leopardstown. I began to feel that there was an awful difference between racing in England and that at home. By the time I did get some sleep, I had come to the conclusion that all the racing journalists in Ireland had built me up for a fierce fall, and within a few hours I was going to look pretty stupid.

Early on Wednesday morning Edward O'Grady set about making up for the errors of the previous day. Charlie Swan partnered both the

O'Grady runners, Time For A Run and Mucklemeg, in a spin on the course. As soon as he got off them, the trainer started talking tactics.

> These two horses were my last shots. Time For A Run was in the Coral Cup, a thirty-runner handicap that was going to be hard to win. I stressed to Charlie in the strongest possible terms how the horse should be ridden. I told him in plain English that he was to sit patiently for as long as possible, and that he was not to hit the front until as late as possible. I said he was to ride with balls of steel. I also said that it wouldn't worry me if he got beaten for leaving it too late but, if he lost the race by going too soon, I would have his guts for garters.
>
> I don't know how many times I said all this but we went through it all again when we got to the races. I have found Charlie to be a great help to me because he is so interested in the races he is riding in. He is a great one for picking up bits and pieces of information in the jockeys' room, and elsewhere, about the other horses. He passed these onto me as we had further discussions about the race and the way we thought it would develop.
>
> We did much the same with Mucklemeg who was running in the Festival Bumper, the last race of the day. We both knew a fair bit about Time For A Run but a lot less about this mare. I had bought her over three months earlier but I had not run her in a race, and nor had Charlie ridden her in one. This made tactics difficult and, as a result, we discussed things in only the broadest terms. But I was determined to try to cover every eventuality. For instance, what should be done if the gallop was slow; or if, on the other hand, it was particularly fast. Fortunately Charlie is usually able to use his own judgement as the race develops to make best use of what he knows about the horse – and of all the information he has gathered about the others.

The Sun Alliance Novices Hurdle was the first race of the afternoon and for Tom Foley, as the clock steadily and agonisingly ticked away towards the moment that would mean either destiny or disaster, the air of nervous apprehension was almost frightening. And the tie around his neck felt like a hangman's noose.

He had hardly ever worn a tie since leaving school, not even to go to church. Just doing up the top button of his shirt made him feel dizzy but one or two of the newspapers had seized on his intended lack of sartorial elegance and, because Foley reads all the columns of newsprint written about him, his wife had also seen what these papers had had to say. Goretti Foley, who had decided she should stay at home with her four children, was horrified to find that her husband was going to be the only man at Cheltenham with his shirt open at the neck. When Tom told her that he would take a tie with him, stuff it in his pocket and put it on if Danoli won, she was furious. No, she insisted, he must wear it when he went into the parade ring, and he was to keep it on. Dizziness, or no dizziness.

When Charlie Swan picked his way through all the other trainers and owners in the parade ring, and touched his cap to an excited Danny O'Neill, Foley told him: 'The chances are I will never be back here again, so I want you to put in as good a run as you can.'

It was not the sort of remark calculated to instil confidence in a jockey but Swan had already realised that the trainer was having doubts, and he set about putting him at his ease. The celebrated Swan charm worked because, within two minutes, a lot of Foley's own confidence came flooding back.

'We are here to win,' he insisted. 'Our problem is going to be to lie up with the pace. But, if you can do that, Charlie, none of the others will be able to come up the final hill as well as Danoli. If you are there at the last, I reckon it will take a good one to beat you.'

As his pride and joy went off with the other runners down the chute between the milling crowds and out onto the course, Foley went to the stands. He used not the section reserved for owners and trainers but the small part used by the stable lads. Whenever the horses were too far away for him to see what was going on, he switched his gaze to the big screen opposite him, gritted his teeth and said his prayers.

Danoli started hot favourite – it was not just the Irish who had backed him – and Charlie Swan discovered to his delight that Foley's fears about the horse's ability to stay up with the pace were groundless.

> He was travelling so well, and jumping so well, that I went to the front at the fourth last at the top of the hill. It was quite a bit sooner than I should have done, but I didn't want to disappoint him. As we swept into the lead, I heard a roar from the stands. It's most unusual to hear anything so far out and it was not until I saw the replay that I realised why. The commentator had called out 'Danoli has hit the front' and the crowd promptly erupted. Once I was in the lead, I was able to give him a breather but, any time any of the others tried to get near him, he changed gear. The

way he did it was unbelievable and in that respect he is different from any other horse I have ever ridden. I had to push him out up the hill to hold off Carl Llewellyn on Corrouge but, really, he was never a horse that was going to win hard held. You had to make him do it. But he would have found more if Corrouge had been able to get any closer. When we passed the post, I punched the air more in relief than celebration. The Irish banker had won. Thank God.

Funnily enough, each time I ride a Cheltenham winner, the thought goes through my mind that I may never ride another and that I should make the most of the excitement, the cheering and the jubilation. The Irish traditionally let out a tremendous roar when their winners are led in. I wasn't there when Dawn Run won the 1986 Gold Cup but I am told that the reception Danoli got was the noisiest since that race.

When Danoli was led through the cheering crowds to the winner's enclosure, Tom Foley was mobbed by well-wishers and by an avalanche of reporters anxious to get another of the quotes for which the County Carlow trainer was rapidly becoming famous. They were not disappointed. One of them asked Foley how good he thought Danoli was. 'How good is he?' Foley repeated the question as he thought about it, his head quizzically on one side. 'I reckon he is too good for me to say how good he is!'

But not all the Irish were celebrating. When Danoli jumped the final flight, Dorans Pride was less than two lengths behind him. The other Irish horse promptly fell and, even though he looked held by Danoli at the time, some of his connections felt he would have gone close – at the very least – if he had not fallen.

Dorans Pride was trained near Patrickswell in County Limerick by Michael Hourigan and was named after Tom Doran, one of fourteen children of a County Mayo farmer. Doran had left Ireland fifteen years earlier to make his fortune in the building industry in Britain, and he had since set up a profitable construction company on the outskirts of London. He managed to choke back his own disappointment to struggle through the huge crowd surrounding Tom Foley and shake his hand. What Foley said in reply still hurts: 'If your horse had stayed on his feet, we would still have beaten you.'

'I didn't think much of him for that,' Doran recalls with traces of bitterness still in his voice. Several of his eight brothers and five sisters were with him at Cheltenham. So were a small army of his friends.

When he told them about his brief conversation with Foley, a feeling of resentment towards the County Carlow trainer rapidly built up, and with it a burning desire for revenge.

One of those who had backed Danoli was John Patrick McManus. JP, as he prefers to be known, had left his father's plant hire business in County Limerick to become a racecourse bookmaker when he was only twenty. He met with some early reverses – twice he ran out of money – before becoming part of racing legend with a series of spectacular gambles, often at Cheltenham and on his own horses. Dark-haired and quietly spoken, he had hoped to celebrate his forty-third birthday five days late with a big double on the opening day of the 1994 Festival. He owned Gimme Five and he had a share in Sound Man. They cost him dear.

McManus tends to be deliberately vague when quizzed about how much he has won or lost but he is reported to have had more than £100,000 on Danoli, simply to recoup his first day losses. He intended getting into profit in a big way with Time For A Run in the Coral Cup, and Charlie Swan found him in a particularly cheerful frame of mind when he walked back into the parade ring in McManus's famous green and orange-hooped colours.

> The first thing he said to me was that he had got all his money back, so I could go out and enjoy myself. He made no mention of having a bet on Time For A Run. Indeed he never says anything about the money being down. But many owners do. They will say, 'We are having a right few quid on this one and there will be something in it for you if you win. Make sure you do your best.' I don't like this at all. I will be doing my best in any case because I want to win. But knowing that you are expected to land a gamble really puts the pressure on, and it makes me uptight.

McManus grinned with wry amusement when Edward O'Grady repeated his 'balls of steel' instructions but the trainer's concern was with winning the race, not with helping his owner cane the bookies.

> I have never regarded what JP does with his money as any part of my job, and nor do I even ask him. Nor did I back the horse myself. This was a crossroads in my career and, in terms of a mid-life crisis, far too important a race for me to want to be bothered with having a bet.

However, the race was almost halfway through before McManus realised he had no bet either. He had instructed one of his brothers to put the money on for him, and he was not to take less than 10-1. This should not have been a problem. It was a highly competitive handicap and Time For A Run opened at McManus's minimum price before drifting out to 14-1. But the owner's brother was betting on credit, not in cash, and therefore he was restricted to a small number of bookmakers who knew him, and were prepared to bet in the sort of large sums favoured by McManus. The best price they would offer him was 8-1, even though the gelding started at 11-1. Time For A Run was still at the rear of the field when the brother reported that he had turned his back on the 8-1. McManus, watching the race in the stands, promptly saw Charlie Swan beginning to weave his way through the other runners and hit the front after landing over the last. The horse who finished second was So Proud, the one Swan had won on at Chepstow four days earlier.

Ironically, McManus did not back his other winner either. Mucklemeg started favourite for the Festival Bumper and Swan swept her into the lead two furlongs out to slam Aries Girl by three lengths with Rhythm Section, who had not raced since winning the same event twelve months earlier, a remote fourth. This success proved to be enough for the Irish champion to clinch the Ritz Trophy for the second year running.

It also brought him rave reviews in the following day's papers, something that was viewed with distinctly mixed feelings by Edward O'Grady.

> I'd landed a double, and had my first Cheltenham winner for ten years. I knew it was going to stand me in great stead but my achievement was totally overshadowed by Charlie riding a treble and, of course, by Danoli. From a public relations point of view, I was unlucky.

But not ungrateful. Some weeks later he presented Charlie Swan with a memento – a small piece of board covered in green baize. Embedded in it were two metal balls. The inscription read 'Balls of Steel. Time For A Run and Mucklemeg. Cheltenham Festival 1994. Thanks. Edward.' The memento has a treasured place in the jockey's sitting room.

Charlie Swan began Cheltenham Gold Cup day on an understandable high but he was determined not to get carried away. He reminded himself of what could happen if he got too cocky. But racing's fickle fates decided it was time to bring him down to earth anyway, and in the big race he took a crashing fall from Ebony Jane. It is debatable whether the previous year's Irish National winner should have even been in the race – she was a brave staying handicapper and she was to follow up her third in the 1994 Irish National by finishing fourth in the Aintree equivalent a mere five days later – but she was so much out of her depth in the Gold Cup that she started at 100-1, and she was towards the back of the main group when she hit the sixth from home so hard that her jockey was pitched out of the saddle.

Swan picked himself up and got into the ambulance feeling sore. But no worse than that. He was able to take his three remaining rides – two for Martin Pipe, and a close second in the Cathcart – and it was only late that night that the pain in his back really began to make itself felt. He thought that perhaps he had cracked a rib.

For the next month he continued to feel a lot of pain. Sometimes it was only painkillers that kept him riding. The agony was always in the same place, in his back by one of the ribs. He became increasingly certain that it was a hairline fracture. He decided that the only thing was to keep going and eventually it would mend itself. But one day on which there was no racing, and after a particularly bad night, he resolved to drive to Nenagh County Hospital and have it X-rayed. The doctor who examined the X-rays called him in and asked him to sit down.

'Mr Swan,' he began, 'do you know what you've done?'

When the jockey shook his head, the doctor continued. 'You have broken a vertebra.'

Charlie Swan chuckled. No wonder it hurt. He glanced up at the doctor and was surprised to see that his expression was deadly serious. He hadn't finished either.

'Mr Swan, you are a lucky man. The vertebra is now nearly healed. But, if you had had another fall on the same place, or received a kick in this area, the piece of broken bone could have spiked the spinal cord. If that had happened, you would have been paralysed for life and you would now be in a wheelchair.'

The Irish champion drove home in a state of shock. He had been far more frightened by the doctor's words than by any normal fall. He mentally ran through the ones he had had since Cheltenham. Miraculously there had only been three – the first in the mud at Tipperary, the next at the first fence in the Power Gold Cup at Fairyhouse. That could have been nasty but fortunately there were only three runners. The third had been in the Grand National. An image of Paddy Farrell in a wheelchair flashed through his mind. The unfortunate Irishman had broken his back when he had fallen at the Chair in the National thirty years earlier. In the 1994 National the Nicky Henderson-trained Henry Mann had jumped the first fence perfectly only to knuckle over on landing. His rider had been pitched forward onto his feet. The speed he was travelling at had carried him on for several strides before he lost his footing. Charlie Swan remembered how he had picked himself up saying a silent prayer that he had not been kicked, rolled on or trampled. If he had known what the touch of a hoof could have done to his back, he would have got down on his knees and thanked God for his safe deliverance. He was still shocked when he reached home and told Tina what the doctor had said. But, beyond those in his immediate family circle, he never told anyone. That is why his official medical record makes no mention of what was, potentially, the most dangerous fall he has ever had.

He was still feeling the pain when he rode Danoli to an impressive win over Mole Board and Fortune And Fame in the Martell Aintree Hurdle and landed Tom Foley's £50 bet. The man from County Carlow had had few bets in his life and this one, at 5-1, was his first on Danoli.

The physical pain had largely gone by the time it came to the Whitbread Gold Cup towards the end of April. But what was still there was the mental agony of the disqualification three years earlier. The only way to remove that was to win the race. He asked Ciaran O'Toole to find him a mount. Maybe one of the lightweights had no regular jockey.

When O'Toole reported back that he had managed to find one – no easy task, considering most of the jump jockeys in England were after the same thing – Charlie Swan wondered what he had let himself in for.

> The horse was Ushers Island, a no-hoper with a terrible record. I'd ridden him on one of his last Irish starts in the days when he was trained by Ted Walsh. He made a dreadful mistake with me in a chase at Fairyhouse. I ended up on the ground with the bridle in my hand while Ushers Island galloped off towards the racecourse stables. In the Grand National, his most recent start, he had unshipped his rider at the third and then managed to fall again when he was galloping loose! He didn't just fall either. He galloped straight through a fence and brought down one of the leaders. When I told Dessie Scahill I was riding Ushers Island in the Whitbread, he said I was mad. That's what I thought too.

Ushers Island was trained in County Durham by Howard Johnson, a blunt-speaking Northcountryman who is also a farmer. Less than two and a half years later, 'the day job' was nearly the end of him. He was worming a cow when the animal lashed out and fractured his jaw in three places. However, the freak accident left him with rather more than just facial injures. He had a seemingly permanent buzzing noise in his head. He said it felt as if a combine harvester was working close by. The doctors told him he should have an operation. But they also told him there was a risk of it going wrong and, if it did, he would be partially paralysed.

At Sandown on 23 April 1994, though, Howard Johnson was surprisingly enthusiastic about the chances of his eight-year-old. He seemed to think that the Aintree fiasco was almost an irrelevance. Charlie Swan was to jump him off with the leaders, have him up there over the first fence and then settle him. He, Johnson, thought the horse could win. Swan was to do his best.

On this occasion, though, the jockey decided that his first priority was to live to fight another day. He privately made up his mind that, regardless of the instructions, he was going to ride the horse to get round. If he succeeded, and some of the others did not, he just might be able to run past tired horses and sneak a minor placing. Fourth would do nicely. It would also be a miracle.

> Not for one moment did I think he had the slightest chance of winning. When they quickened away from me going down the back straight for the final time, I decided to let them go. The horse was jumping better than I had expected but he was going right at his fences. As we neared the third from home, those in front started to slow. At the same time Ushers Island was showing signs of really staying on. I was astonished. At the last the villain of three years ago, Docklands Express, was in the lead. He was ridden by Norman Williamson, and Philip Hide on Fighting Words was almost level. I was on their heels. I switched my mount to the inner, he quickened and we were in front. And this time I knew the stewards could not take it away from me.
>
> When I was presented to the Queen Mother, I mentioned that it made up for Cahervillahow and, much to my surprise, she both remembered the race and sympathised with me. 'That was terrible,' she said. I was struck by how much on the ball she is.

12

Playing Poker

At the San Marino Grand Prix at Imola in Italy on 1 May 1994 the Williams-Renault driven by Ayrton Senna careered off the track out of control, and one of the best racing drivers Formula One has ever known was killed.

The world of motor racing was plunged into mourning and at Haydock Park the following day jump racing had a tragedy of its own when Declan Murphy was injured so badly that it was thought he would not survive. If he had not done so, Charlie Swan would have had Murphy's death etched on his heart, and his conscience, for the rest of his life.

It was a Bank Holiday in Britain with meetings all over the place, and I flew there primarily to partner Cockney Lad for Mark Roper in the Crowther Homes Swinton Handicap Hurdle, but I also had a couple of rides at Southwell in the evening. The journey was less then 100 miles but, because it would be a nightmare with all the holiday traffic, I arranged to share a helicopter with Richard Dunwoody and Martin Pipe.

I won the first race at Haydock on Admiral's Well for Reg Akehurst and I thought Cockney Lad had a big chance in the Swinton. In the jockeys' room before the race several of us started talking about Ayrton Senna. Declan and I knew each other well from the days we shared digs in Rowanville, and we had been jokingly giving each other a bit of stick. When Senna's death was mentioned, however, Declan became serious. He said how the Brazilian had repeatedly risked his life and got away with it, and the next minute he was dead. He added, and he was still extremely serious, that people did not seem to realise the dangers jump jockeys went through on almost every ride. We all agreed with him. Although none of us liked to think about this sort of thing, we knew he was right. But it did not occur to any of us that little more than fifteen minutes later he would be on the verge of death.

When we came to the last, Michael Hourigan was in front on Dreams End and Declan was chasing him on Arcot. I was behind Declan. I didn't think I could win by this stage but I was hopeful I might run into a place, and it was a valuable race. Arcot hit the hurdle hard, and I could tell by the way he was going down that he was falling. I had a split second to decide whether to go to the right of him, or the left. I steered Cockney Lad to avoid Arcot but he had flattened the hurdle, and Cockney Lad ducked sideways to go through the gap. Not until he was going through it did he see that Arcot was crumpling directly in his path. Somehow he managed to get his hind legs under his hocks and propel himself into the air. But it wasn't enough. Declan was on the ground in front of the fallen horse. Cockney Lad couldn't manage to clear both of them, even though we were going a tremendous lick on the fast ground. I felt a dreadful clunk as Cockney Lad's hoof struck Declan's helmet.

I looked back. Declan was motionless. When we pulled up and turned round, I knew that it was serious. When I got back to the weighing room, and I found out how serious, I thought, 'Oh my God. I have killed him.' I was in a terrible quandary. Somehow I felt I owed it to him to go on to the hospital – he was taken to Liverpool's Walton Hospital, the one where the jockeys used to go when they were hurt at Aintree. But I had committed myself to riding at Southwell. I couldn't just turn round and say I am not going to ride. That would have been letting down the owners and trainers of the horses concerned.

In the helicopter I prayed that he would be all right. On my way back to the airport, though, I rang Walton Hospital. I was told that Declan's condition had deteriorated and that he would not survive. Again I thought of abandoning my travel plans and going straight to Walton. But the more I thought about it, the more I realised there was nothing I could do. The following morning I managed to get hold of his brother, Eamon, who had been at Kevin Prendergast's when I was there. He was now riding for Josh Gifford, for whom Declan was first jockey. I was hoping against hope that he would tell me Declan was improving. But he wasn't. He was still critical, and still not expected to live. I felt awful.

Murphy's skull was fractured when Cockney Lad's hoof hammered into it. He also suffered internal head injuries, and a blood clot formed on his brain. The surgeon had to cut a piece out of his skull to remove the clot. He also had to move the optic nerve to get at the clot and the doctors believed that, if the jockey lived, he would lose the sight of his right eye. Amazingly, not only did he survive, but he made a complete recovery. He even rode again although, very soon after he resumed, he decided to give up race-riding and go into television. He joined the new Racing Channel as a presenter, a job for which the articulate, talkative Murphy was eminently suited.

The first time Charlie Swan saw Declan Murphy after the Haydock fall, Murphy had been out of hospital for several weeks, but the man who had so nearly killed him was horrified at what he saw.

> Declan had changed completely. I had expected him to look frail and shaky after such a dreadful fall and such a major operation. But it wasn't just his head and his body. It was his mind. He just wasn't the same Declan Murphy. He had a totally different outlook on life. Whether it was the fall that did that, I just don't know. It may have been the operation, or what went through his mind during the long convalescence. But when I saw him the next time, he was a little bit more like his old self. I saw him several times more over the next year, and on each occasion I noticed an improvement – as if he had taken another step towards returning to the person he used to be. Perhaps his recovery took a lot longer than people thought.

Early in August 1994, Charlie Swan decided to dispense with his agent. Ciaran O'Toole had expanded his business since setting up Ireland's first jockeys' agency nearly two and a half years earlier and his clients now included both rising star Paul Carberry, and Richard Dunwoody for his rides in Ireland. Both figured among Swan's main rivals and, when the agent booked Dunwoody for two Galway festival winners that Swan reckoned should have been his, he saw red.

> It was not just a question of conflict of interest. I had already made a loose arrangement with Aidan O'Brien whereby I would

ride his horses whenever I was not required by Edward O'Grady and, since he looked like having runners in the majority of the races, there was no point in paying Ciaran ten per cent of my earnings from rides that I was going to have whether I had an agent or not.

In the 1993/94 season only fifteen of Swan's ninety-nine winners had been for Aidan O'Brien, who had provided just sixty-three of the now five-times champion's 496 rides. But O'Brien was fast attracting new owners and his stables, near Piltown at the southern end of County Kilkenny, were expanding rapidly. The previous season's bumper winners were going hurdling and things were really beginning to click into place. As the month wore on, Charlie Swan began to view his commitment to Edward O'Grady with increasing concern. The Ballynonty trainer would again have some big race mounts for him but Swan was fast coming to the conclusion that he had attached himself to the wrong bandwagon. In September he plucked up courage to visit O'Grady, explain the position and ask for his release. The trainer, though, was in no mood to lend a sympathetic ear – and into Swan's he put a sharply delivered flea.

> I pointed out to Charlie that, under our agreement, he had already gone well past his sell-by date for the current season. The agreement had re-started at the beginning of June and it was a bit late to come along in September to say he wanted to change it.

As Charlie Swan drove back to Modreeny with O'Grady's words still burning his ears, the trainer reflected on just why – apart from the agreement – he was so adamant that there could be no parting of the ways.

> He may not be as stylish as some jockeys but I could live with that. I met Mercy Rimell (widow of Fred Rimell, former champion jockey and brilliant jumps trainer) at Cheltenham on the evening after the Time For A Run–Mucklemeg double and she said, 'He is a bit loose.' I thought it was a good description. Like many brilliant people, he would not necessarily be an ideal role model. But he has his own way of doing things, and it is tremendously effective. He also reads a race terribly well and he never gives a horse an unnecessarily hard race. Furthermore he is totally dedicated. I have never known a jockey in Ireland to have

the same appetite for work that he has, and another big plus is that he is terribly good with the owners. He does not fill them with bull but, at the same time, nor does he dash their hopes.

If Charlie Swan had been privy to these thoughts, he might have made the drive home in a rather more cheerful frame of mind. But instead he found himself preoccupied, not only with the air of realism he now had to inject into his relationship with Aidan O'Brien, and indeed with how he was going to have to work to maintain it, but also with how he was to cope with another problem connected with the O'Grady agreement.

Tom Foley was training Danoli for the Champion Hurdle, even though many good judges felt two miles in top company was too sharp for the horse who had become Ireland's favourite. The best four-year-old hurdler in the country the previous season, at least on paper, was Balawhar, trained by O'Grady, and he too was being aimed at the Champion. If Charlie Swan had put all his cards on the table when he visited Ballynonty, he would have pointed out that a major conflict of interest was looming – and how could he be expected to sever his links with a horse that had such huge public appeal? But Swan had chosen to involve himself in a mentally torturing game of equine poker. He intended to keep the ride on Danoli, and not fall out with either Edward O'Grady or Aidan O'Brien in the process. This meant playing some of his cards close to his chest – and praying that somehow they would all miraculously fall into place when the crunch came.

> In this game you never know what is going to happen. Jump racing takes a high toll on horses, and many of them suffer strains and injuries that put them on the sidelines. I tend to try to keep the ride on several so that, if one does get hurt, I still have others to fall back on in the big races. But this means bringing in a fair bit of politics and diplomacy.

The diplomacy included reassuring Tom Foley: 'Charlie told me that he would make sure he was always available to partner Danoli throughout that season.' But a phone call the County Carlow trainer received at the end of November shattered Foley's peace of mind.

> It was from somebody connected with the Dorans Pride people, although it wasn't from Michael Hourigan or Tom Doran, and it

was about the Hatton's Grace Hurdle at Fairyhouse at the beginning of December. Apparently this person seemed to think that Dorans Pride might have beaten Danoli if he had not fallen at the last in the Sun Alliance Hurdle. The caller said he wanted to make a challenge out of the Fairyhouse race. I wasn't standing for that. I told him that I was not interested – and that I was going into the Hatton's Grace to win it, not to get the better of one particular horse.

I got the impression that the Dorans Pride people felt their horse was better than Danoli. I could not see how they could have got that idea into their heads. I felt that Danoli would always have the upper hand over Dorans Pride over hurdles, and in the Hatton's Grace I was more afraid of Atours, who was sent over by David Elsworth after easily winning his previous starts at Ascot and Cheltenham. This was a race that I had planned to take in my stride because, with the Champion Hurdle being my target, December was too early to have my horse at his peak. But the phone call put pressure on me, and I stepped up Danoli's preparation. I drove up to Fairyhouse on the Sunday morning of the race determined to beat Dorans Pride. The race had become so important to me that, if I had been told I could win either the Champion Hurdle or the Hatton's Grace, but not both, I would have opted for the latter.

Both Michael Hourigan and Tom Doran are emphatic they had nothing to do with that phone call. Doran said: 'There was a lot of press talk and a lot of gossip. I feel that the newspapers blew it up into a rivalry that never really existed. But I also suspect that all the press about the matter somehow got to Tom Foley.' Charlie Swan, though, had heard all about it well before the Fairyhouse meeting, and he was dismissive of those responsible.

A lot of silly talk went on. When people have a decent horse, they should be thankful instead of trying to say their horse is better than somebody else's. Dorans Pride would never have beaten Danoli in the Sun Alliance. If he had stood up and tried to tackle Danoli, my mount would have simply pulled out more and gone away again. I was pretty sure Danoli would come out on top in the Hatton's Grace too, and I thought so throughout the race, even though he ran lazily. Pimberley Place went off in front, and much too fast for me and Danoli. He was soon so far clear that, as far as Danoli was concerned, he simply didn't count and it was as if Danoli was making the running himself. Hence the laziness. Pimberley Place fell back beaten before the third last but in the straight there was so much noise coming from the crowd that I thought something was trying to challenge. In fact there wasn't, and we beat Dorans Pride by four lengths with Atours a length back third.

The big Dorans Pride contingent was left licking its wounds, particularly after Tom Foley rubbed salt into them by declaring: 'There was so much talk about what happened at Cheltenham in March that I said I would let my horse do the talking this time. He did just that and I got a lot of pleasure out of this. I am not naming any names but thank God nobody fell today!'

Amid all the excitement, Swan's impressive eleven-length win on Sound Man in the Drinmore Chase half-an-hour earlier went almost unnoticed. But it augured well for Cheltenham and seemed to justify Edward O'Grady's decision to hold on to his jockey. Six days later, though, the pull of Aidan O'Brien's gathering strength was underlined at Punchestown. When Common Sound won the relatively minor Cappagh Hurdle, Charlie Swan passed Joe Canty's 1925 total of 117 Irish wins – Flat and jumps combined – in a calendar year. He had done it with twenty-one days to spare. However, so far as Swan was concerned, what was every bit as relevant was that this was O'Brien's ninetieth success of the season. No trainer had ever had as many winners as this in an Irish National Hunt season, and the 1994/95 campaign was little more than halfway through. Swan knew where his future lay. He also knew that, despite the big guns in Edward O'Grady's stable, he could not afford to let himself be talked into staying put next time round.

Tom Doran and his entourage refused to give in. They decided to take on Danoli a third time, in the Christmas Hurdle at Leopardstown three and a half weeks after having their noses rubbed into the dirt at Fairyhouse. Revenge, when it finally came, tasted sweet, even if it was gained in controversial circumstances.

On Christmas Eve, and again on Christmas Day, Tom Foley noticed Danoli give a few coughs, normally a sure sign that a horse has picked up a debilitating virus. When he called in his vet on Boxing Day evening to scope Danoli – examine his throat and lungs with the aid of an endoscope – traces of phlegm were visible on the lungs. Most trainers would have taken heed of this as confirmation of an infection, and have withdrawn the horse. But Foley decided to risk it. He made, as he was the first to admit, a disastrous mistake. The Christmas Hurdle was run less than forty-eight hours after that veterinary examination and Danoli trailed in a distance behind his old rival, but only after his jockey had been put through agonies of indecision.

> Danoli seemed well in himself at Leopardstown, even going down to the start and for most of the race. Tom Foley had made public the news of the coughing and the phlegm found by the vet. But he told me that it was probably nothing to worry about. These sort of infections, though, often don't really show up as serious until the horse comes under pressure. It was not until after the third last, when I was disputing the lead with Dorans Pride, that I found out Danoli really was suffering from something. The minute I asked him to quicken, he emptied. I was in a quandary. Although Dorans Pride went away from me, I was still in second place a long way clear of the rest. I felt it would be wrong to pull him up. He was a 2-1 on favourite, and I could tell he could keep going. Obviously I could not stop riding him but, equally, I couldn't bear to be hard on him. I seemed to spend the rest of the race alternatively looking round to see where the others were, and urging him to keep clear of them.

Michael Hourigan, surrounded by pressmen egging him on to get his own back on Tom Foley, sportingly refused to do so. He pointed out that this was not his way of operating. He also said that he had learnt this the hard way after going through his first six years as a trainer without a winner. However, Tom Doran, reflecting nearly two years later on what had happened, commented cryptically: 'I read the reports that Danoli was sick. But, in that case, What A Question must have been sick too because she finished a distance behind Danoli.'

Charlie Swan's poker-playing paid off when Balawhar was ruled out for the season and when Montelado, another in his Champion Hurdle deck, had his reappearance repeatedly delayed. The way seemed clear for him to ride Danoli. But Foley was having desperate problems. The horse was put on antibiotics after his Leopardstown flop, and after losing his place at the head of the Champion Hurdle market, and a new vet was called in. Foley refuses to name him.

> The owner brought him in, and this vet wanted Danoli to be laid

off for the rest of the season. He couldn't tell me what was wrong with the horse but he prescribed various different medicines. I did not give Danoli half of them. I was convinced he didn't need them. Indeed, he returned to some right good form, but the vet would not give me the go-ahead to run him. One day I decided I would ring him to try to get to the bottom of it. I resolved to make him say why he thought the horse was not ready to run. But he did not give me the answers I wanted.

I felt I had reached the stage where the owner should step in and either say the horse should run, or the vet should take him over. When I discussed things with Danny O'Neill, he asked me what I would like to do. I asked for one of the top vets from the Curragh to come down and check out the horse. We decided on Kieran Bredin. He said there was nothing wrong with Danoli and that we should go ahead with him. But we had missed the Irish Champion Hurdle and the alternative, the Red Mills Trial Hurdle at Gowran Park, had to be postponed for ten days when the course became waterlogged. I then decided the ground was too heavy, and that the race was too close to Cheltenham.

Danoli had to make do with a schooling hurdle, enterprisingly laid on by the Leopardstown management, before racing at its meeting run five days after the Gowran Park meeting eventually took place. But Foley was lucky to have Charlie Swan on board, and indeed the jockey was counting his blessings that he was still in one piece after a horrific fall at Gowran.

I had arranged to ride Never Back Down in the Red Mills Trial Hurdle if Danoli was withdrawn. There were only four runners but she was a long way last and dead-tired by the time she fell at the final flight. She rolled as she fell, and I was trapped underneath her. She tried to get up. When she found she couldn't, she panicked and started to lash out. It was one of the few times I have really been frightened. My head was by her hooves and, try as I might, I could not pull my legs out from under her body. I put my arms round my head to try to protect myself. The hooves were hammering my arms and I yelled to Liam Healy for help.

The burly racecourse photographer, father of Pat Healy, ducked under the rails, rushed across the course and deposited his not inconsiderable bulk on the horse's head. Never Back Down suddenly had something else to think about other than her panic-stricken difficulties in getting to her feet. Apart from the weight on her head and neck, her vision was blanked out. Healy knew from previous experience that this, far from making a horse even more frightened, would have a temporarily tranquillising effect. But Charlie was still trapped. It was Healy's turn to shout for help. Two of the rapidly growing number of onlookers stepped forward and, following the jockey's instructions, bravely took hold of the mare's hind legs. She did not resist and two more people, encouraged by the first two and by Swan's urgent shouts, took hold of her front legs. They were able to roll her over and so release the by now ashen-faced Swan.

On the Saturday evening before the Cheltenham Festival Adrian Maguire's mother died. David Nicholson's brilliant young stable jockey was devoted to Phyllis Maguire, who was only fifty-six. The funeral took place in County Meath on Tuesday, the first day of the meeting, but Maguire soon decided he should not ride on any of the three days. He was so stricken by grief that he felt he would not be able to do himself justice. David Nicholson immediately started hunting round for replacements. It was no easy task with most of the top jockeys already booked. Charlie Swan had ridden Putty Road to win at Leopardstown before the horse had been sold out of Aidan O'Brien's stable but he was obliged to tell Nicholson, with no little regret, that he was committed to O'Brien's Trickle Lad whose chance in the Sun Alliance Hurdle was nothing like so obvious. However, he had no ride in the Queen Mother Champion Chase and he was delighted to get the call for Viking Flagship, who had won the race the previous year.

But for the Irish champion, hoping to win the Ritz Club Trophy for the third successive year, the first day of the Festival proved a nightmare. On Edward O'Grady's Ventana Canyon in the opening Supreme Novices Hurdle, he was beaten two lengths by Tourist Attraction. It was a winner that, had it not been for the O'Grady agreement, could have been his. He had ridden the mare to victory at Navan two months earlier. Then came the Arkle Trophy, and he was second again. This time on Sound Man who was outbattled up the run-in by Klairon Davis even though Frank Woods had lost his whip.

The Champion Hurdle was next and Danoli started joint favourite with Large Action.

Graham Bradley on Mysilv set a cracking pace. It was so fast that, if I had wanted to make the running, I would have been off the bridle just to get to the front. Even so, I was half flat-out almost throughout the race. We made good progress to join the leading group coming to the third last but, just when I thought I was in with a chance, Danoli struck the hurdle hard. Instead of landing running, he hit the ground on all fours and lost his momentum. It was quite the wrong time for this to happen. Whether it was just the way he landed, or something worse after hitting the hurdle so hard, I still don't know. But from that point on he hung desperately. I could never get him out to challenge. In the end I had to let him try to make up his ground on the inside. A lot of people said afterwards that the two mile trip was too short for Danoli and, while he is definitely better over further, I do believe he would have been second instead of third if he had not made that mistake. Tom was disappointed. In some ways he is his own worst enemy because he hypes the horse up so much. He thinks Danoli is unbeatable and, when the horse does meet with defeat, it's a big downer for him.

Foley, as Swan suggested, was unwilling to accept the result at face value. Nor was he prepared to concede that all the critics – who had been so adamant that Danoli was not fast enough to win a Champion Hurdle – had a valid point.

I left the tactics to Charlie, but I would have preferred it if he had ridden the horse up with the pace. Danoli does everything better when he is up there. Charlie told me afterwards that he wanted to wait until after jumping the third last before making his move in earnest. He pulled the horse back a bit coming into the hurdle, and Danoli thought he was being asked to take off. But the horse was a bit too far away, and he realised he was wrong. He put down again, hit the top of the hurdle and almost fell.

Charlie Swan had been beaten on all his six mounts by the time it came to Wednesday's showpiece, the Queen Mother Champion Chase. As he had feared, the Sun Alliance Hurdle had turned out too hot for Trickle Lad but not for Putty Road, who proved a fortunate chance ride for Norman Williamson, enjoying the sort of Cheltenham that most jockeys have only in their most far-fetched dreams.

David Nicholson, son of Frenchie, who had given Mouse Morris his grounding in the art of race-riding, had been a highly successful jump jockey for more than twenty years when he retired in 1974 and decided to concentrate on training. A tall, sometimes haughty-looking man, he was nicknamed 'The Duke' by one of his father's stable lads when he was still at Haileybury. The lad was referring to the public schoolboy's accent and his self-imposed air of superiority. But the nickname stuck, and these days the Jackdaws Castle trainer is conspicuous by his insistence on wearing red socks and a curious-looking sheepskin coat, almost regardless of the weather. He is incredibly superstitious – hence the attire – but for a long time the Cheltenham Festival seemed to be a personal bogey, and he had been training for eighteen years before he finally broke his duck.

However, he had won the Triumph Hurdle as well as the Champion Chase the previous year and, with the Sun Alliance Hurdle already in the bag, he was more than optimistic that Viking Flagship could do it again.

> Viking Flagship had run badly when starting favourite for the Victor Chandler Handicap Chase at Ascot in January, and he then tipped up when 5-2 on for the three-runner Game Spirit Chase at Newbury the following month. He would have won if he had stayed on his feet but I was running out of time and he needed the outing when I sent him to Kempton for the Emblem Chase a fortnight later. The ground that day was deplorable. It was like a gluepot and he was beaten a length by Thumbs Up. But I thought he would have won if he had not made a mistake at the last. I was bullish about his chance at Cheltenham.

Charlie Swan had never ridden the horse before but he had spent much of the previous evening going through the videos of the gelding's previous races. He had come to the same conclusion as Nicholson. So had the punters. Viking Flagship started 5-2 favourite. Swan listened carefully to the trainer's instructions – 'buck him out, give him a bit of light and ride a race on him'. He also took the precaution of talking to the horse's lad as he was led round the paddock. What he learned was something that Nicholson had not told him, but it was to prove every bit as relevant as the riding instructions. Swan also had his own ideas about how the horse should be ridden.

> Viking Flagship had been in the limelight for some time and I

had been watching him a lot on television. I'd come to the conclusion that the two miles of the Champion Chase was a bit on the sharp side for him and so I made up my mind that, if I was going in any way well, I would kick on quite some way from home. Warren Marston on Egypt Mill Prince made the running. I had my horse just where I wanted him to be and he was travelling smoothly. At least he was until we got onto the dead ground in the back straight when he suddenly started to make a noise in his throat. Something was obviously wrong. But then what the lad had said came back to me – 'Sometimes he will gurgle for no reason. Leave him alone and he will come back on the bridle for you.' I sat still and, as we reached the top of the hill where the ground was better, whatever was troubling him cleared itself and he was back on the bit. He was soon travelling so strongly that I decided to go on. We had only a narrow lead over Deep Sensation coming to the final fence but I could tell, from the way Norman Williamson was niggling, that we had him beaten. We flew the last and quickly opened up a five-length advantage.

A few brief words with the Queen Mother preceded Time For A Run's attempt to win the Coral Cup for the second year running. But this time there was no happy ending, and the balls of steel of twelve months earlier somehow seemed to shrivel – and with fatal consequences. Swan again rode the horse from well back but, instead of waiting until he had jumped the last before hitting the front, his mount was going so strongly that his rider let him take it up well before he reached the final flight. What happened after that showed just why Edward O'Grady had been right to insist on waiting so long the previous year. Two other Irish horses, whose jockeys had ridden with rather more patience, swept past on the run-in and Time For A Run was only third.

O'Grady found the three defeats hard to take, particularly after his first day disasters had turned into glorious triumph within twenty-four hours a year earlier.

Charlie went a bit soon on Time For A Run but I blame the way the race developed for that rather than the jockey. On Ventana Canyon he had hoped for a lead to the final flight, but he was tracking Callisoe Bay, who collapsed after the second last and left Charlie in front. As regards the Arkle Trophy, subsequent history has shown that Sound Man was up against a future champion in Klairon Davis. But a total of six lengths cost us three Cheltenham races. If we had won just one of those three, I feel it would have been justice. Since when, though, has justice been any part of racing?

13

The Call of O'Brien

Tom Foley decided Danoli should be allowed to try to make up for his Champion Hurdle failure by attempting to win the Martell Aintree Hurdle for the second successive year. But, when he heard that Dorans Pride was to be among the opposition in the Grand National curtain-raiser, the County Carlow trainer took it almost as a personal insult.

> The same people who said Dorans Pride might have beaten Danoli if he had not fallen at the last in the 1994 Sun Alliance Hurdle, and who said their horse could prove it in the Hatton's Grace, now seemed to think they could beat us at Aintree. They were clearly hard men to convince and I don't know what they thought they were going to prove. Dorans Pride was always second best to Danoli over hurdles. But we had to go out and show them all over again.

However, Dorans Pride had won the Stayers' Hurdle with incredible ease and, for Tom Doran and his entourage, it was not so much a matter of proving anything as a question of principle: 'It's all right for Tom Foley to make comments like that but the fact is I never shied away from a challenge against Danoli. Indeed, there is rivalry in every sport, and quite right too.'

The fast ground, though, was all against Dorans Pride. It was against Danoli too, and for most of the race Charlie Swan was convinced it was taking its toll.

He was hanging in – leaning left towards the rails – the whole way round and, when we went past Mysilv coming to the second last, Danoli hung in even worse. From the stewards' point of view, we were probably far enough in front of Mysilv for them not to take any action, but she was a little bit blinded for a vital few strides, and she took a heavy fall. Norman Williamson on Boro Eight was challenging strongly but Danoli battled on with his usual bravery to hold them off and win, with Dorans Pride only fourth. I gave Danoli a pat as I pulled him up. But, the minute I turned him round to canter back towards the stands, I noticed he was lame.

Tom Foley believes he saw the horse nod as he was pulled up. When he rushed up to Swan, to be told 'I think he has cracked something', Foley's immediate thought was not that a bone had been fractured but that the horse had damaged a tendon and had broken down. Surprisingly, Swan did not dismount.

I told Tom that I would get mobbed if I did. It's a long walk to the unsaddling enclosure at Aintree and the crowds were massive. I was afraid that, if I got off and led him in, people would come surging round me and some of them would get hurt. Danoli gets uptight when people crowd round him and I knew he would start firing himself all round everywhere. I felt that the damage to his leg had already been done, and it would not get any worse simply by having me sit on him for another five minutes. The opposite, if anything, because he would be able to walk back quietly. But it was not until just before I left the course that evening, when I bumped into Jim Treacy, that I realised how serious the crack was. I immediately thought back to that mistake at Cheltenham when he had hit the hurdle so hard. It was then that he had started to hang. I am inclined to think that it was there that the crack first developed. Sometimes a horse can incubate an injury and it does not show itself until he actually races again. The Aintree race, and the fast ground, probably aggravated it. This would also account for him hanging from the start in the Martell. When I heard the following day where the crack was, and that it would mean an operation, I felt that Danoli would never race again.

The crack turned out to be a severe fracture in the near-fore fetlock joint, between the cannon-bone and the long pastern. This joint, roughly equivalent to the ankle in a human, takes much of the strain of a racehorse's half-ton weight when he is galloping and jumping. That it could be repaired as good as new, and just as strong, seemed inconceivable. Certainly, had the injury happened to a human athlete, there would be doubts about him or her ever being as good again. There are further problems in operating on horses. At one time many did not come round from the anaesthetic and, although the fatality rate has been improved out of all recognition, the after-care still involves major difficulties. Horses cannot be expected to understand that they are required to stand with a leg in plaster for weeks on end because it is the only way they will recover; nor can they be made to understand that the enforced inactivity is for a limited period only. Some simply lose the will to make a full recovery.

Indeed, it is frequently considered kinder to put a horse out of its misery than subject him to an operation and a doubtful future. Danoli was fortunate to be owned and trained by men prepared to do anything to save his life, and also to come under the care of a veterinary surgeon as skilled as Chris Riggs.

Dr Riggs, although still only thirty-two, was the professor in charge of the equine unit at the Leahurst Veterinary College in the Wirral in Cheshire. The College is part of the University of Liverpool and it was to Dr Riggs that Danoli was sent, with the help of a police escort, shortly after the Grand National had been run. Riggs had X-rays taken and found that 'the fracture was a nasty one and that there was quite a bit of damage to the joint'. After carrying out an operation to repair the fracture by inserting screws into the bones, he was optimistic that the horse would survive. But he warned that there was a danger of arthritis setting in at a later date, and he privately told Tom Foley not to build up his hopes – 'only a handful of horses who have had this sort of injury have made it back to the racecourse, and most of them were two-year-olds. The chances of a seven-year-old racing again, particularly over jumps, are no more than fifteen per cent.'

Charlie Swan, out of luck in the Grand National – the ground was too fast for Riverside Boy – fared even worse in the Irish equivalent. He jumped the first fence perfectly on Jassu but, as the horse landed, another cannoned into him and knocked him down. Events at the end of May, though, proved of far more significance and Swan found himself forced into taking prompt action in a bid to keep his position at the top of the tree.

He finished up the season with a new record of 118 winners in Ireland from 542 rides. No less than 248 of these, plus more than half the winners, had been provided by Aidan O'Brien, but Swan could see a dark shadow closing in. The shadow was the by now frequently gaunt figure of Richard Dunwoody. As the British season drew to a close with Dunwoody landing his third successive championship, he let it be known that he had had enough of chasing titles, and chasing winners from one end of the country to the other. From this point on, he was going to aim for quality rather than quantity. Furthermore, and this was what gave Swan sleepless nights, he was going to ride more in Ireland.

When Martin Pipe rang to offer him the job as his stable jockey, Charlie declined. He next had to end the O'Grady arrangement. Aidan O'Brien had made it clear that he would like to have first claim on him. He did not put it in as many words, but the jockey gained the impression that he would no longer put up with having somebody who was not going to be available for all his best horses. Swan rang O'Grady and arranged to go over to see him.

He explained that, although some of Edward's horses were better than those of O'Brien, the latter had so many horses that riding for him would guarantee the championship – and that was the option he wanted to take. What he did not tell O'Grady was that he was frightened that, if he did not say yes to O'Brien, Richard Dunwoody would be asked to take the job. O'Grady replied that Charlie should go away and think about it before committing himself. A week later Charlie was back at Ballynonty. This time his resignation was accepted. A few weeks later he heard that O'Grady had fixed up a replacement. It was Richard Dunwoody!

Aidan O'Brien was not yet twenty-six and he had held a licence for only two years. Yet he had established a new prize money record for an Irish National Hunt season in his first twelve months, when he was also the champion amateur rider, and in the 1994/95 season he had sent out an incredible 138 winners. He was also training a phenomenal number of horses and had run 165 of them in the season just ended. The trainer with the next biggest hand, Michael Hourigan, had run ninety-eight. Nobody else in Ireland had run more than sixty under National Hunt rules that season.

The son of a County Wexford farmer and permit holder, he decided he wanted to become a trainer when he was still at school. When he left, at the age of sixteen, his father entrusted him with his six point-to-pointers. But the young O'Brien's ambitions far exceeded his knowledge. Each of the six went wrong, and not one of them made it to the course. The farmer decided that it was time his racing-mad son had a proper job. He found him a temporary one picking strawberries and, when the season was over, another in the Waterford Co-op. There was no closed season for sweeping floors but the quietly-spoken farmer's son proved good at this, so good that he was promoted. To driving a fork-lift truck.

After eight months, though, he decided to try racing again. A friend fixed him up with a job with P.J. Finn on the Curragh. The flamboyant PJ is a son of the legendary Tipperary hurling captain, Jimmy Finn, who is now a farmer near Cloughjordan. PJ's brother, Jimmy junior, married Charlie Swan's elder sister, Natasha, and they now live next door to Modreeny. But after Aidan O'Brien had been with P.J. Finn for two months, his boss decided to move on. The would-be trainer was still only seventeen and he found employment with Jim Bolger at Coolcullen in County Carlow. Bolger expects his staff to work every bit as hard as he does. Not all of them have been either willing or able to stand the pace but O'Brien, brought up on a farm, already knew that working with animals was an almost round the clock affair.

He went to Coolcullen as a stable lad but his lack of experience meant that, for the first three weeks, he was not allowed to ride out. He stayed there for three and a half years and, by working tirelessly from dawn until dusk ('I often started in the dark and finished in the dark'), he became one of his boss's most trusted aides. He also became an extremely capable amateur rider and in August 1989, when he was two months short of his twentieth birthday, he met his future wife at Galway. They were both riding in the same race. He won it on Jim Bolger's appropriately named Midsummer Fun, but what he remembered most about the race was the dark-haired girl who finished fifth, and the few words they had exchanged when they were circling round at the start.

The attractive Anne Marie Crowley was a part-time model. She was four months older than Aidan and the eldest of the six daughters of Joe Crowley, who farmed and trained a few horses – many of them bred by himself – at Piltown in County Kilkenny. Anne Marie also had ambitions to train and at the beginning of 1991 she took over her father's permit. She traded this in for a full licence and in August that year her boyfriend left Jim Bolger to help his future wife. They became a wonderfully successful partnership although, as the winners mounted and the patronage increased, Anne Marie seemed to prefer to take more and more of a back seat in the winner's enclosure. She deflected most of the questions put by the press to her husband. He was dreadfully shy, and he found this part of being a trainer every bit as difficult as his wife did.

At the end of the 1992/93 season, when Anne Marie became Ireland's first woman champion trainer and also a mother, Aidan took over the licence and stepped the operation up a gear. The winners snowballed and, to the amazement – and indeed horror – of many of his rivals, he showed that he had mastered the art of running his horses often without them losing their form. He had learnt this, as so much else of his training knowledge, from observing how Jim Bolger had run his operation. There was a hill behind the stable yard O'Brien and his wife had built on Joe Crowley's farm. The young couple constructed an all-weather gallop up this hill, similar to the one at Coolcullen but much steeper. In the first seven furlongs it rises 300 feet. There is also an extra furlong, beginning with a sharp right-handed turn, and it climbs so steeply that few human beings could even walk up it without becoming out of breath. O'Brien reserved this final grueller for bumper horses making their debut. If they were fit enough, and strong enough, to continue up the last furlong without much effort, they were ready to win a two mile Flat race at the first time of asking.

The uphill gallop makes a lot of sense. The horses take less work to get fit than they do on conventional flat, or flatter, gallops. They also do not have to gallop as fast so the strain on their legs is nothing like as great. Furthermore, because the horses do not have to work so often, they can race more frequently. It is no coincidence that Martin Pipe, who has also shown that he is able to make his horses run often without loss of form, uses an uphill gallop. But there is more to getting horses to stand up to frequent racing than simply working them uphill, and O'Brien had carefully observed the painstaking attention that Bolger paid to ensuring the horses overcame the effects of the dehydration caused by racing, and by travelling to and from the racecourse. O'Brien worked out how much water each of his own horses got through in a day, and how much more they needed to drink to put back the effects of a hard piece of work. When they went away to race, he instructed the lads to tell him how much the horses had drunk on the journey. When they returned home, he monitored the level of the water bowls. He also put electrolytes into the feed. These replace the body salts a horse loses in a race. They also contain vitamins C and E, as well as protein. Once the liquid, and the salts, had been replaced, the horses were ready to run again. O'Brien maintained they were happier kept on the go.

'If you took the weekend off,' he reasoned, 'you might not feel like going back to work on Monday. You would be better off if you kept working. It's the same with horses.'

Not everybody would agree with O'Brien's logic. But it was an approach to life that he certainly applied to himself. He worked even harder than he had done at Coolcullen. By 6.30 a.m. he was feeding every horse in the yard. When he was not away racing, he did the lunchtime and evening feeds too. He also rode most of the work in his first year. He seldom finished his rounds of the stables before 10.00 p.m. Often it was nearer midnight. He never took a day off, let alone a holiday.

However, success in racing's small world is invariably greeted more with envy and resentment than with recognition and praise, at least among the professional element. Many of those whose horses were beaten by the O'Brien runners, and most of those who lost horses to the new training sensation, refused to believe that a shy, bespectacled and baby-faced youngster of twenty-four could possibly be doing so well. Word went round that it was really O'Brien's father-in-law who was doing the training. Credence to the rumour, which spread like wildfire and which was treated as gospel in many quarters, was given by the fact that Joe Crowley helped to look after one of the three yards that O'Brien operated on the Crowley farm. The gossips conveniently forgot that it had not been Crowley's idea to build such a testing gallop, that he had never run his horses at such frequent intervals, and that he had never chosen to train huge numbers of them. In fact the small, white-haired farmer did play a significant part in the operation. Not so much in the training, although his son-in-law appreciated the older man's advice, but in buying the bumper horses. It was Joe Crowley who attended the sales, studied what was on offer and used his expertise to select which ones to buy.

One man who ignored the rumours was John Magnier, the boss of the huge Coolmore Stud operation. When the legendary Vincent O'Brien, Magnier's own father-in-law, decided in October 1994 that at the age of seventy-seven it was time for him to give up training, Magnier immediately asked Aidan O'Brien to take over the stables and training grounds at Ballydoyle. Furthermore, Magnier said that he, and other owners associated with him, would give O'Brien a string of superbly bred Flat horses to train. Ballydoyle is, arguably, the best training establishment in the world. To make such an offer to a man so young, and who had held a licence for less than eighteen months, was an incredible act of faith. But it was also recognition by the shrewd, calculating Magnier that he had spotted genius at work. Significantly Magnier made the offer to O'Brien, and to O'Brien alone. There was no mention, not even an implied one, of any part Joe Crowley might, or might not, play in the new operation.

Remarkably O'Brien elected to use the Magnier offer, not as replacement for all the hard work he was putting in on the jumpers at Piltown, but to add to it. He simply got up a little earlier and drove the twenty-five miles to Ballydoyle once, and sometimes twice, a day. He soon became almost as effective a force on the Flat as he was in jump racing. As Ballydoyle began to take up more of his time, he decided to uproot Anne Marie and their fast-expanding family from their small house in the middle of the main stable block to a bungalow on the Ballydoyle estate. It used to be occupied by Elizabeth McClory, Vincent O'Brien's eldest daughter. But the change to Aidan O'Brien's punishing routine was minimal. There was no let-up in either the numbers at Piltown, or in the demands on the trainer's time. Instead of travelling to Ballydoyle each day, he simply made the same journey in reverse.

There is no uphill gallop at Ballydoyle – at least not with the sort of gradient as the one at Piltown – but O'Brien had already decided on a switch to the quality races with his best horses. The ordinary ones were still run often but the good ones were raced far less frequently. It is a measure of O'Brien's brilliance that he has been able to produce results every bit as good from a training establishment run on conventional, albeit superbly equipped, lines as he has with the one he still runs in tandem. It is also a measure of his willpower, constitution and dedication that he has been able to stick the pace.

It was Vincent O'Brien who transformed Ballydoyle from an ordinary agricultural farm into a superb training establishment and throughout the years he was there – he moved his operation from Churchtown in County Cork in 1951 – he was always trying to improve the place. When he was driving round the estate, he would frequently spot something that he thought should be changed and stop for a closer look. Aidan O'Brien does much the same and in 1996 widening the access roads was one of the aspects that he felt demanded his attention. He has also made other changes there, including a schooling ground, complete with Grand National fences, on the land across the road from the gallops.

He seems just as proud of the latter as his predecessor, and visitors lucky enough to be taken on a conducted tour are shown the replica of Tattenham Corner, the four-and-a-half-furlong two-year-old gallop which runs parallel to the main drive, and the Ascot gallop. This, as its name suggests, is where the horses going to Royal Ascot complete their preparation and O'Brien first made his mark on this meeting in 1997 when Harbour Master won the Coventry Stakes. Just twelve days later the young trainer stunned the racing world by winning the Budweiser

Irish Derby with Desert King and becoming the first since Paddy Prendergast thirty-four years earlier to make a clean sweep of Ireland's first three classics. The most significant difference since his predecessor's day, the schooling ground apart, is that there is now a row of hurdles alongside the back straight of the Derby course. The jumpers are not necessarily confined to Piltown, and indeed those Flat horses thought to benefit from the gruelling all-weather climb are boxed over to work up it. The staff are expected to be equally as versatile and, although they no longer call the boss 'Sir', the respect they showed under the old regime is still very much there.

O'Brien denies that he had Richard Dunwoody in mind for the job if Charlie Swan had not severed his link with Edward O'Grady.

> I knew about Charlie's visit to Ballynonty in September 1994 to ask to be released from his agreement, and obviously I knew about him going back again the following summer. If he had stayed with O'Grady, I would have had to get somebody else for my horses for the 1995/96 season but I had not given much thought about who that might be because I felt there was no need. The way I looked at the picture, it made no sense for Charlie not to agree to be my first jockey with all the winners we have. And I was certain that Charlie would do the sensible thing.

Aidan O'Brien has a knack of being able to improve horses sent to him from other trainers, sometimes by incredible amounts. The most notable case was Life Of A Lord, and Charlie Swan's doubts about his boss's ability to keep on improving the horse were to cost him dear.

Life Of A Lord was a nine-year-old when his owner, Michael Clancy, who owned and ran the Bridge House Hotel at Spiddal in County Galway, decided to transfer him from Tom Costello to the young trainer who was making all the headlines. The gelding had shown a fair bit of ability and had won three of his final four starts in 1993. But, before he joined O'Brien, he had run twelve times on the trot without reaching the frame. What he had reached, when Clancy decided to make the switch, was the age at which steeplechasers are believed to reach their peak. There would obviously be a race or two in him if O'Brien could bring him back to form, but the scope for sustained improvement appeared distinctly limited. The gelding had an official handicap rating of 116 which meant he was more than three stone below the best chaser in the country, Merry Gale.

When Life Of A Lord had his first start for his new trainer at Gowran Park at the end of June 1995, he was set to carry 11st 13lb. Charlie Swan decided it was too stiff a task and elected to partner O'Brien's other runner, Kelly's Pearl. Tony O'Brien, no relation to the trainer and a jockey who had few opportunities, was given the mount on Life Of A Lord. The pair won by more than five lengths, much to the surprise of the stable jockey, who managed only third.

Swan rode Life Of A Lord, though, when he led throughout the Galway Plate trial at Tipperary three and a half weeks later. But this win meant a penalty for the Plate and the handicapper decided to give the horse 7lb. It looked as if he was taking the easy way out by ensuring that Life Of A Lord could not make it three in a row. After all, Life Of A Lord's winning margin had only been two lengths and he had had to be ridden to win the race. Swan did not see how the horse could succeed in the famous Galway race.

> Life Of A Lord had not beaten all that much when he won at Tipperary, and he might not have won at all if Desert Lord had not fallen and broken a leg at the final fence; he was challenging me at the time and was going every bit as well. If Desert Lord had won, then Life Of A Lord would not have been given a penalty in the Plate. Instead, he had the equivalent of seven lengths. Aidan also ran Kelly's Pearl and Loshian in the race but, to be sure I was not making a mistake, I waited until I had ridden all three in their final work-outs on the Saturday before the race before finally deciding which to ride. I opted for Loshian, even though she had not raced since the Irish National at Easter, but I felt she was well handicapped. Certainly she was a lot better treated than Life Of A Lord.

Loshian did not enjoy the best of runs – she was hampered at the first and again before the ninth – but her jockey, to his considerable chagrin, was obliged to watch from way behind as Trevor Horgan sent Life Of A Lord to the front after the ninth, and then drew further and further away to beat Kelly's Pearl by twenty lengths with Loshian only third. It was one of the biggest winning margins in the 126-year history of the race and, so far as anybody could tell, the first time that a trainer had sent out the first, second and third in the Plate.

The result gave almost as much satisfaction to Noel O'Brien as it did to Aidan O'Brien. The former, again no relation, had taken over as senior jumps handicapper from Ted Kelly earlier in the year, and he had been widely criticised for giving Life Of A Lord such a big penalty for his Tipperary win. However, when O'Brien put the horse up a further 15lb to 142 after Galway, there was not even a murmur of protest. O'Brien, the handicapper, had proved he knew almost as much about his job as his namesake did about training horses. Indeed, Life Of A Lord went on to make it four in a row in the Kerry National at Listowel. None of the huge crowd who cheered the gelding to the echo as he passed the post – with the champion jockey saluting the packed stands – thought, even in their darkest dreams, that they would witness his death at virtually the same spot twelve months later.

The horse, his jockey and his trainer were riding the crest of an almost continuous wave of success that seemingly knew no bounds. But for Charlie Swan one of the smallest fish was the sweetest. On 15 August he won on all his three rides at Tramore. It was almost exactly twelve years since his first visit to the tight County Waterford switchback – when Zimuletta had slipped up with him, and when Christy Roche had abruptly decided that a former champion jockey would live longer if he opted for discretion rather than valour. What was special about this particular treble was that one winner was in a hurdle race, another on the Flat and the third in a chase. The two successes over jumps were for O'Brien but the Flat winner was for his old guv'nor, Dessie Hughes, still barely able to believe the heights to which his former pupil had reached.

O'Brien went from strength to strength. In the valuable Tattersalls Breeders Stakes eighteen days later, he was responsible for nine of the twenty-nine runners. They took four of the first five places and almost eighty per cent of the £150,000 prize fund. For good measure, he also won three other races on the card, to complete the first four-timer of his brief, but mercurial, career. At Punchestown, less than two months later, he became the first Irish-based trainer to send out 200 winners in a calendar year when Charlie Swan rode Kaldan Khan to victory in a hurdle race. Only a handful of Irish trainers had sent out more than 100 winners in a year before this. O'Brien was presented with a magnum of champagne to mark his achievement, and he promptly confessed that all he would drink would be a cup of tea, and even that would have to wait until he got home!

At Fairyhouse on 3 December it was Charlie Swan's turn to ride into the record books. He landed a double for O'Brien to record his 100th winner of the season. To ride 100 jumping winners in an Irish season is an incredible achievement – and no one else has ever got near it – but to do it with almost half of the season still to run was unbelievable.

What is more, he reached his century faster than any jump jockey in Britain had ever done. Until 1995 the British season did not start until late July or early August, but there is far more racing in that country and at that stage the fastest century had not been achieved until 20 December – by Peter Scudamore in 1988 and again on the same date the following year.

Aidan O'Brien is convinced his stable jockey warranted much more than a few newspaper paragraphs.

> What Charlie did is very much underestimated, and indeed he does not get the recognition he should for all his achievements. There was a tremendous fuss in Britain in 1996 when Tony McCoy broke the record for the fastest century there – he did it on 21 November, but he had all June and July, whereas his predecessors did not – but Charlie did it in Ireland where there is only half as much racing.
>
> Furthermore, he manages to get some terrible horses to win. To my mind, he is the best jump jockey in the world. I have seen plenty of his rivals but I have no doubt whatsoever that he is better. None of the others have the same racing brain. He also has a great pair of hands and, while he can be as hard as necessary when a horse is not doing enough, he is basically kind to his mounts. He is a good horseman as well as a great jockey. He has a gift for this game, and he is able to assess horses simply by riding against them. Even when he does not win a race, he picks up valuable knowledge that he can put to use to beat the opposition the next time.

The press coverage might not have been all that Aidan O'Brien would have liked but Charlie Swan was careful not to get carried away by the column inches that he did get. He had had a painful reminder of what fate could have in store for him at Galway five weeks earlier.

> I was riding Lucky Salute in a beginners' chase. We went fast into the first and he fell. Either him, or one of the other horses coming up behind, thumped his hoof down onto my stomach. Often the back protector deadens the impact of such blows because it goes round to your front to protect the ribcage. But this one landed a bit lower, and it was horribly painful. I was rushed to hospital and the doctors found that I was bleeding internally. They were worried that the bleeding could get worse, and that the damaged

tissues might become inflamed. Fortunately, a night's rest went a long way towards putting me right. I was released the next day and I was able to resume, with the help of a few painkillers, the day after that.

But Swan, as he half-feared, had been riding high for too long. Racing's cruel fates struck him down at Clonmel just five days after he had reached his century. Again it was the inexperience of a novice chaser that put him into the care of the doctors.

Flawless Finish fell heavily, and on top of me, at the sixth fence. I put my right hand out to save myself as I was about to hit the ground. But it was at this point that the full half ton weight of the mare slammed down on top of me. I knew immediately that I had broken a bone and I thought, 'Oh my God. Not my arm again.' I knew how long a broken arm takes to heal and the big Christmas meeting at Leopardstown was less than three weeks away. But when the X-rays were taken, I was a lot more optimistic. There was a crack in the bone two or three inches below the elbow. The doctors seemed to think it would heal quite quickly and that, if it did, I would be back for Christmas. I promptly told everyone that I would be. If I had kept my mouth shut, and been a little more patient, I would have saved myself a lot of pain – and an operation.

14

Returning Too Soon

At Navan on 4 November 1995 the highly regarded Moon Man broke his near-foreleg as he came to the second last in the lead in a good novice hurdle. The racecourse vet informed a disconsolate Tom Foley what he had already realised. There was no hope. The horse had to be shot with a humane killer.

His trainer made the journey back to County Carlow in torment. His mind was as black as a funeral shroud. Moon Man was not just a horse. He was, for Tom Foley, a symbol of the hope that he had had to abandon with Danoli. Moon Man had looked potentially brilliant when winning his two bumper starts the previous season. More recently he had proved himself a good jumper, good enough for Foley to aim him at Cheltenham. His death was, for his trainer, a tragedy.

That night Foley tossed and turned. When a sleepless midnight passed, it was officially his forty-ninth birthday. But there was nothing happy about it, and nor could he see anything that was going to bring any happiness. In the early hours, when things always seem at their worst, he looked into the future. What he saw was a small-time trainer who, like many others before him, had once had a good horse and who, for the rest of his life, was going to have to make do with his memories as he struggled to stay in business with a handful of moderate animals. Foley convinced himself that he had never been destined for anything other than a life of hardship, a life in which the reward for hard work was nothing more than survival: 'I realised I had fallen all the way down to the bottom of the ladder. I was going to find it horribly difficult to climb even one rung.'

He got up the following morning and went out into the stable yard. Moon Man's box was as empty as the trainer was of hope. Foley went, as he had done every day for more than four years, to look at Danoli. Despite what Chris Riggs had told him, Foley for several months had refused to accept that the horse who had taken him to such heights could be finished. Indeed, he had long remained stubbornly optimistic about racing him again in that current season. However, little more than a fortnight before Moon Man's death, he had finally bowed to the inevitable.

His vet, a German called Heinrich Zieg who was based on the Curragh, told him that Danoli needed two months of slow work before he could attempt anything faster. Foley had had the horse ridden out as soon as he reasonably could after his return home from Leahurst, partly to try to stop arthritis setting in, but also because he was determined to race him again. But Zieg warned Foley that, if he worked the horse before he was ready, the arthritis was almost certain to take a grip. And, although the vet did not have to spell it out in so many words, if that happened then any last lingering hopes of Danoli returning to the racecourse would be destroyed.

But, that Sunday morning, the doors were closing in on Tom Foley's world. Much like a once-rich gambler down to his last few chips, Foley decided he had to make an all-or-nothing throw. He would get Chris Riggs to fly over from the Wirral and make the brilliant veterinary surgeon tell him whether the horse was out for good. If he wasn't, Foley was going to train him for the Irish Champion Hurdle in January and then the Champion at Cheltenham.

Once he had decided on a plan of action, Foley felt a lot more at ease with himself – and he was able to accept the birthday wishes of Goretti and their four children. The following day, though, he ran into a major snag. When he rang the Leahurst Veterinary College, he was told that Dr Riggs was touring Australia and could not be contacted. All Foley could do was leave a message that he had rung, and that it was vital for Riggs to ring him the minute he was in touch.

It was almost a month before Riggs was able to travel to Ireland and have X-rays taken. When he went back to Leahurst to study the evidence, he rang a vet he knew in America who specialised in injuries to the fetlock joint. The vet wanted to know what the X-rays had revealed. When he was told that the bone had mended, and was showing neither signs of stress nor of anything that might give way under stress, he discussed the arthritis situation. He said that, in his view, there was a greater danger of arthritis setting into the fetlock joint if the horse was put on the easy list until the following season than if he resumed training. Three days before Christmas Riggs flew over to Ireland a second time, and drove down to County Carlow. Heinrich Zieg also travelled to Tom Foley's stable that Friday. Riggs informed the trainer what the American expert had said. He then gave his own cautious go-ahead and, when the German vet backed him up, Foley was overjoyed. The following morning Danoli was boxed over to Jim Bolger's all-weather gallop to begin his preparation for the Irish Champion Hurdle four weeks later.

Tom Foley assumed that Charlie Swan would ride the horse, as he had in the past. It was no idle assumption. Swan had told him months ago that, no matter what other arrangements he might make, he would have it written into any agreement that he would be free to ride Danoli if the horse returned to racing. But, when Foley contacted him only to be told that the jockey was not sure – he might have to ride Hotel Minella – Foley was both surprised and annoyed.

> I believe Charlie thought my horse would never race again, and that was why he felt able to give me that commitment. Charlie is a fine jockey but his one real fault is that he did not stay freelance. Richard Dunwoody got fed up with being tied down to the same stable and he decided not to continue like that. As a result he rides here, there and everywhere and really enjoys himself. Charlie could have done the same. As the Irish Champion Hurdle drew nearer, I could not get a straight answer out of Charlie. I was getting browned off and I let it be known that I was going to go looking for a jockey. Early on in the weekend before the race both Adrian Maguire and Tony McCoy were on to me to say they could ride Danoli but, at that stage, I still was not sure whether Charlie would be free. I said I would let them know within twenty-four hours because on the Sunday I was going to Navan where I knew I would see Charlie. I told him I wanted a straight yes or no. The answer was no. He felt committed to Hotel Minella. But Maguire and McCoy were no good to me if they could not ride the horse in the Champion Hurdle as well. Neither could give me that commitment. I told them to forget it. I then rang Tommy Treacy and he told me he would love to ride the horse again.

Adrian Maguire and Tony McCoy both found other mounts in the AIG Europe Irish Champion Hurdle at Leopardstown on 21 January.

Maguire teamed up with Montelado, whose huge frame was still giving Pat Flynn reason to worry, and who had not raced since winning the Irish Cesarewitch at the Curragh over three months earlier. McCoy rode Absalom's Lady, one of the two British challengers. Montelado started hot favourite, Absalom's Lady was a 9–1 chance and Danoli started at 10–1. The money for him was primarily based on loyalty and patriotism. None of the professionals thought he had a hope – not after breaking a fetlock joint and being off the course for over nine months. It was only down at the start that Charlie Swan realised otherwise.

> Danoli was terribly fit – certainly a lot fitter than Tom had let on – and, from what I could see, he was ready to run the race of his life. In a way, he did. I was beaten a head on Hotel Minella, and Danoli finished half a length behind us. But he should have won. He can be a bit ignorant down at the start. He tends to drag his head forward and try to pull you out of the saddle. Sometimes he will attempt to barge his way through the tape. This time he whipped round and lost several lengths. As we passed the winning post for the first time, he was really tanked up and Tommy Treacy was having to battle to hold him. If Tommy had known how fit Danoli was, he could have let him stride along and the horse would have gone better for him. But I suspect he had been told to save him, and to ride for a place. I also suspect Tommy had not been told just how fit Danoli really was.

As Danoli stayed on strongly up the run-in, the cheering could be heard for miles around. When he was led into the unsaddling enclosure, he was greeted like the Messiah. The winner, the English-trained Collier Bay, was virtually ignored. The only horse the public wanted to see was the one who had finished third – and the only trainer the press were interested in was the man who trained him. If Danoli could finish so close after overcoming injury, and being off the course for so long, what could he do in the Champion Hurdle, except win it? As Aidan O'Brien was also going to run Hotel Minella in the big race at Cheltenham, Charlie Swan realised he had lost the ride on a legend, and that he had almost certainly lost it for good. He was sad.

> Danoli is a bit of a freak, and this is what sets him apart from other horses. He has a relatively short body and, although he is by The Parson, he is built more like a sprinter than a National

Hunt horse. He is also something of a character. If there is a horse in front of him, he will pull your arms out to try and get past him. But, once he is in front, you have to push him to keep him there. When you hit him, he will sometimes swish his tail. With some horses this can mean a reluctance to battle. Not with Danoli. He has tremendous determination and he loves a fight. I expect the tail-swishing is his way of saying 'There is no need to hit me, I am going to give it all I can.' I was thrilled at the idea of his going to Cheltenham with a chance but desperately sorry that it would not be me on his back. But I didn't say anything. I just bit my lip and did my best to accept it.

He had to bite his lip a second time when his poker-playing went wrong again and cost him an even more valuable card at Leopardstown three weeks later. In December the previous year, he had been approached by Fergie Sutherland about riding his horses. Sutherland had trained at Newmarket for five years, and had earned a reputation as a shrewd man who knew how to get the best out of his horses. He won the Queen Mary Stakes at Royal Ascot in his first season in 1958, but he seemed to gain far more satisfaction from winning a string of handicaps with an old gelding called Fox King, and he was fond of telling people that 'Any fool can train a two-year-old. Winning sixteen handicaps takes a bit of management!'

In 1967 Sutherland left England to join his mother on her estate on the banks of the River Lee near Coachford in County Cork. There he became a farmer and also turned his hand to training jumpers, mostly on the point-to-point circuit. Anything that was any good was normally sold before it graduated to the racecourse. Despite his upper-middle-class background, and very British upbringing – Eton, Sandhurst and the Guards – he rapidly assimilated himself into the local way of life and, equally rapidly, became recognised as something of a character. He has a rolling gait – the result of having the lower part of his left leg blown off by a land mine in the Korean War in 1952, wears the countryman's flat cap, uses a huge sheep's crook to help his artificial leg and has a colourful turn of phrase.

He was sixty-four when he approached Swan about riding his horses. He said that things were not working out too well between himself and Gerry O'Neill, who normally rode for him. Sutherland had only a handful of horses but the reason the jockey happily agreed to ride them was that they included some really promising animals, including Go Go Gallant and two half-brothers, Lisselan Prince and

Imperial Call. The last-named was held in high regard by Sutherland, who had used Richard Dunwoody when Lisselan Prince won at Thurles in mid-December when Swan was out of action. The Sutherland horses would obviously clash with some of Aidan O'Brien's runners, but Swan was optimistic that this would not happen often enough for the County Cork trainer to decide to abandon the agreement and go back to Dunwoody.

Swan seemed to have made the right decision when it came to Ladbroke day at Leopardstown in January. O'Brien, who had only a limited number of good chasers, had nothing in the McCain Handicap Chase and so his stable jockey was free to partner Imperial Call. Swan gave the horse a forceful, vigorous ride to beat Strong Platinum. Since the runner-up was conceding 12lb and hated the heavy ground, the performance was nothing to get excited about. But Fergie Sutherland told Swan that he was going to run the horse in the Hennessy Cognac Irish Gold Cup on the same course four weeks later and, if Imperial Call won that, he would run him in the Cheltenham Gold Cup. If Aidan had nothing in the Leopardstown race, he would definitely ride Imperial Call, Swan told Sutherland.

When O'Brien decided that Life Of A Lord should run in the Hennessy, Swan rang Sutherland. 'Not to worry,' the deep, gruff voice came back down the line. 'The ride is yours if my fellow goes to Cheltenham, no matter whether we win, lose or draw at Leopardstown.' Sutherland contacted Dunwoody whom he had originally booked to ride the horse in the Ericsson Chase at the Leopardstown Christmas meeting. Swan had been due to ride Life Of A Lord. But frost set in and the race was abandoned. However, Dunwoody knew that John Mulhern was planning to run Flashing Steel in the Hennessy, and that Mulhern wanted him to ride the horse. Dunwoody, in Sutherland's words, 'kept humming and hahing'. The hesitancy was to cost him dear. The County Cork trainer then turned to Conor O'Dwyer, who was enjoying a good season but was still considered something of a journeyman jockey, the sort of rider who will go anywhere to ride anything. But Sutherland had come to the conclusion that the ever-cheerful, wafer-thin but tremendously brave O'Dwyer was a rather better jockey than people had been giving him credit for.

> Conor had ridden a horse for me just over a fortnight before the Hennessy at Gowran Park. It was an animal I thought a lot of, called Tempo. He had never run before, and he was not fit enough to win. But sometimes a good horse will surprise you and

I had £50 on him at 100-1. He ran out of puff at the last and finished fifth. I was impressed with Conor. Even more so when I watched him riding in a chase. I saw that he had one hell of an eye for a stride, and that he rode his mount into the fences the way a man ought to. I knew he would suit Imperial Call.

Imperial Call defied his relative inexperience in the Hennessy Cognac Irish Gold Cup to trounce the opposition. Richard Dunwoody, to his considerable chagrin, finished a long way last on Flashing Steel, while Swan was forced to pull up Life Of A Lord, who proved totally unable to cope with the soft ground. But, for him at least, there was compensation. He mentally ran through that 'win, lose or draw' conversation. Fergie Sutherland was a gentleman of the old school. If he gave you his word, he would stick by it.

Sutherland, despite being showered with more acclaim than at any time in his long life, had not forgotten the promise he had made. But he also felt a deep loyalty towards the jockey who had stepped in when the best in Britain and Ireland had said no, and who had ridden his horse so brilliantly. As the trainer left the racecourse, crook in hand, and slowly made his way over to the car park, he silently battled with his principles and his conscience to try to find an answer that was both equitable and just.

In my book, this game is a matter of do as you would be done by. I could not go back on a promise but, after the way Conor had ridden Imperial Call, I felt that taking him off the horse would be a bad way to say thank you. As I reached the jeep, I knew what I had to do. I got on to Conor and told him he was not to say a word to anyone until I had telephoned Charlie first thing the following morning.

When the phone rang at The Cobs, and the jockey heard that deep voice saying 'Charlie', Swan's heart sunk to his stomach. He knew who it was – and he knew what was coming.

As I drove home from Leopardstown the previous night, I kept thinking about that conversation – and the more I thought about it, the more the doubts crept in. By the time it got to the following morning, I was praying that the phone wouldn't ring. Fergie began by explaining that he could not very well jock Conor off. After that, I was only half taking things in. I muttered something about understanding his position. What else could I say? There was no point in trying to hold him to his promise. His mind was made up, and Fergie is not the sort of person you can persuade to change his mind. But I was upset. I knew Imperial Call could well win the Cheltenham Gold Cup. He had One Man to beat but, over the final two furlongs, Imperial Call was the horse I would have picked.

One Man was hot favourite and Swan had seen him in action at first hand in the King George VI Tripleprint Chase, which is normally run at Kempton on Boxing Day, but which that season had been postponed to Sandown eleven days later. Norman Williamson, who had won the previous season's Cheltenham Gold Cup on Master Oats, was out of action recovering from a broken leg and so Kim Bailey asked Charlie Swan to fly over and take the mount. Pat Healy decided to go with him to take some photographs. Williamson, who comes from County Cork, also went, as did Richard Hughes.

The four travelled in the same car from Heathrow to Sandown, and Williamson drove. Because the sun was shining when they were stuck in traffic in Esher, he reached up to open the roof. The four men passed the time by eyeing, and commenting on, the girls walking past the car. Hughes had his wallet in his hand. When his attention was distracted by a particularly striking-looking blonde, Healy reached over, grabbed the wallet and tossed it through the sun-roof. It landed on the pavement, credit cards scattering everywhere. Most people would have cursed the perpetrator and jumped out of the car before anybody had a chance to make off with the wallet. But Dessie Hughes's jockey son is as sharp as a surgeon's knife. He reckoned he knew what was coming. He hastily cast around for insurance. He grabbed Williamson's diary. By the time he had picked up his wallet and restored the credit cards to safety he found, as he knew he would, that the doors were locked. He marched round to the driver's side and informed Williamson that, if they were not unlocked immediately, Williamson's diary – and all the telephone numbers it contained – was going down the nearest gutter. The doors were promptly unlocked.

Fifty yards further down the road Williamson, doing his best to keep a straight face, complained that the leg he had broken at Sedgefield three months earlier was hurting him. Did anybody have any painkillers? Charlie Swan, sitting in the back, said he had some in his bag in the boot. He got out to get them but, when the good samaritan tried to return to his seat on the pavement side of the car, Williamson pressed the automatic door lock. The traffic started to move, not fast but at walking pace. For the best part of half a mile, a red-faced Swan was forced to walk along the pavement, repeatedly trying the door handles and shouting to those inside to let him in. Those inside, particularly Hughes, gesticulated at the by-now fascinated and amused Saturday-morning shoppers, and shouted through the sun-roof at them 'That's Charlie Swan. He is riding Master Oats in the King George this afternoon.' The occupants of the car thought the whole episode was hilarious. For Swan, the joke had worn thin after the first few yards.

When Moon Man met his death on that fateful day at Navan, the race was won by Thats My Man, a five-year-old owned by J.P. McManus, trained by Aidan O'Brien and ridden by Swan. This was the fourth consecutive hurdle race the gelding had won and, when he made it five out of five in a valuable race at Fairyhouse the following month, O'Brien decided to put him away for the Supreme Novices at Cheltenham. He was clearly an exceptional horse and was widely regarded as an Irish banker.

Rather than risk him on a racecourse in the testing going in the early part of the year, O'Brien opted to prepare him for the Festival on the gallops at home and on 21 February he sent him by horsebox from Piltown to work on the trial grounds at Ballydoyle. It seemed a sound idea. The journey in the horsebox, and the new surroundings, were sure to wake the horse up and encourage him to work with real relish. But it turned into tragedy. Thats My Man, ridden by Swan in a gallop over a mile, broke his off-hind for no apparent reason with a furlong still to travel. The break was below the hock and, although O'Brien called in the vets and had the leg X-rayed, far too much damage had been done for the horse's life to be saved. Swan was devastated.

> I love horses – I don't think I would even be in racing if I didn't – and I get upset whenever one of those I ride is hurt or killed. When that happens to a horse who has been good to me, I find it almost unbearable. I rated Thats My Man as potentially the best hurdler I had ever ridden, and he was my best hope for Cheltenham. I could not believe it when I felt the leg go. He was still on the bridle, and he was just about to overtake his lead horse, when the bone suddenly cracked. As I took the saddle off him, and held his head while we waited for the vet to arrive, I had to fight to hold back the tears.

Not even victory on Lo Stregone (unkindly christened Slow Stregone by some members of the media!) in the valuable Greenalls Grand National Trial at Haydock three days later could take away the pain and, with the notable exception of Urubande, the Cheltenham Festival proved a disaster for the Irish champion. His decision to join forces with Aidan O'Brien cost him victory on Ventana Canyon in the Arkle Trophy – Richard Dunwoody rode the Edward O'Grady-trained seven-year-old to a twenty-length win – and, far worse, it also cost him the most treasured prize of all, the Cheltenham Gold Cup, on Imperial Call. In addition, it resulted in him employing the wrong tactics on Viking Flagship in the Queen Mother Champion Chase.

> Adrian Maguire again missed the meeting, this time through injury, and so David Nicholson booked me. When I saw Klairon Davis making a bad mistake at the open ditch at the top of the hill, I thought he was out of contention. Richard Dunwoody was in front on Sound Man and, having ridden Sound Man several times before, I thought the best way to beat him was to take him on. I drove Viking Flagship up to him but my horse made mistakes at the third last and the next – the previous year he had pinged both – but this time the ground was a bit dead, which didn't suit him. I felt I'd been right to take on Sound Man, and I'd got the better of him by the time we headed into the last. But I had underrated Klairon Davis. Just when I thought I had the race in the bag, Francis Woods loomed up on my outside on Arthur Moore's horse. He didn't half give me a shock, and I got another one when he quickened away from me up the hill. I should have kept something in reserve.
>
> Things had worked out much better on Urubande in the Sun Alliance Hurdle forty minutes earlier, but he is a headstrong horse, and he gave me some anxious moments. Because he has a high cruising speed, I led for a lot of the way but, going down the back straight, he suddenly saw some parked cars and swerved away from them. I had more problems going down the hill towards the second last. He had his ears pricked so I knew he had plenty left. But he spotted a gap between the hurdle and the rails, and he swerved left towards it. I had to fight to get him back on course, and to stop him running out. I then had to ride him hard after the last to hold off Mark Dwyer on Go-Informal. But it was great to win. It was just a shame that Aidan's first Festival winner should be accompanied by so much controversy.

The controversy began when O'Brien left Hotel Minella in the following day's Coral Cup at Tuesday morning's final declaration stage. It had been widely assumed that Hotel Minella had been sent to Cheltenham to run only in Tuesday's Champion Hurdle. In his absence, the weights for the Coral Cup would go up by a stone. The majority of trainers with runners in the race had worked on this assumption and, when Hotel Minella was left in, two-thirds of the field were out of the handicap. When O'Brien withdrew Hotel Minella on the day of the Coral Cup, several of the trainers cried foul, some of the officials were convinced they could smell a rat, and many of the press accused Ireland's youthful champion trainer of committing racing's equivalent of high treason. They called for his head.

O'Brien, who reported that Hotel Minella had failed to eat up after running in the Champion Hurdle, said that he had no alternative but to withdraw the horse. He had little idea that his decision to leave the horse in at the declaration stage would provoke such a furore. It used to be commonplace for Irish trainers to run horses more than once during the course of the three-day Festival. In 1984, for example, five Irish horses ran twice and in 1980 ten of them did so. O'Brien, who had run Hotel Minella on successive days at Punchestown the previous April, would have followed suit with the same horse at Cheltenham if he thought he had recovered from the previous day's exertions. He was incensed at the accusatory attitude adopted by the stewards.

> It was as if they were trying to say that I was lying. Certainly they did not appear to believe what I told them. They produced flight schedules and booking lists. They said Hotel Minella was not on the flight back to Ireland that he was meant to be on.

The stewards refused to accept O'Brien's explanations, or those of John Nallen who owned the horse, and both men were summoned to appear before the Jockey Club's disciplinary committee in London the following month. They were then absolved of all blame. But Charlie Swan did not escape so lightly after the Triumph Hurdle. As the leaders galloped towards the final flight, he and Magical Lady were fighting it out with Carl Llewellyn on Mistinguett. Just behind them, seemingly travelling best of all, was Paul Carberry on Embellished. At long last Noel Meade's dreams of winning a race at the Cheltenham Festival looked like being realised. But the tall County Meath trainer, along with the thousands in the stands and the millions more watching at home on television, looked on in horror as Swan's mount veered left and squeezed up Embellished, who lost his footing and fell. As the announcer called the result – Paddy's Return first, Magical Lady second and Mistinguett third – most of the onlookers were already speculating what the stewards would do to the Irish champion. The penalty the stewards imposed was a six-day suspension for irresponsible riding.

Many critics thought Swan had got away lightly. The jockey was as white as a sheet when he walked out into the parade ring for the next race. But neither the ghostly palor, nor his uncharacteristically grim-set expression, had anything to do with feelings of guilt. Swan was livid at what he regarded as the greatest injustice he had suffered since the loss of the Whitbread Gold Cup nearly five years earlier.

> There was no running rail for part of the way between the last two hurdles and you had to go past the second-last fence on the chase course. As we did so, Magical Lady ducked slightly away from the fence. I had no idea Paul Carberry was close behind me. Obviously I wasn't going to look round – I had a race to try and win – and nor did I hear anything coming. Not until I moved to my inner. By then it was too late. But it was not this that caused Embellished to fall. That was Carl Llewellyn's fault.
>
> He had gone over onto the chase course in a bid to save ground, and get up my inside in the process. He was trying to be smart. Too smart. When he moved off the chase course back onto the hurdles course, Embellished swerved away from his mount and caught Magical Lady's heels. On the patrol film, and on television, it looked as if it was me who was doing the damage. I knew it was Carl's manoeuvre that had caused the fall but I could not prove it, not from the evidence in the stewards' room. It was only afterwards, when I watched the aerial view on the Channel 4 re-run, that I saw the proper picture. This showed the incident quite clearly. It also showed who was at fault.
>
> But when I was called into the stewards' room for the inquiry, they already had their minds made up. It was like the Whitbread all over again. As far as the stewards were concerned, a horse had fallen and they had to put the blame on someone. Because I was in front of Embellished, and because I moved off a straight line as Magical Lady ducked away from the fence, it was me they blamed. When I tried to explain what had happened, they didn't want to know. They said I was guilty. They also heard evidence

from Carl and Paul. The latter didn't say much and Carl was intent on trying to make sure he got second. He did because the stewards disqualified Magical Lady. It was only afterwards that Paul said to me that the fall was Carl's fault. I saw Carl again at Punchestown the following month. He admitted then that he was to blame.

Charlie Swan had ridden 135 winners in Ireland at this point in the season. Six days on the sidelines, despite the burning sense of injustice that accompanied them, seemed unlikely to stop him riding remorselessly into the record books with another thirty or so victories before the season's end on the last day of May. Yet, within six weeks of the Cheltenham fiasco, he had picked up three further suspensions. All were for excessive use of the whip. The first was at Fairyhouse, and on the day he returned to the saddle at Punchestown he was given another. The following day he picked up the third. They totalled fourteen days but he had been suspended for the whip only three times in the previous thirteen years. Something had clearly gone wrong. Either the stewards were after his blood, or he was suddenly riding with a total disregard for his mounts.

Swan dropped a few hints that it was the former, but he did it half-heartedly and unconvincingly. He told the press he would devote the 'holiday' to improving his golf. He spent most of it worrying about the problem. He knew what it was. An ugly growth had appeared on his right arm, where he had cracked it at Clonmel the previous December, and it was causing him a lot of pain. The growth was bone, and it was big. It looked like a second elbow a few inches below the real one. It also made him appear deformed. He was careful to keep the arm covered up. He now knew what a dreadful mistake he had made attempting to return to the saddle without giving the crack time to heal.

I should have taken the hint when the doctor examined me at Limerick on Boxing Day. When I tested it by riding out a few days earlier, the arm had hurt me a bit even though I rode with it strapped up. But I was determined to get back to ride Urubande at Leopardstown. Ironically, Leopardstown was called off because of frost until New Year's Eve but Aidan O'Brien also had runners at Limerick. I felt I couldn't very well say that I was all right to ride at Leopardstown but not at Limerick. Also Fergie Sutherland wanted me to ride Go Go Gallant in a chase at

Limerick. I felt I couldn't let him down either.

When you have been injured, you have to pass the doctor before you are allowed to return. I was waiting for the doctor to appear at Limerick when Dr Lyons, whom I knew, walked in. I asked him if he was the doctor on duty. He said he wasn't but he could pass me. He made me do all sorts of movements with my right arm, and it hurt so much I felt he was trying to break it. But I gritted my teeth and tried not to let on I was in agony. He eventually passed me fit to ride but I had to take painkillers after he had finished with me.

From then on I was in pain most days, and after Cheltenham it became really bad. The growth was getting bigger. It seemed that, instead of the bone knitting over the crack, it had taken on a will of its own and grown outwards. I became terribly depressed. Apart from the pain, I knew it was affecting my riding. It hurt me to push a horse, and it was too painful for me to slap him down the shoulder. You are allowed to do this provided you keep the whip in the carry position, and it's an accepted way of urging on your mount. Because I couldn't do it, I was picking up the whip and hitting the horse behind the saddle. But I was starting to do this much too early in a race and I had to keep on doing it to keep the horse going. This is why I was suspended at Fairyhouse and Punchestown.

He then had a fall on the gallops at home. He landed on the injured arm. The pain was even worse than that caused by Dr Lyons in his examination at Limerick. And this time painkillers were not enough. Swan drove to Navan to see Fred Kenny, and early in June the surgeon operated.

Part of the problem was that the Clonmel crack was in a piece of bone that had been broken in the Chamois Boy fall at Galway. Kenny removed the remaining plate he had inserted that August night and replaced it with a more rigid one. He used several screws to fix it to the bone. He also cut away the growth. Three weeks later the arm was as good as new. At least it was, if you averted your eyes from the long scar left by the surgeon's knife.

15

Devastated

The gloom of the whip suspensions, and the worries about the arm, had been briefly lifted two days after Punchestown when Life Of A Lord became the first Irish-trained winner of the Whitbread Gold Cup for thirteen years.

Aidan O'Brien and Charlie Swan had hoped that the ten-year-old would win the Grand National, but he made two mistakes just as the tap was beginning to be turned on – at the fence after Becher's on the second circuit and at Valentine's – and he managed no better than a well-beaten seventh. O'Brien expected the horse to feel the effects of his exertions for quite some time after he returned to Piltown. Two days later, though, he was astonished to find the horse as well as he had been before the National. He remembered what his jockey had said earlier in the season, that this was a horse who could win the Whitbread. When Swan drove over to Piltown and saw the horse jumping out of his skin, he repeated his earlier prediction. O'Brien promptly decided to aim the gelding at the rich Sandown race.

However, he decided against flying to England to supervise Life Of A Lord's saddling. He had six runners at the Curragh on the same day and, just as much to the point, the O'Briens' third child was due at any moment. If Anne Marie needed him, it would be easier to get back from County Kildare than from Sandown. Swan flew to Heathrow on his own. He was in a confident frame of mind.

Some people said Life Of A Lord did not get the trip in the National. I know he appeared to tire on the run-in, but I was convinced it was those two mistakes that had cost him the race. He was always travelling well at Sandown and, going down the back straight on the final circuit, I let him move upsides the leader, General Rusty, ridden by Richard Dunwoody. He shouted across at me, 'Take your time. You're going a bit quick.' His horse was empty and he was hoping that I would wait for him. I ignored him, and sent Life Of A Lord clear five fences from home. Proud Sun, ridden by Dean Gallagher, ran on well in the closing stages but I never had any doubts about holding him.

Victory was greeted with jubilation by all the lads at Piltown, particularly when they heard that the sponsors were to give forty crates of beer (960 cans) to the stable staff of the winner! For Swan it was another chance to get to know the Queen Mother.

I was invited up to the Royal Box, and I spoke to her at length. The subject of Norman Conqueror came up. He belonged to the Queen Mother but he had to be put down after fracturing a bone in his knee in the Irish National less than three weeks earlier. It was a sad ending for her first runner in Ireland for almost a quarter of a century. I said how sorry I was. We talked about her other horses and she said how much she loves jump racing. I was again struck by how on the ball she is. To talk to her, you would not believe she is in her nineties.

Next stop for Life Of A Lord was Galway at the end of July. Aidan O'Brien again ran Kelly's Pearl but for his stable jockey, who had managed to finish up the 1995/96 season with a new record of 150 winners despite all those suspensions, there was no question of deserting the ten-year-old even though he faced a formidable task. No horse had won the Galway Plate in successive seasons since the Stan Mellor-partnered Ross Sea thirty-one years earlier, and only one in the past twenty years had been successful with as much as twelve stone on his back. O'Brien, worried that the handicapper would give Life Of A Lord a penalty for the second year running, had not dared to give him a preliminary outing – and for much of the race Swan was convinced this was going to prove the horse's undoing.

I was flat to the boards the whole way, and from a mile out I was niggling at him. It was not until I gave Life Of A Lord a couple of cracks going down the hill towards the second last that I felt I was in with a chance of winning. Bishops Hall was in front at this point. Richard Dunwoody was riding him but I knew that the tough, uphill finish would not be in his favour. I'd ridden Bishops Hall a few times. He is such a good jumper that he is always at his best when he has another fence in front of him, and at Galway there is an awful long way between the last fence and the winning post. As we turned into the straight, I knew I had him. My only worry was that something was going to come from behind. Thankfully, though, there was nobody within striking distance.

As Swan returned to unsaddle, he went past Pat Healy. 'Get your camera ready for the winner's enclosure,' he told the photographer. 'I am going to do it.' Healy, who had been plotting this for months, was overjoyed. Like other photographers, and indeed just about everybody else in racing, he had been taken by Frankie Dettori's flying dismounts. When he drove to Cheltenham with Norman Williamson on the morning of the 1995 Gold Cup, he persuaded his great friend to emulate the Italian if he won the big race on Master Oats. The resultant photograph is Healy's pride and joy.

At Cheltenham twelve months later, he succeeded in talking Charlie into doing the same if he won a second Queen Mother Champion Chase on Viking Flagship. But defeat put the leap on the backburner. Healy knew that none of the other photographers at Galway would be prepared for what Swan was going to do. With a bit of luck, he would be the only one to get a good picture. But he left the winner's enclosure as disappointed as if he had been one of the bookmakers who had to pay out on Life Of A Lord. Swan, feeling a growing sense of embarrassment, chickened out halfway through the leap. What should have been a supremely athletic-looking victory salute turned into an ungainly, crab-like gesture that had him staggering to stay on his feet when he hit the ground.

At Tralee in August Swan broke a collar-bone for the first time in his long career. He also had a lot of bruising on his chest, and he drove to Navan concerned that this could be another fractured rib bone. However, X-rays, and Fred Kenny's examination, revealed that the only fracture was in the clavicle, and Swan was confident he would be out of action for only two and a half weeks. A collar-bone is a minor break by racing standards, but the jockey was unpleasantly surprised to find that this one took nearly four weeks to mend. Two days after his return, he tried to win a second Kerry National on Life Of A Lord. But this time, though, things went horribly wrong from the beginning.

There was a false start and, as we jumped off, Life Of A Lord stumbled and went down. I trotted him round to make sure he was all right. He seemed sound but I later had an uneasy feeling that he might have somehow damaged himself. Once the race got under way, I was never happy on him. Also he was slipping all over the place. There had been a lot of problems with the slippery surface earlier in the meeting. The grass was a bit long but he seemed as if he was too big for such a tight course. I remembered him slipping with me when he won there twelve months earlier.

I had him well placed, though, when we jumped the last with a circuit to go and galloped in front of the stands. Suddenly, and tragically, I felt his leg go. Possibly he slipped into a slight hole made by a hoof print on the previous circuit. His off-fore fetlock joint was broken. Obviously he had to be put down. We found out afterwards that the joint was completely shattered. I was terribly upset and, as with Thats My Man at Ballydoyle seven months earlier, I was close to tears. This time, though, I was more upset than I had been with the death of any horse. He was a really kind individual without an ounce of badness in him. Never would he kick or bite, and the youngest kids in the yard were able to ride him. He used to cough every day, and after doing a piece of work he would cough his head off. To begin with, I thought he was sick and I would feel sorry for him. I felt that it was all a terrible strain for him. In fact, it was just something in his throat that tickled and then cleared itself. But he had done so much for me, and now he was dead. I was devastated.

At Clonmel on 1 November 1996 Danoli made his chasing debut. It was a Friday, traditionally a poor day for attracting the racegoing public in Ireland, but those who did make the journey to the County Tipperary course were treated to some high drama.

In the opening maiden hurdle Oxford Lunch broke a leg and Tommy Treacy, who rode Tom Foley's ill-fated four-year-old, fractured his collar-bone in the fall. At least that was the verdict of the racecourse doctor who put the arm in a sling and instructed Treacy to go to the nearest hospital for X-rays. In fact, the injury proved to be nothing more serious then damaged ligaments.

But Foley, finding himself without his stable jockey, was plunged into turmoil. He paced up and down behind the weighing room as he wondered what to do. He would dearly love to have withdrawn Danoli, but he was acutely conscious of those who had paid to see the famous gelding race over fences for the first time. He decided that the answer was to get the jockey who knew the horse best. Charlie Swan was due to ride Consharon for Aidan O'Brien in the same race but Foley, now that his mind was made up, was not to be put off by what he clearly regarded as an irrelevance. Danoli was the people's champion. Consharon was just a horse.

The trainer quickly tracked down Swan, and asked him if he could get off his intended mount. Charlie should have said no. His agreement with Aidan O'Brien was clear cut. There was no way he could do what Foley asked. Not if he possessed even the slightest sense of honour. But, instead of standing up to Danoli's trainer, he hesitated. He was not sure, he replied. He would have to speak to Aidan O'Brien and see what he thought.

Swan retired to the jockeys' room, picked up his mobile and rang the trainer who was at Ballydoyle. O'Brien was surprised by the request but, amazingly, he did not turn it down. He simply said: ' If you want to get off Consharon, Charlie, there is no problem so far as I am concerned.'

O'Brien's ultra-reasonable reaction – most trainers would have erupted in fury – finally made Swan see sense. He then used O'Brien as a sounding board for his thoughts. He explained that he had told the owners of Consharon, after she had fallen with him at Limerick on her previous start, that she should run next at a minor track like Clonmel. They had taken his advice, and had travelled to the course to see him ride her. Besides, what would the other owners in the stable think if they heard about him getting off one of O'Brien's runners at the last minute, just because he had been offered a better mount? Finally, and this was the clincher, supposing he rode Danoli and Consharon won? He would look the biggest fool in Christendom.

'Do what you want to do, Charlie,' O'Brien replied. 'Whatever it is, it will be fine by me.'

Swan put away his phone and went in search of Foley. 'I am afraid I can't, Tom. It would not be fair on the owners.'

'What you mean is that it's Aidan O'Brien. He won't let you off.'

'No, Tom. It's not Aidan. I simply can't let the owners down. If you had owners in the same position, they wouldn't like it either.'

'This is different. This is Danoli.'

Danoli duly won, ridden by top amateur Philip Fenton, and Consharon was second. But Foley was not content to bury the hatchet.

He promptly accosted Swan and told him bluntly, 'You should have made the effort to get off that horse.'

Tony McCoy, sixty-six winners clear in the jockeys' table, fractured two bones in his left shoulder in a fall at Wincanton on 23 January 1997. The tall Northern Ireland-born champion had been riding many of Martin Pipe's horses, and the Somerset trainer was forced to cast his net wide in search of replacements. One of those he decided to turn to was Charlie Swan. Early the following month, the Irish champion received a phone call from Pipe asking him if he could ride many of his runners at Newbury on 7 and 8 February. These, Pipe said, would include White Sea on the Friday and Make A Stand in the following day's Tote Gold Trophy.

Swan replied that he would be only too happy to fly over for the rides on the first day of the meeting, but Aidan O'Brien had several runners at Navan on the Saturday, and under his agreement he would have to ride them. Clonmel, although he did not say so, had taught him when to say no.

White Sea was the first of Swan's three Newbury mounts for the champion jumps trainer. The filly, owned by Tim Hely-Hutchinson, a well-known London publisher, had shown signs of both nerves and mulishness on the Flat, but she had won her only previous hurdles start in fine style at Newbury in November. She started 2-1 favourite, and Swan sent her straight to the front.

The filly was a long way clear as she jumped the second last, and she was still travelling strongly. Just about the only movement her jockey made was to look round to see how far back the others were. He did this several times, but he somehow failed to spot that Kerawi was closing on him. It was not until he landed over the last that he realised he was in trouble. But, by that time, White Sea had lost her momentum. Kerawi swept past and, despite the frantic and belated efforts of her rider, White Sea was beaten a length and three-quarters.

Those who had backed her were furious, and the Irish jockey was greeted with jeers and catcalls as he returned to unsaddle – 'Swan makes punters Sea sick' proclaimed the headline on the front page of the next day's *Sporting Life*.

The following week the *Racing Post* printed two letters from irate readers. Dave Sugarman from Cardiff wrote:

> Am I alone in being outraged at the disgraceful ride given to White Sea by Charlie Swan in the Stroud Green Hurdle at Newbury last Friday? Martin Pipe's filly was fully ten lengths

clear and cruising at the second last, needing only to be pushed out with hands and heels for victory, before Swan inexplicably decided to ease her down.

This episode has once again highlighted the inconsistency which is rife throughout our sport. Last year, Willie Carson was crucified by the press and given a seven-day ban by the stewards for dropping his hands on Kamari at Lingfield Park. Less than nine months later, Swan commits an almost identical offence without penalty. It's barely credible. Week in, week out, jockeys are given lengthy bans for trying too hard to win races. And yet here is an example of a rider who threw a race away and got off scot-free. Such incidents make a mockery of the game.

Neil Wilby of Chesterfield had this to say:

> It was a performance of mind-numbing mediocrity. We all make mistakes in our work and, in Swan's case, he too could have been forgiven for the lapse, except for the pathetically lame excuses he produced to the stewards, implying that the horse rather than rider was responsible. Also, his flippant comments to the press afterwards were dismissive to the point of being offensive.
>
> Worse still, the stewards accepted his explanations instead of standing him down for fourteen days. Any half-competent race-reader will tell you Swan was not aware of Kerawi's rapid progress until after the last. In my view, he was guilty of not riding to obtain the best possible placing and should, therefore, have been punished accordingly. The case was little different to that of Willie Carson at Lingfield last summer.
>
> So wake up, Portman Square, and invite Mr Swan in for a little chat. Offer him the chance of a holiday so that he can concentrate his mind for Cheltenham. And an apology to the racing public would not go amiss either.

Charlie Swan confined his apologies to Martin Pipe and Tim Hely-Hutchinson, not least because he was all too well aware that the stewards might try to give him the 'holiday' that the Chesterfield reader was convinced he deserved.

> When I went out for the race, Martin told me that White Sea stayed well and was a good jumper. I should therefore either have her handy, or actually make the running. But there was not a lot

of her – she is a narrow sort – and she sweated a fair bit, and got herself worked up. As a result, she was pretty keen early on, and I decided she might relax more if I rode her out in front. After I jumped the second last, I looked round. I was between ten and fifteen lengths clear, and everything else was off the bridle.

As we went into the last, I felt I was just as far in front, and so I could afford to let White Sea fiddle it. She made a slight mistake, and I got one of the shocks of my life when Carl Llewellyn swept past on Kerawi. I got my filly going again, but it was all too late. There were a few boos from the crowd when I returned to unsaddle, and I heard somebody shout 'What a Charlie'. But, before Martin or the owner could say anything, I put up my hands and said, 'I messed up. I am very, very sorry. It was an error of judgement on my part. She should have won. She is good enough to pretty nearly win the Triumph Hurdle.'

Martin simply said, 'Okay, Charlie. Just don't say too much when you go in.' I think he wanted to get a price on her for the Triumph! Some of the press tackled me and asked me if I should have won. But I wasn't going to admit to them that I had boobed. I already knew the stewards wanted me, and I could see myself getting days. In the stewards' room I defended myself. I had to. I didn't want a suspension. I explained about White Sea sweating up, running free early on and making that mistake at the last. I also said that Kerawi had me held at the line. Fortunately they accepted my explanations.

It wasn't a good day. In the next I rode Eudipe for Martin in a novice chase. He started odds-on, and he was beaten too. The only good thing was that Tim Hely-Hutchinson was with the horse's owner when I went out into the parade ring, and he asked me to ride White Sea in the Triumph. The next day I watched on the television in the jockeys' room at Navan as Make A Stand galloped the opposition into the ground. I discussed with Aidan and J.P. McManus which race we thought the horse would go for at Cheltenham. When I got home that night, I rang Martin.

I congratulated him on winning the Tote Gold Trophy, and I asked if White Sea was all right after her run the previous day. Some papers on the Monday said that I had rung to ask for the ride in the Triumph. But I didn't, because I knew I had already got the mount. What I did say, though, was that I thought Make A Stand could win the Champion Hurdle. When people are making up their minds about whether or not to go for a big race, they sometimes need a push. I felt what I said was true, but I also wanted Make A Stand out of the Supreme Novices so that Finnegan's Hollow had one less of the good ones to beat!

An hour after Make A Stand annihilated the Tote Gold Trophy field, Cyborgo won his second successive chase. A fortnight before the Cheltenham Festival, Pipe rang Swan to ask him to ride the horse in the Gold Cup. He was not to say anything to anyone until nearer the time – Pipe wanted to wait before announcing Cyborgo a definite runner, just in case anything should go wrong in the interim. He rang again later in the week. If Charlie could spare the time, he would like him to fly over to school the horse. He did not want this to be too near to Cheltenham, so the pair agreed on Monday, 3 March.

Swan caught the 7.50 a.m. flight to Bristol. He was met by Pipe's son, David, and the latter's girlfriend, and he arrived at the yard at ten o'clock. He schooled not just Cyborgo but several other horses, had lunch with the trainer and his wife Carol, and then watched the Racing Channel with them before being driven back to Bristol for the 4.00 p.m. flight to Dublin. When the girl at the check-in desk told him the flight was cancelled, Swan thought she was pulling his leg! She directed him to a coach which would take him, and the other unfortunate Dublin-bound travellers, to Heathrow.

> The journey was a nightmare. Just about every other person on the coach kept asking the driver to stop because they wanted to go to the loo. It took more than three hours to reach Heathrow. I was due in the centre of Dublin for the opening of an Italian restaurant at 6.30 p.m. I finally got there at 10.45 p.m. I stayed the night in the Westbury Hotel, but I had to get up at 5.15 a.m. because I was due to ride work at Ballydoyle at 7.30 a.m.

On the Saturday, Swan again left home early to catch the 7.50 a.m. flight to Bristol. He was riding What's The Verdict for Aidan O'Brien in the 2.15 p.m. at Chepstow. He was also booked for Tony Mullins's Lady Daisy in the Imperial Cup at Sandown at 4.05 p.m. He and a number of other jockeys riding at Chepstow – including Richard Dunwoody and Tony McCoy – had booked a helicopter to take them to Sandown. Three-quarters of an hour before the helicopter was due to arrive, Dunwoody's mobile rang in the Chepstow jockeys' room. It was the helicopter company. The caller was apologetic, but the helicopter was grounded by fog and could not take off for Chepstow.

Dunwoody passed on the bad news to his fellow travellers and, while they were still debating how they could raise a replacement chopper, he grimly informed them that they would have to drive.

What's The Verdict won but, instead of walking him back to the winner's enclosure, Swan trotted him all the way. The minute he weighed in, he ran to Tony McCoy's Ford Probe. So did Dunwoody and McCoy who had also been riding in the race. Their valets had already loaded their saddles and other equipment. Bob Bray, McCoy's driver, had the engine running.

> Norman Williamson and Dean Gallagher went with Johnny Kavanagh in Johnny's Nissan Primera. They agreed that Norman would do the driving. Johnny was not riding until the last race at Sandown, and the other two felt he wouldn't give it the same sort of kick that Norman would. We went like hell. Whenever I looked at the speedometer, we seemed to be doing between 120 m.p.h. and 130 m.p.h. I remember saying to the others, 'If we get killed, we will have plenty of publicity. Two British champion jockeys and an Irish champion all smashed up in the same car!'
>
> Then I looked at the petrol gauge. We were going so fast you could see the needle moving. And it was moving too fast. At halfway we realised we had to stop for diesel. We were quite near the course when we received a call from Johnny's car to slow up. There was a police patrol car on an overhead bridge. But, even with further delays caused by traffic lights and roundabouts, we still managed to average nearly ninety miles an hour. The journey, somewhere between 112 and 120 miles, took seventy-eight minutes, and we weighed in at Sandown with two minutes to spare.

Cheltenham would have been a disaster for Swan if it had not been for Istabraq, and Finnegan's Hollow in the opening Citroen Supreme Novices Hurdle left the favourite's jockey as dejected as his owner.

> I have never been travelling so easily down the hill at Cheltenham as I was when I approached the third last on that horse. He got in close and, although he did not hit the hurdle hard, his hindquarters were a bit high as he landed. The weight behind him and the impetus, particularly going downhill, was too much for his balance, and he tumbled. I took a heavy fall. I was lucky nothing galloped over me, but I got to my feet feeling

as sick as if the whole lot had hammered into me. I knew it wasn't my day when Theatreworld, the horse I had rejected, finished second in the Champion Hurdle. I was delighted for the staff – Aidan had put £250 each way on for them at 40-1 – but I would have felt ill if the horse had won. I remember saying to Tina that night, 'I just hope Istabraq makes up for all this tomorrow.'

In the author's opinion, the Istabraq ride ranks as Swan's finest hour. This was a horse who could not win, not after sweating up to such an extent beforehand. Although nobody has ever tried to quantify it, there is a direct link between the amount of liquid a horse loses in sweat before a race and the number of lengths he runs below his best. The sweat produced by Istabraq would have filled a decent-sized mug, and the effect on his nerves was every bit as devastating.

Yet the favourite's jockey, himself subject to supreme pressure, was able to turn certain defeat into victory by coolly rejecting conventional tactics, and riding the horse as if he had not a care in the world – and for much of the race as if he had not a hope in hell. He then had to overcome a nasty bump at a crucial stage. It was a bump that would have put a lesser horse on the floor, and that would have made a less skilful jockey lose his head. Swan, though, sat tight for as long as he dared to give his mount the chance to recover both his wind and his momentum. However, he is still sore about what happened.

I expected the stewards to call an inquiry, and I was very surprised when they did not do so. Richard Johnson knew I was on his inner and, having watched the video time and time again, I am convinced he moved across deliberately. He was entitled to do that if he wanted – he was race-riding and he was trying to win every bit as hard as I was – but the stewards should have asked him what he was doing.

The ground proved to be too fast for Cyborgo in the Gold Cup and White Sea, far from making amends for the Newbury fiasco, went lame jumping the second last in the Triumph Hurdle. The one that got away, though, was All The Aces in the Mildmay of Flete. Swan rode the J.P. McManus-owned ex-Irish horse for Jonjo O'Neill. Martin Pipe was represented by both the favourite, the Tony McCoy-ridden As Du Trefle, and an apparent no-hoper called Terao who Swan had ridden at Haydock on his previous start. The Irish champion decided that he should give a few words of advice to Timmy Murphy, even though the young rider had partnered the horse twice before. Swan explained that Terao could be a dodgy jumper. He would go best if he was left alone at his fences. But at the last it was All The Aces who made a mistake – he had also lost a lot of ground when hampered twice inside the last half mile – and he was beaten just over a length by Murphy's mount.

J.P. McManus was taken aback when Pipe went up to him and said, 'We would never have won if it hadn't been for Charlie!'

For the first time in its 160-year history, the Grand National was delayed by two days because of a terrorist bomb warning. At 2.49 p.m. on 5 April 1997, less than an hour before the world's greatest steeplechase was due to start, a telephone call was received at Fazakerley Hospital to say that a bomb had been placed at nearby Aintree. The caller used a recognised IRA codeword. Three minutes later a second call, saying much the same thing, was made to the Merseyside police control centre in Bootle. Little more than a quarter of an hour afterwards, the police ordered the course to be evacuated.

Aintree racecourse became the subject of some bizarre scenes that were transmitted by satellite around the world as 70,000 people were directed towards the middle of the course. Some were well protected by coats and scarves but many female racegoers, a few with even shoulders and thighs bared, were soon frozen almost to the marrow by the biting wind. For the most part, the evacuation was orderly but dozens of lager louts, egged on by their equally drunken friends, attempted to jump some of the fences and then pull the furze off them.

At 4.20 p.m. a loud bang was heard as the police carried out the first of two controlled explosions, and just over an hour later the police announced that no one would be allowed back into the car parks until the following day. Those who had driven from all over Britain were left to find their own accommodation and, with every hotel within a fifty-mile radius rapidly becoming booked out, thousands had to be put up in schools, sports centres and church halls.

Charlie Swan was fortunate in that he put on his overcoat before leaving the weighing room. Some, like Robbie Supple, went out onto the course in just their silks, boots and breeches, erroneously believing that they would soon be allowed back into the warmth. The Irish champion was among a group of jockeys ushered into an area by the stable yard by Michael Caulfield, the secretary of the Jockeys Association of Great Britain. When he became too cold, Swan took refuge in Peter Niven's car. Then, when hunger assumed a greater priority, he begged a couple of sandwiches from a picnicking racegoer.

After the police ordered him, and everybody else, to leave the car parks, he waited outside the stables with several other riders for the best part of two hours. When Conor O'Dwyer informed him that he was returning to the Moat House Hotel in the centre of Liverpool, Swan asked him to book himself and Tina in for a further two nights. His mobile phone was in his suit pocket in the weighing room. But it would not have been of much use even if he had had the foresight to bring it with him. All the airwaves were blocked.

Swan adjourned to a nearby house where a hospitable lady called Eadie was treating everybody to tea, coffee and sandwiches. He then walked – still in his racing boots – in the direction of Liverpool until he found a taxi. He had packed three suits before leaving home for the meeting. That Saturday night he lent one to Norman Williamson and another to David Casey. But, when the trio walked up to the Adelphi Hotel, they were amused to find many of their rivals intent on dancing the night away in their boots, breeches and racing colours!

The race was finally run at 5.00 p.m. on Monday, and for much of the first circuit Wylde Hide's jockey was convinced that the wait was going to be worthwhile.

Arthur Moore had told me to be no nearer the leaders than mid-division until the race began in earnest. But Wylde Hide jumped the first few fences so quick and well that I was soon about fifth. I felt the pace was not as fast as it usually is in the National, and so it was just as well to be handy. I had been a little worried that Wylde Hide would find the ground too fast for him. Not a bit of it. He was travelling so easily that I thought this was going to be my year, and my National.

Coming to the thirteenth, the first fence after re-crossing the Melling Road, Jason Titley on Nahthen Lad was on my inside and he was clicking his tongue at his horse to make him go faster. I shouted at him to stop because he was making Wylde Hide a bit too keen. My horse got in close for the first time in the race. He did not get high enough and he landed steeply. His front legs crumpled, and I thought he was gone. Somehow he scrambled up as I sat tight, and his head struck me hard in the face. By the time I recovered, both reins were on the right side of his neck. I had no steering, and I tried desperately to get the reins back. We had jumped the next fence, and were heading for the Chair, before I was able to do so.

I had lost a tremendous amount of ground and my chance was gone. In an ordinary race, I would have pulled up. But this was the National. There might be a pile-up. But, as we jumped the first few fences on the second circuit, the doubts began to creep in. Supposing he was injured through me continuing? I was still debating whether to pull up, when he made another bad mistake at the fence before Becher's. I suspect my indecision got through to him and caused him to misjudge it. At Becher's the horse in front of me blundered, unseated his rider and then veered sharply left. I had given Wylde Hide plenty of rein because of the drop on the landing side. When his head came up, and he too veered left, I fell off!

16

Falls, Fractures and Fear

Falls are an unavoidable, frequently painful, and sometimes damaging part of a jump jockey's life. They eventually force most National Hunt riders into retirement, and occasionally they are the cause of their death.

Hitting the ground at over 30 m.p.h. is, for a super-fit sportsman with youth on his side, not usually that much of a problem. Admittedly, if the ground is firm, it will hurt and bruise. But it won't normally break anything. It's the horses behind who do that. Sometimes you will see a horse roll on a fallen jockey or, far worse, turn a somersault on landing and bring his whole body weight crashing down on the hapless rider. When this occurs, he is in trouble and in serious danger of ending up in hospital.

The really bad falls, though, tend to come in large fields and often in hurdle races where the pace is faster than in a chase. Racehorses have an in-built sense of self-preservation and they will avoid a fallen jockey if they possibly can. Not because they don't want to hurt him but because they realise that, if they trip over him, they will fall and hurt themselves. But in a big field of hurdlers everything often happens too quickly, with the horses too tightly bunched, for them to take avoiding action. A jockey unfortunate enough to fall near the front will be galloped over, and suffer as much damage as if he fell in front of the Charge of the Light Brigade. He will become a human football as aluminium-tipped hooves hammer into him with the force of a pile-driver. If he is lucky, his helmet and his back protector – a padded vest – will come between him and the aluminium, and he will probably escape with nothing worse than bruising. But there is no protection for the face, arms and legs. When the blows hit these parts of the body, something has to give. It is never the aluminium.

Hooves break bones but bones mend. It is the spirit that in the end proves incapable of doing the same. For much of a jump jockey's career the bone-breaking, and more particularly the fear of it, is buried in the subconscious by the adrenaline-surging excitement of winning. It is only in the final weeks of the career that the fear takes over, and that the nightmares prove impossible to bear.

If a jockey can avoid it, he will not let his mind dwell on the almost inevitable consequences of his chosen way of life. An overactive imagination is a positive drawback in such a dangerous occupation and the cynic might say that Charlie Swan, not bright enough to even sit his exams at school, let alone pass them, is supremely well equipped for his accident-filled profession.

In fact, although he never normally admits to it, Swan knows apprehension – if not actual fear – despite having had comparatively few falls in recent seasons. He hit the ground only twenty-five times during his 538 rides in Ireland in the 1995/96 campaign, whereas most jump jockeys reckon that on average one in twelve of their mounts will fall. Swan's ratio was better than one in twenty and in the 1996/97 season it was only marginally worse with twenty-nine falls from 528 rides in his native country. But he also averaged one broken bone per season, and many times he travelled to the races knowing that he had to steel himself to be brave. He has developed his own way of driving his mind through the nerve-barrier.

> Any jockey who says he is never nervous is a liar. We all get a bit apprehensive before a big race, particularly so in the Grand National, or when we know the horse we are riding is a dodgy jumper. And I have to admit that the last-named bothers me. The ones I know to be really bad, I refuse to ride. But you can't refuse to partner everything that might fall – you would soon have no rides if you did – and I sometimes find myself on horses that are dicey. Before going out for the ride on a horse like this, I will psych myself up. I tell myself this one is dodgy and that, therefore, he can't prove to be any worse at the fences than I think he is going to be. I then turn the race into a challenge to get him round. I become determined to do so. If he does, I am thrilled to bits.

If he doesn't, he falls – and Swan has become adept at taking avoiding action.

Normally everything happens pretty quickly, and so you have to act fast. I try to pitch myself forward away from the horse so that I roll clear of him. If I can do that, there is little risk of him rolling over on top of me, or kicking me. The second I hit the ground, I roll myself up into a ball to protect myself, or as much of myself as I can, from the horses behind who I know are going to gallop over me. People say you should lie still, curled up like this, until all the horses have gone but I usually have a quick look to see if I have time to get out of the way before the next one comes. If you stay put, sometimes a horse who is tailed off will gallop up and kick you all over the place. By the time he reaches you, you could have been in safety on the other side of the rails. The more falls you get, the better you become at avoiding danger.

Of course, a jockey's best chance of avoiding danger is to keep his horse on his feet, and that means getting him to meet the obstacles spot on, and making sure he jumps them cleanly.

Every horse is different, and each one has a slightly different way of going about things. For example, some dislike you touching their mouths with the bit and you have to hold the neck strap. Dessie Hughes taught me to ride with the ball of my foot on the stirrup iron so that, when the horse makes a mistake, you do not pull his mouth as much as you would if you had the stirrup against your heel. Other horses are less easy to help. They may hang, or they are lazy. Others are too excitable and you have to concentrate on making them relax, and so conserve their energy. Some like being in front, others don't. You never get two exactly the same.

Most of them are quite intelligent. They can tell who is riding them, and they will go better for a jockey who understands them than for one who doesn't. I will often talk to them in the course of a race to give them encouragement and confidence. If I am on a bit of a rogue, I might shout 'Go on' at him. If I sense that he is a bit cowardly, and may try to jam on the brakes going into a fence, I will growl at him to stop him slowing. Normally, though, I would not say anything to a horse going into a fence when both he and I are trying to measure the right stride. Twenty strides out, I know if I am going to meet it right. When we are going very fast, particularly in a two mile chase on firm ground, it can be hard to get the horse right in time. I have to decide whether I am going to shorten him up a bit, or get him to put in a long one. Shortening means easing him back a notch, perhaps half a stride, so that he then meets the fence right. Alternatively you can squeeze the horse with your legs, and get him to extend his stride, so that he reaches the take-off point a bit sooner. On fast ground you can sometimes get the horse to stand back and wing almost every fence. But if you do this in heavy going, you might not make it and the horse will fall.

I adopt a similar approach when riding over hurdles but, because the obstacles are not so unforgiving if you hit them, you don't have to be so exact. You sometimes see jockeys kicking away – the ones Dessie Hughes calls the brave jockeys – at every fence and hurdle. But there is more to riding over jumps than being brave. Indeed, bravery can sometimes prove stupid. You run the risk of getting the horse hurt – and brave jockeys can often lose races that a more careful jockey might win. Really, you have to learn when to be brave, and when not to be.

Sometimes, though, no matter how many precautions I take, I meet the fence or hurdle wrong. If I get away with it, I feel a great sense of relief and I will mutter a heartfelt 'Good lad'. When I realise the horse is not going to stay on his feet, I often find myself saying, 'Jesus. I am going to go here.' Then I have to protect myself as best I can. But what bothers me most about falling is that it means I have lost the race. It's only if it happens when I am already beaten that I become more concerned about what the horses behind might do to me.

The horses behind, and indeed his own mounts, have done a lot of damage to Swan over the years. On the inside of his lower left arm is the scar left by the operation to insert a plate following his fall from Irish Dream on his first ride at Cheltenham in March 1987. On his lower right arm there are two scars, running almost parallel and both seven inches in length. They are the legacies of more plate-inserting operations. The lower one owes its existence to Chamois Boy at Galway in August 1990, and the other to the operation carried out in June 1996. Between the two there is a noticeable bump, either an unnatural bone growth or the consequence of the plate that lies beneath it. He also has a scar on his forehead from the Saracen fall at Gowran Park in May 1988.

Other breakages have left no marks. At Tipperary in October 1991 he broke a bone in his right hand. Just over two years later he broke one in his left hand. There is no mention of this on his official medical record filed with the Turf Club. He simply bandaged up the hand and carried on. Frequently it hurt like hell – Swan reckons it was one of his most painful injuries – and it was nearly a year before he felt able to ride without the bandaging. He has also broken ribs on a number of occasions, and again he has managed not to have them recorded. Indeed, hardly anybody has known about them.

I have been to Fred Kenny on occasion with painful bruising in my chest only to be told that I have cracked or fractured ribs. So far I have been able to keep riding when this has happened. But I have had to take painkillers, usually Froben, to deaden the agony. I prefer to keep riding if I possibly can. It hurts me more to miss out on the rides on good horses in good races. As a result, I am often riding either with a slight injury or feeling the effects of something that I have not really given time to heal. Indeed, there are few weeks in the season when I don't feel sore, or in pain, from some injury or other. Often it's something that cannot be traced, directly, to a broken bone. I often feel pain in my back and my neck. This is why I frequently don't look as stylish as I should. Even now, I study the videos a lot to try to improve my style but, when you are riding partly in pain, you tend to adopt a style that will not put pressure on the part of the body that is hurting.

When the injury has been so bad that I have had to take time off, I am always a bit worried that I am going to fall or get kicked on the bone I have damaged. On my first fall after that operation in 1996, I was kicked just where the plate had been put in, the one place I was trying to protect.

In the jockeys' room over the years I have noticed the odd rider whose nerve has gone. I can see he is actually frightened of race-riding, almost terrified of what he is going to have to face. I never say anything in such circumstances, but I silently sympathise. I can see how it might happen. I was frightened at Gowran Park in February 1995 that day when I was trapped under Never Back Down. A similar thing happened to me at Thurles in January 1994. Rose Appeal fell at the last, absolutely knackered. As I was going through the air, my stirrup leather somehow wrapped itself round my foot. I knew I was in trouble before I hit the ground. If the horse had got up and galloped off, I would be dragged, kicked and injured. Possibly even killed. Again it was at the last

hurdle, and again Liam Healy was there. He answered my shouts
for help and ran over to sit on the horse's head. Fortunately Rose
Appeal was winded and Liam was sitting on him before he got
his breath back. But I had a terrible job getting my foot free. It
took me the best part of five frightened minutes. As at Gowran
Park thirteen months later, I returned to the weighing room as
white as a sheet. After both those incidents, I had to force myself
to put them out of my mind. I told myself that they were freak
accidents, and they should never happen again.

But such a simple-sounding philosophy cuts no ice with his wife. For
Tina Swan, every racing day is fraught with danger and, when it is
safely over, she says a silent prayer of thanks. When she first became
engaged to Charlie, her friends and relations wondered how the
nervous Tina would cope with the accidents the man in her life was
bound to suffer. The fact that she has not been able to do so has come
as no surprise to many of them, and her years of living on edge have
whittled away much of their sympathy.

'I was with Tina one day in a bar at Galway. We were watching a
race on the television and Charlie had a fall. It wasn't a bad one but
she started crying,' says younger sister Paula, almost incredulously. Her
tone suggests that if she, not Tina, had married Charlie, falls would
never have become a reason for tears.

Sister-in-law Natasha Finn remembers being with Tina at the
Cheltenham Festival where the long queues to use the lavatories can
assume a nightmare scenario for female racegoers: 'Tina would dash
off to the loo a few minutes before the race, knowing full well that she
would still be in the queue when the race was ending. Sometimes she
finds the risks Charlie takes almost too hard to bear.'

For 'sometimes' substitute 'always'. Many jump jockeys' wives do
their best to blank out the dangers by not going racing. Tina is
different. She feels it is her duty to be at the racecourse. But in the
process she tightens the rack, increasing her self-imposed mental
torture to almost impossible levels.

When we first went out together, I wasn't at all conscious of the
dangers Charlie was facing. Then I began to go to the races with
him. I immediately started to get nervous, and to worry. People
told me: 'There is no need to worry; it will get easier.' But they
were wrong. If anything, it has got harder. I worry about Charlie
the whole time and, if he is going to have a fall, I would rather

be there to see it than hear about it at home. In fact I only half watch the actual races. I can't manage to do more than that. If I see him coming back in safely – it doesn't matter that much to me if he has won or not – I am happy. If he has a fall, then I must rush off to see he is alright. Or at least see him get to his feet, and see that he is not seriously hurt. Occasionally he is knocked unconscious and, for me, that is terrible.

In some ways I will be glad when the day comes when he retires. But I also think it's a bit sad when a jump jockey is forced to retire, although I wouldn't dream of trying to stop Charlie before he was ready to do so. Racing means everything to him. For example in June 1996, after he had the operation on his right arm, we went to Portugal for a fortnight's holiday. He was glad of the break but, as it always does, it took him a few days to unwind. For the rest of the first week he relaxed. But in the second week he was off scouring the shops to buy *The Sporting Life*. He was looking for the racing results. The problem was that the paper did not come in every day, and he then had to ring Dessie Scahill to find out who had won. Horses were winning that he would have been on. By the end of the holiday, he was dying to get back to Ireland and to his racing.

Dessie Scahill is a failed jockey who found his real vocation, as a racecourse commentator, almost by accident. He comes from north County Dublin as his accent – his voice is loud, deep and at times almost rough – vividly testifies. He was apprenticed to Dermot Weld's father, the late Charlie Weld, in 1974 when he was sixteen. But he was only given two rides. After three and a half years he left, a little disillusioned, to work for Paddy Prendergast. After a further year, by which time his dreams of becoming a jockey had disappeared for good, he left racing to do office work for his brother, who ran a garage in Dublin. But the pull of the turf was too great. Little more than ten months later he was back on the Curragh, this time working for Mick O'Toole. He became the stable's travelling head lad. At Galway four years later, when he had just left O'Toole but had held on to the stable staff identity card that got him free admission, he was watching a race from the roof of the weighing room when the loud-speaker system broke down. Scahill, who had done the odd commentary as a party-piece in pubs, took over for the benefit of those around him. At least he did until an official came up to him and asked him what he thought he was doing up there.

When he received a letter some weeks later asking him to audition for racing commentaries, he thought somebody was trying to wind him up. But, when Tony O'Hehir gave up his job as racecourse commentator in 1986 to become the Irish correspondent of the newly-formed *Racing Post*, Scahill took over from him. Apart from his commentaries, he is perhaps best known for being the most ardent Manchester United fan in Ireland. He has even called his Kildare home Trafford House. However, perhaps because of his own unfulfilled aspirations, he has also taken a keen interest in the careers of up-and-coming jockeys. Those on the Curragh know that a lift to the races will always be available in Dessie Scahill's car, and that they can turn to him for help and advice. When things go wrong for any of them, he feels the hurt almost as much as they do. He broke down in tears when Johnny Murtagh's brilliant career looked like being destroyed in 1992. He has also gone out of his way to help jockeys' wives – particularly Charlie Swan's wife – cope with the mental agony they are put through.

When she does not go racing, Tina Swan rings the commentary line for each race her husband is riding in. This line relays Scahill's commentary and, whenever a horse falls, Scahill will make a point of including in his broadcast the fact that the jockey concerned has got to his feet. He leaves his mobile phone switched on throughout the afternoon so that wives and girlfriends of fallen jockeys can contact him to make sure their loved ones are all right. If Swan has a fall, and has not stood up by the time the race is over, Scahill knows his phone will ring. He also knows who will be on the other end.

A generation ago, jump jockeys were far less subject to medical supervision than they are now. When they returned to action after breaking a bone was more or less up to them, and many of those long since retired have – when they can be persuaded to tell them – some horrific tales about how they resumed far too soon, and what they had to do to overcome the pain of the still-not-mended bones. Swan's account of riding with broken ribs pales by comparison. But these days jockeys have to pass the doctor before they are allowed to return.

A major point of contention between some jockeys and the medical profession, though, is concussion – or more particularly how long a rest is necessary after being knocked out. Racing doctors tend to err on the side of caution and Walter Halley, the Turf Club's medical officer, is regarded by the jockeys as being over-careful. But he is adamant that he is right, saying: 'The most worrying injury a jockey can suffer is concussion. The danger is repeated concussion which can lead to post traumatic encephalogy, a condition known in the boxing world as punch drunk. I always insist that any jockey who suffers dizziness after a fall is stood down for the rest of the day, and all the following day. If he is knocked out, even if only for a few seconds, he is off for a week. If he is concussed, and suffers any sort of amnesia or memory loss, no matter how temporary, he has to go to hospital and he is not allowed to ride again for three weeks. However, what worries me most of all is concussion that happens off the course and is not reported.'

No jockey is going to report such incidents, and indeed most do their utmost to avoid the bans that follow racecourse concussion. Charlie Swan is among those convinced that the racing doctors – in Britain the Jockey Club's medical advisers adopt much the same stringent approach as Halley – go over the top.

> In cases of bad concussion a week is more than enough to get over it, and indeed for the system to recover completely. Three weeks is ridiculous, and totally unnecessary. I also do not agree with the punch drunk scenario, at least not for routine minor concussions. One day I had a fall at Clonmel and I was knocked out, but the racecourse doctor didn't realise this and I got away without any sort of lay-off. A week later, I was concussed again and stood down for a week. But three or four days later I was perfect. I know some medical opinion states that you may feel fully recovered while the brain may not be. But my experience, and that of the other jockeys I have discussed this with, is that this viewpoint is unnecessarily over-cautious.
>
> When you have been concussed, the other jockeys will often help you to beat the system if there is time for them to do so before you are seen by the doctor. They know the sort of questions the doctor is going to ask. While you are sitting on the bench in the jockeys' room, not having a clue where you are or what is going on, they will make you tell them what racecourse you are riding at and the name of the horse you were riding. If you don't know, they tell you – and they go on telling you until you have got it right. The doctor may also want to know the names of the horses you have ridden in earlier races. The jockeys will go through these with you too. They know that three weeks could cost you a fortune and they will go out of their way to make sure that, if at all possible, you keep any lay-off down to a minimum.

Another area in which Charlie Swan believes the rules are too harsh on jockeys is the whip. Few issues in racing are more controversial, with some veterinary opinion pointing to the damage that overuse of the stick can do to certain horses, while the cruelty aspect arouses dire passions among animal lovers. Swan, though, is convinced that even the stewards – who allow the whip to be used far more than organisations like the Royal Society for the Prevention of Cruelty to Animals would like – have got it badly wrong.

I totally agree with punishing any jockey who abuses a horse, particularly when the animal concerned is out of the placings and is obviously not going to finish any closer. But there are any number of occasions when the whip rules are too restrictive, and when the stewards are over-protective. The situation is not that bad in Ireland but in Britain the stewards are so anti-stick, and have become so ridiculous over the way they frame and interpret the rules, that they are in danger of ruining racing. They also make life impossibly difficult for jockeys because they leave you feeling far too conscious of the fact that you must not hit the horse more than a certain amount.

The last thing in the world I would want to do is to be cruel to a horse. I try to win without hitting my mount if I can, and so I confine myself to hands and heels if possible. If it's not, I will give the horse a slap down the shoulder, and also wave the whip at him. Some horses will pick up and quicken when they see the whip. Others have to feel it. Some horses will produce a bit more each time you hit them, but others soon come to the point where they have no more to give. A good jockey can tell if they have given their all, and he will not continue to hit them. Indeed, there are some horses who won't go at all for the stick, and with them you have to put your whip down and drive them with your hands and your heels.

However, when you are fighting for the lead in a close finish, I think it's fair enough to be able to give the horse a few extra cracks to try and win. This can mean hitting him a few times more than the stewards, and many of the public, think you should. But I honestly believe that horses don't feel it as real pain. When I was playing rugby, I would get a lot of bangs and kicks but they hardly hurt when I was warmed up and giving it all I'd got. Certainly the horses don't bear any resentment, either at the time or afterwards. If they did, they would lay their ears back when you next get on them. But they don't.

17

One Break Too Many?

Racing stables traditionally make an early start to the day and, on work mornings at Piltown, Charlie Swan is at the wheel of his BMW by 5.30 a.m. The seventy-five-mile journey takes him through Moneygall, Thurles, Clonmel and Carrick-on-Suir. With the early morning roads almost empty of traffic, he will reach his destination by 7.00 a.m.

On the days when Aidan O'Brien requires him at Ballydoyle, he has the luxury of an extra hour in bed. The staff there come in a bit later and the journey takes little more than fifty-five minutes. Those mornings on which O'Brien does not need him are spent riding work or schooling for trainers who do. When Swan has no commitments, though, he is in his father's yard by 7.30 a.m. and, unless he has to leave early to go racing, he will ride out two lots. But O'Brien's demands can be considerable.

> The way I operate is that everybody is held responsible for their particular aspect of the job. It is the jockey's duty to ensure that the horses jump properly, and Charlie must be able to go to the races satisfied that the horses he is riding know enough about their job to be able to produce their best. I discuss with Charlie and the other jockeys what needs to be done with each horse and, if there is an animal that needs schooling five days on the trot, then Charlie will drive over to school him on every one of the five mornings.

A lot of the schooling at Piltown is done in a huge barn – it is approximately fifty yards long and the same in width – and the horses are normally jumped, without anybody on their backs, around a schooling lane. The O'Brien practice is to send them two at a time, with an experienced horse accompanying a novice, so that the latter has an example to follow. Most of the obstacles are stiff hurdles and small fences. There are also some with poles and, if a horse gets in too close, the poles will be moved back to make sure he stands off when he jumps. The idea is to teach horses, not just how to jump, but how to measure the right stride without having to be told by the jockey.

Horses cannot be loose-schooled like this at racing pace, so there are more sets of hurdles and fences on the gallops. The stable jockey, who takes a close interest in how the horses get on inside the barn, will partner them over the jumps outside – and go on doing so until he and O'Brien are happy that they have got it right. It is part of the painstaking, time-no-object method that has brought the young trainer such amazing success, and won the admiration of his jockey.

> When you look at Aidan O'Brien, with his almost-baby face and glasses, you would never think that this was one of the great trainers of the modern day. Nor would you when you speak to him. He is shy, quiet and modest. Sometimes, though, he gets rattled. The public don't see this because it is usually with the staff. If somebody takes a horse up the gallop too fast, for instance, he will really give it to them.
>
> His runners are supremely fit but in fact he does not give them as much work as people seem to think. The horses usually trot or hack canter up the first four or five furlongs of the gallop, walk down again and then do a nice swinging canter over seven. The bulk of the work is short and sharp. But it's a method that works, and he is able to bring about massive improvement in the horses that he takes over from other people. I think the reason for this is that the horses enjoy life under his care. He spends an awful lot of time with them, and frequently he does not go to the races because he has so much to do in the yards. He has so many horses that it surprises me that he can recognise each one. But he does, and it's far more than simply recognising them. He has an intimate knowledge of every single one of them, and he is able to understand their individual characteristics. It's this understanding of horses, coupled with his total dedication, that makes him such a brilliant trainer.

Swan is a jockey who does not like being tied down to instructions. He believes that all a trainer needs to tell him are the basic necessities – whether the horse stays or not, whether or not he likes being in front, plus any individual quirks. The tactics should be left to the jockey. Aidan O'Brien suits him admirably. He gives no riding instructions at all!

We will discuss the race, and I more or less know how Charlie intends to ride it by the time he goes out onto the course. But often he will hear things down at the start – for instance that the race is going to be run differently to the way we thought – and he will completely change his plans. Like all good jockeys, he hates being beaten and, when he is, his expression as he passes the post would make you think somebody had stuck a knife into his side. He normally manages to be reasonably cheerful by the time he returns to the unsaddling enclosure. But not always.

He has a reputation for being good with the owners. When he does finish second, he will often apologise to them for getting beaten. He will have thought of some way in which he could have won the race. Nobody else will have noticed it, but it has occurred to him immediately. He wouldn't dream of keeping that to himself. He feels he has a duty to tell me and the owners. Some jockeys will blame the horse when they are beaten. Charlie never does.

Swan has not forgotten a painful early lesson:

I rode a horse for Andrew McNamara one day when I was still pretty green. When I got off him, I said he was useless and he would never win a race. Next time out the trainer put somebody else up and the horse won. Apart from learning to be more polite about horses, this also taught me that I can be wrong. Since then I have learned that very few horses are no good. If they run badly, or appear to be ungenuine, there is normally a reason. They may have a heart problem, or something could be hurting them. It costs people a lot of money to own horses, and they normally think the world of them. The last thing they want to hear is that the horse is a dog. I try not to add to their disappointment. Although I endeavour to tell them the truth, I do my best to let them down gently if I have to dash their hopes.

Swan is fortunate in having almost no weight problems but breakfast, even a working one spent discussing horses and their running plans with Aidan O'Brien, is usually restricted to a bowl of cereal. On non-racing days, when he gets home in time, his main meal is lunch – meat, potatoes and other vegetables, plus pudding. When he gets back to The Cobs too late, or goes racing, lunch consists of a sandwich and he will have his two-course meal for supper. Otherwise he just has something light, like an omelette, in the evening.

Only when he is riding below ten stone, does he have to think about losing weight. He has a sauna in the house but he prefers the old jockey's trick of spending an hour in a hot bath after pouring in liberal quantities of either table salt or bath salts. He passes the time reading a newspaper, repeatedly turning on the hot tap to keep up the temperature, and sipping a cold drink. By the time the hour is up, he will have lost four pounds.

On days spent with Aidan O'Brien, he frequently does not return home until 3.30 p.m. There are no children to greet him. Just a wife, a West Highland terrier, an Alsatian and a cockatiel. The last-named was christened Tootsie. When the Swans acquired it, they had no idea what sex it was. But they had just seen the film in which Dustin Hoffman plays an out-of-work actor who dresses up as a woman in order to get a job in a soap opera. Tootsie is still of indeterminate sex but has developed a limited vocabulary. Its favourite trick is to summon the dogs by calling out their names.

When Swan gets home, one of the first things he does is to turn on the Racing Channel. You might imagine that a man who has been thinking, talking and working horses since dawn would want a rest from them. Not this one. He avidly watches the events on British racecourses, plus all the interviews that the programme relays. From this he picks up valuable information about big race mounts he might be offered and, every bit as important, about horses he may meet in races at Cheltenham and elsewhere. He does not simply put his feet up in front of the box, though. Frequently he has the Irish form book in his hand and he works his way through the races in which he is riding the following day.

> I spend a lot of time on the form book, and I always try to ride the race well before I go out into the parade ring. I work out what I can about the opposition, their strengths and their weaknesses. I also try to work out which horse is likely to make the running, and I balance the sort of pace my mount wants with the pace the principal opposition does not. I also want to see how

the race could be run in such a way that it does not suit the other fancied horses. But I always have a plan B in mind in case things don't go the way I expect.

When the homework is done, Swan will often turn to his finances, and the VAT returns and other paperwork they involve. By the standards of jump racing, he makes a lot of money. In the 1995/96 season, for example, his riding fees grossed £42,750 and his share of the million-plus earned by his mounts brought him a further £77,000. Out of that he had to pay valets' fees of nearly £3,000 and Turf Club handling charges of more than £4,000. The Turf Club takes four per cent for debiting the accounts of owners with jockeys' riding fees and percentages, and crediting the accounts of the jockeys. Weatherbys, who perform the same service in Britain, charge only a fraction of this – just 40p an entry – and in Swan's case their total bill was a mere £20. But his telephone bills are high, as is the cost of the fuel and insurance for his BMW. Pat Keogh, the Limerick car dealer, provides the car free of charge and pays the other running expenses in return for having his name, and Swan's, on the driver's side door panel. However, the balance of the jockey's income does not go anything like as far as he believes it should.

> I pay some of it into a pension scheme but I find it hard to put away the money I am going to need when the time comes for me to give up race-riding. The reason is that my tax bills are staggering. When I pay them, it feels as if I am buying a new Mercedes and giving it straight to the government. They leave me with almost nothing – and I am the lucky one who gets all the rides he wants. I don't know how the less fortunate jump jockeys survive.

A major outlay, and one which Swan never mentions, is his generosity to those who look after the horses he rides. The stable lad or stable girl of a big race winner ridden by the Irish champion can expect a cash present. Every Christmas he writes out a handsome cheque to Aidan O'Brien for distribution among his stable staff. He is not the only jockey to do this – it is a long-standing tradition in racing – but few jockeys are as generous as Swan.

He is also different from most of his rivals in that he does not drink. Many teetotallers are against the whole idea of alcohol and are convinced it does people no end of harm. This one simply does not like the taste. Gin, whisky and brandy, even diluted with a mixer, have him grimacing in disgust. To be sociable at a party, and to avoid looking too out of place, he will sip at a glass of wine or beer. But he would not dream of doing so in his own home.

In the evenings he relaxes by watching television. Tina is an avid fan of both *Eastenders* and *Coronation Street*. Her husband watches them with her but he prefers the films on Sky Movies. His mind, though, is never that far away from the horses and sometimes he finds himself unable to resist the temptation of the telephone at his elbow. The person he rings is normally Aidan O'Brien, and the calls are often made at a time when most trainers are fast asleep.

> I have a private line, and the number is known only to a handful of people. Charlie is one of them. Sometimes the phone will ring at midnight. Then it's invariably Charlie. He has been lying in bed thinking about the horses, and he has come up with an idea about how we might improve one of them, or improve his chances of winning. He thinks I ought to know. I don't mind. Quite the opposite, in fact. I am glad he thinks about the job so much because that helps me to do mine.

However, sports other than racing do attract his attention. He has been an Arsenal supporter since he first went to school at Headfort, even though he has never been to Highbury or seen the Gunners other than on television. He also takes a keen interest in the rugby internationals, and he is glued to the television whenever his racing commitments allow him to watch the Formula One Grand Prix races. He plays tennis and squash, but his real non-racing activity is golf. His busy schedule, and the limited hours of daylight, mean that he can play only about once every three weeks during the winter months, but in the summer, when evening racing takes over, he will be on the course three times a week. He plays to a handicap of thirteen and achieved his greatest success in 1996 when he won the captain's prize at Nenagh, his local course. Nearly 200 people crowded round the eighteenth to watch the final stages and the jockey, who will play in front of an audience of 40,000 at Cheltenham, found it nerve-wracking!

There are other sharply contrasting, and difficult to understand, aspects to his character. A man who dedicates his life to winning races, and who is so successful, could be expected to be something of a prima donna – at the very least difficult to deal with. But Swan is the opposite. He is always approachable, and always available to answer questions.

Even when things are clearly not going well for him, he is able to put politeness and decency above his own personal difficulties. Indeed, one of the most difficult aspects of this book was to find anybody with a bad word to say about him! His insistence on almost burying his own feelings beneath the interests of everyone else's amazes his relations and his rivals alike.

Sister-in-law Valerie says: 'Sometimes, when Charlie is riding in the Kildare or Dublin areas, he will drop off Tina to spend the afternoon with the family. When he returns to collect her, he will always find time to come into the house and ask how we all are. I know several jockeys who would be boasting when they have ridden three winners or won a big race. When that happens with Charlie, he never mentions it. He just sits in an armchair sipping his tea. He seems more interested in what we have been doing than in his own achievements.'

Conor O'Dwyer has been struck as much by Swan's sense of fair play as by his modesty: 'He is a straightforward person, with no pretence to airs and graces. He would neither attempt to pinch your ground on the course, nor go behind your back off the course.'

Richard Dunwoody, who has often proved an arch-rival, has been impressed most by Swan's ever-present cheerfulness: 'As a jockey he is ultra-competitive and he is as determined as they come but, surprisingly, he is rarely in bad humour. Even when things go wrong, he will always put a brave and cheerful face on it.'

Not quite always, however. In August 1996 Melissa's husband, Brian Kenny, a London commodity broker, died after a long battle with cancer. Her brother-in-law was devastated.

> Brian's cancer had been in remission for several years and, although we all knew it might come back, it was a shock when it did. We are a close family and I would often talk to Brian on the phone. His death meant that Melissa was left to bring up their two young children on her own. I felt as sad for her as I did for Brian. I did not ride for three days, even though it was the start of the Tralee festival.

The problem of what to do when the time comes for retirement is one to which most jump jockeys happily adopt a head-in-the-sand approach. Swan, though, has had his future mapped out for some time and in May 1998 he announced that he was to embark on a new career, albeit in tandem with his existing one.

We started the Charlie Swan Equestrian Centre at Modreeny a year or so earlier. The idea is that people use it to improve their riding, and indeed to learn to ride. My father runs it, we have qualified instructors and I am often around to give advice. There is a cross-country course and a showjumping ring. That will continue but I have agreed with my father that I will take over the licence, and he will act as my assistant. I have had this move in mind for the past year and it was a matter of finding the right time to start it. But, when I heard that Aidan might not have as many jumpers in future, I felt I should act. We have some superb facilities at Modreeny, and I have built more boxes so that I can accommodate forty or more horses.

Few people manage to combine riding with training for long. The demands the two jobs make are considerable. They also tend to pull in conflicting directions. Most who try soon find they have to give up one of them, usually the riding. Charlie Swan is fully aware that his long career in the saddle is drawing to a close.

It will be hard work, particularly as I will continue to go to Piltown and Ballydoyle to ride work. But for some time I have been choosier and choosier about what I ride, and so taking out a licence to train was in some ways an inevitable progression. However I am still enjoying life as a jockey and I don't want to say that the 1998/99 season will be my last. I would love to make it ten championships. But that is not really the point. What is, is that the excitement of riding good horses is like a drug. It's hard to switch off from it. If the likes of Istabraq are still winning big races, I might find it impossible to turn my back on them – and all the thrills they bring me.

18

Champion Glory

Istabraq was favourite for the 1998 Smurfit Champion Hurdle for most of the winter, partly because he did nothing wrong but more particularly because there was no outstanding challenger of comparable class.

Aidan O'Brien geared the horse's whole preparation towards the opening day of the Cheltenham festival. He said at the beginning of the season that the horse would have just four races before the Champion, and that they would all be in Ireland. Nothing from England came to take him on, and there was nothing in Ireland good enough to test him. He started favourite for all four, he was odds-on for all except the first and he did not have to be asked a serious question. The going was testing on each occasion except in the Avonmore Waterford Hatton's Grace Hurdle at Fairyhouse at the end of November. Then it was only yielding but the distance was two and a half miles, widely considered to suit Istabraq better than the two miles of the Champion Hurdle. Indeed this was believed to be a major chink in the favourite's armour. No winner of the Royal & SunAlliance Hurdle had ever won the Champion – and for good reason. The novice event, run over two miles and five furlongs, is for horses with abundant stamina. You need speed to win the Champion Hurdle.

Charlie Swan, like almost everybody else in jump racing, listened carefully whenever people discussed whether Istabraq had sufficient pace. When he was asked for his views, the questioners were given much the same line as they got from O'Brien – 'I don't think distance matters to this horse. He has plenty of pace.' But Swan was being economical with the truth. Indeed, had his soul been called upon to give evidence in the witness box, opposing counsel might have thought the Swan statements closer to perjury!

> Whenever I spoke to JP McManus, he was always confident that two miles was Istabraq's trip. Christy Roche, who had ridden the horse at Ballydoyle, also thought he had enough pace to win a Champion Hurdle. And Aidan was adamant that Istabraq meant speed. I had my doubts. I kept them to myself but I intended to ride him for stamina rather than pace. No matter what I said in public, I thought two and a half miles was his best trip.

Those who went to Cheltenham on St Patrick's Day determined to back Istabraq, and those whose money was already on, had double reason to call on Ireland's patron saint for help. In the opening Citroen Supreme Novices Hurdle, His Song started favourite on the strength of his second to Istabraq in the AIG Europe Champion Hurdle at Leopardstown nearly two months earlier. Mouse Morris's novice let the form down by being slammed seven lengths by French Ballerina.

Just as bad, the Cheltenham atmosphere again got to Istabraq. The favourite coped with the paddock well enough, but the parade in front of the packed stands was too much for his nerves. He started to sweat and, by the time he was allowed to break away and canter down to the start, his neck was awash with lather. His jockey's mind was filled with conflicting thoughts.

> There was tremendous pressure on me but, even though this was the Champion Hurdle, it wasn't anything like as a bad as it had been twelve months earlier. The sweating wasn't as bad either. I remembered what Aidan had told me about all the good horses trained by Vincent O'Brien. Several of those sweated up before their races. Aidan had also insisted that it meant their minds were on the job in hand. But, if you get beaten when a horse sweats up, you have a ready-made excuse.

Charlie Swan also mulled over tactics as he made his way to the start, and he did the same when he was circling round waiting for the starter to call the horses into line.

> John Durkan, who had bought Istabraq for JP out of John Gosden's stable, always said that the horse liked to be up there in his races. John would have trained Istabraq but he found he

had leukaemia and, tragically, he died of it just under two months before the Champion Hurdle. Apart from the two and a half mile race at Fairyhouse, I'd been dropping Istabraq out in his races in Ireland. But this time I was going to jump him off smartly because I was worried about the trip being too short for him. What John had told me helped me to believe I was doing the right thing by the horse. I made up my mind to lead over the first hurdle, or at least be upsides over it. Ideally I would then like a lead. If they went a cut-throat gallop I would be able to afford to have one. If not, I might well have to make the running.

The canter to the start had given Swan encouragement. It had also reminded him of a conversation at Ballydoyle the previous week.

Istabraq felt sharp in himself, much sharper than he had done before his races in Ireland. I could tell he had been trained for the day, and that he was absolutely spot on. Immediately after Istabraq won the AIG, Aidan told the press that he was now going to start training the horse. People laughed at him when they heard that. But I realised that he had proved them wrong. This was a different horse.

I suppose I should have known that already. I rode him out at Ballydoyle a few days earlier. The horse seemed in incredibly good form. I said as much to Aidan.

He replied: 'Istabraq will destroy them next week.'

I was surprised to hear him make such a bold statement. It was out of character. He normally qualifies his remarks with things like 'Hopefully' or 'Please, God.' I said: 'But, Aidan. This is the Champion Hurdle.'

'I don't care. He'll destroy them.'

Istabraq drifted from 9-4 to 3-1. The bookies had opened him short, fearing an avalanche of McManus money. But it never came. It was Lady Daisy, a 100-1 outsider ridden by Jason Titley, who cut out the early running. Richard Dunwoody on the fancied I'm Supposin came next and Swan settled Istabraq in third. The favourite was travelling easily but, coming to the fifth hurdle, the one near the top of the hill, his jockey started riding.

This hurdle comes at a crucial stage. If you make a mistake at it, you can lose the race. You're still going uphill for a bit after you jump it and, if you land awkwardly, you lose momentum. Trying to regain it can take an awful lot out of a horse. I saw a stride some way before it, and I wanted to make sure Istabraq winged it.

When we got to the top of the hill, I started to niggle to get upsides I'm Supposin who was in front. The next thing I knew I was in the lead. I couldn't believe he had gone past I'm Supposin so easily. What I didn't know, though, was how the others were going. I had an uneasy feeling that a lot of them were queuing up behind me.

In fact they were all stone cold but I didn't know this. I felt I had to go for it and make it a real test of stamina. When we jumped the second last, I got him to pick up again. He was spot on at the last and, sixty yards after it, I looked to my right. I seemed to be miles clear. But the crowd was making a tremendous noise. That could only mean one thing. Somebody was coming. I got my whip out and waved it. Then I looked round again. But this time to my right. I got a real shock. There was nothing there.

I raised my right hand into the air in my excitement, and waved the index finger to signify victory. I was winning the Champion Hurdle. One of the biggest ambitions of my life was turning into glorious reality. I stood up in the irons, and waved my finger at JP's box. For the past year all he had wanted was to win the Champion Hurdle with Istabraq. Now he had done it.

Charlie Swan made racing history on the opening day of the Listowel festival on 22 September 1997. He rode Rainbow Frontier to win a three-year-old hurdle race and in the process took his career total – Flat and jumps combined – to 1,000 winners. No Irish-based jump jockey had ever ridden anywhere near as many.

But the next landmark was 1,000 jumping winners – his total included 59 on the Flat – and he had to wait until the first Saturday in May. In the meantime Rainbow Frontier – a fast and efficient jumper – had been sold for a six-figure sum by the appropriately named Crock of Gold Syndicate to join Martin Pipe.

Rainbow Frontier had fallen in the Triumph Hurdle and been beaten when starting favourite at Aintree. His next target was the Crowther Homes Swinton Handicap Hurdle at Haydock on May 2. This was the race in which Swan had nearly killed Declan Murphy four years earlier. On the day before the 1998 race, he was walking across one of the fields at Modreeny to put a head-collar on one of the horses when the phone in his pocket rang. It was Graham James who books his rides in Britain.

'Martin Pipe has just been on. He wants to know if you can ride Rainbow Frontier at Haydock tomorrow.'

Surprisingly, Swan's answer was not an immediate yes, even though there was no jump racing in Ireland to stop him taking the ride. He wanted to know why Tony McCoy was not riding the horse, as he had done on the gelding's two previous starts. Pipe, James explained, had three runners in the race. McCoy would have trouble doing ten stone and had opted for Potentate who had won the Welsh Champion Hurdle on his most recent outing. The next morning Swan flew to Manchester and then took a taxi to Haydock. He arrived at the course an hour before the first race. He finished fifth in that on Pipe's Diwali Dancer. The Swinton was next.

> Everything went according to plan on Rainbow Frontier. I took it up after jumping the second last and we held on to win by half a length. To complete the 1,000 winner-double was a big thrill and to do it on the same horse was almost unbelievable, particularly given the change of stables.

Swan took a taxi back to the airport. He wanted to watch O'Brien's King of Kings in the Sagitta 2,000 Guineas which was run two hours after the Swinton. But, when he got there, he discovered to his chagrin that all the television screens in the airport showed only flight times. Eventually he found somebody with a radio who he persuaded to switch to the Newmarket coverage. When he listened to the Ballydoyle colt win the classic, he thought his day was complete. He was wrong.

He arrived back at Modreeny at 7.30 p.m. Tina was on a boat on Lough Derg with Melissa and a few friends. Charlie was to join them at Garrykennedy, a little village on the lake shore and little more than half-an-hour away. When he got there, he found a crowd of people packed into Larkin's pub. Many of his father's owners were there. So were Pat Keogh who provides his BMW, and Andrew McNamara on whose Martinelli he had come so close to death at Killarney fifteen years earlier. They were holding a party. It was in Charlie's honour.

Appendix A

CHARLIE SWAN'S WINNERS

FLAT

	Ireland	Australia
1983	3	
1984	14	
1985	12	
1986	17	1
1987	4	
1990	1	
1995	6	
1996	1	–
	58	1

NATIONAL HUNT RULES

	Ireland	Britain
1985	1	
1986	4	
1987	26	
1988	23	1
1989 to 3 June	12	1
1989/90	73	1
1990/91	59	1
1991/92	79	2
1992/93	104	7
1993/94	99	7
1994/95	118	5
1995/96	150	5
1996/97	126	6
1997/98	90	4

Appendix B

CHARLIE SWAN'S BIG RACE WINS

FLAT

SEASON	COUNTRY	RACE	HORSE	TRAINER
1984	Ireland	Hennessy Handicap – Listed	Ash Creek	P. Mullins
		McDonogh Handicap – Listed	Ash Creek	P. Mullins
		Waterford Crystal Nursery – Listed	Rising	K. Prendergast
		Naas November Handicap	Picadilly Lord	K. Prendergast
1985	Ireland	Craddock Advertising Stakes – Listed	Jazz Ballet	K. Prendergast
		Birdcatcher Nursery – Listed	The Bean Sidhe	J. C. Hayden
1986	Ireland	1,000 Guineas Trial – Group Three	The Bean Sidhe	J.C. Hayden
		Hardwicke Cup – Listed	The Bean Sidhe	J.C. Hayden

NATIONAL HUNT

SEASON	COUNTRY	RACE	HORSE	TRAINER
1988	Ireland	Troytown Handicap Chase	Bean Alainn	D. O'Connell
	Britain	Bula Hurdle	Condor Pan	J.S. Bolger
1989/90	Ireland	Troytown Handicap Chase	Bean Alainn	D. O'Connell
		Champion Novice Hurdle	Vestris Abu	J.S. Bolger
		Tattersalls Gold Cup	Mixed Blends	M.F. Morris
	Britain	Stayers' Hurdle	Trapper John	M.F. Morris
1990/91	Ireland	Findus Handicap Chase	Rawhide	M.F. Morris
		Black And White Whisky Champion Chase	Cahervillahow	M.F. Morris
		Irish Champion Hurdle	Nordic Surprise	J.S. Bolger
	Britain	Long Distance Hurdle	Trapper John	M.F. Morris
1991/92	Britain	Long Distance Hurdle	Trapper John	M.F. Morris
1992/93	Ireland	Dennys Juvenile Hurdle	Autumn Gorse	Mrs A.M. O'Brien
		Bookmakers Hurdle	Novello Allegro	N. Meade
		Irish Grand National	Ebony Jane	F. Flood
		Champion Four-Year-Old Hurdle	Shawiya	M.J.P. O'Brien
	Britain	Supreme Novices Hurdle	Montelado	P.J. Flynn

SEASON	COUNTRY	RACE	HORSE	TRAINER
		Gold Card Final	Fissure Seal	H. de Bromhead
		Triumph Hurdle	Shawiya	M.J.P. O'Brien
		Stayers' Hurdle	Shuil Ar Aghaidh	P. Kiely
1993/94	Ireland	Galway Hurdle	Camden Buzz	P. Mullins
		Troytown Handicap Chase	King Of The Gales	J.E. Kiely
		Leopardstown Chase	High Peak	E.J. O'Grady
		Champion Four-Year-Old Hurdle	Glenstal Flagship	A.P. O'Brien
	Britain	Sun Alliance Novices Hurdle	Danoli	T. Foley
		Coral Cup	Time For A Run	E.J. O'Grady
		Festival Bumper	Mucklemeg	E.J. O'Grady
		Martell Aintree Hurdle	Danoli	T. Foley
		Whitbread Gold Cup	Ushers Island	J.H. Johnson
1994/95	Ireland	Drinmore Novice Chase	Sound Man	E.J. O'Grady
		Hatton's Grace Hurdle	Danoli	T. Foley
		Champion Novice Hurdle	Hotel Minella	A.P. O'Brien
	Britain	Champion Chase	Viking Flagship	D. Nicholson
		Martell Aintree Hurdle	Danoli	T. Foley
1995/96	Ireland	Kerry National	Life Of A Lord	A.P. O'Brien
		Troytown Handicap Chase	Gimme Five	E.J. O'Grady
		Royal Bond Novice Hurdle	Thats My Man	A.P O'Brien
		Dennys Gold Medal Chase	Double Symphony	A.P. O'Brien
		Leopardstown Chase	Royal Mountbrowne	A.P. O'Brien
	Britain	Greenalls National Trial	Lo Stregone	T.P. Tate
		Sun Alliance Novices Hurdle	Urubande	A.P. O'Brien
		Martell Aintree Hurdle	Urubande	A.P. O'Brien
		Whitbread Gold Cup	Life Of A Lord	A.P. O'Brien
1996/97	Ireland	Galway Plate	Life Of A Lord	A.P. O'Brien
		Royal Bond Novice Hurdle	Istabraq	A.P. O'Brien
		Punchestown Chase	Royal Mountbrowne	A.P. O'Brien
		Champion Novice Hurdle	Istabraq	A.P. O'Brien
	Britain	Sun Alliance Novices Hurdle	Istabraq	A.P. O'Brien
1997/98	Ireland	Drinmore Novice Chase	Private Peace	A.P. O'Brien
		Hatton's Grace Hurdle	Istabraq	A.P. O'Brien
		AIG Europe Champion Hurdle	Istabraq	A.P. O'Brien
	Britain	Smurfit Champion Hurdle	Istabraq	A.P. O'Brien
		Swinton Handicap Hurdle	Rainbow Frontier	M.C. Pipe

Index